Dictionary of 4,573

Crucial Cross Words

and their

Clues

Kemp, Curby and Bulten

Published by
CROSSSTAR
5334 S. 74 E. Ave
Tulsa, OK 74145

Dictionary of 4,573 CRUCIAL CROSS WORDS and their CLUES

ISBN 0-9619077-0-3

Cover Design: Barbara Newcomb

First edition

Dedicated to the memory of my beautiful Swiss wife
Verena Henry Kemp (1942-1987)
who loved puzzles
and was the first to suggest
that a book be made
of the words she couldn't remember.

TABLE OF CONTENTS

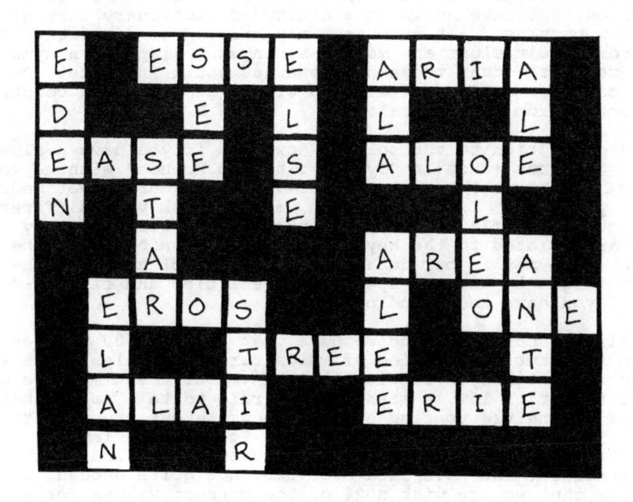

This unique crossword dictionary was conceived to give the novice puzzler a foothold by providing the words and clues that will be met most often in a given puzzle. The authors ran a computer check on the frequencies of words in over 600 puzzles and found that words of nine or more letters in length rarely repeat from one puzzle to the next. Why list them then? Puzzles are solved by completing the easily recognizable words and then guessing the letters of the longer phrases or words until the appropriate word is discovered.

The simple basis for our dictionary is a list of words (see page 125). If you master the first 21 words (on the cover) and their clues, you are usually assured of finding one word in a daily puzzle (of approximately 75 words). If in addition you learn the next 28 words on the list, you will usually complete another word in the puzzle. Learning the entire list of 719 words enables you to complete one-fifth of a puzzle.

As to the claims on the front cover, although we cannot say that every single crossword will contain one of the top 21 words, it is true that on the average one of these words will occur, and the puzzles that do not have one of the words are few and far between. Again, even if a crossword puzzle has less than half of its words in this book, it is a rare case, for our research shows that on the average, 57% of the words (i.e., 43 in a daily, 15x15 puzzle) will be in this book.

In our dictionary, the only words listed are those which occur in at least three different puzzles out of the more than 600 analyzed. The words in the lists beginning on page 125 occurred nine or more times. The word "area", the most frequent word, was found to be in forty-six different puzzles! But among all the more than 600, only six words of nine or more letters qualified for our book. They are:

Adam's apple
Drop in the bucket
Elementary
Entertain
Evanescent, and
Open-handed.

However, in one major dictionary, we found that, on a page selected at random, 99 words out of 342 had nine letters or more, or better than one out of four. But we estimate that the average puzzle has about six of these long words, about 5 to 10% of it. Thus, 25% of that dictionary is devoted to words that appear less than 10% of the time.

Another advantage this dictionary has over others is its usage of complete clues. We have not seen a crossword dictionary that gives actual clues from puzzles. Although some may boast over a quarter of a million words, their clues are mostly synonyms. Simple synonyms occur much less frequently than these dictionaries would indicate. Our dictionary captures the actual wit and wisdom of crossword constructors, quoted directly from their puzzles.

A word of caution to the solver, however: if you have a clue with two or more keywords (such as "Syrian city, to French" with keywords Syria, City, and French) you may not always find your answer under the first place you look. If this happens, merely look up a different keyword. If you do not find the answer under any keyword, you may also try words that are related to the keywords. It is possible that the specific clue you have was not in our data, but a similar clue was in the data. Also, don't forget to use the special abbreviation and fill-in-the-blank sections, if you have that kind of clue.

What kind of confidence do we have that in only 600 puzzles we have homed in on the true frequencies of words for all puzzles? The word "area" occures 46 times, a little less than 8% of the time. We use the binomial distribution law, a mathematical rule to tell us how many puzzles we need to analyze to find out how accurate our probability estimates are. If we want to be 95% sure (the "confidence level") that our estimate, 8%, is within 2% of the true frequency, we find that about 700 samples are needed. We have used over 600, not quite enough, but we can be quite sure that we are within 2% of the correct values for all other words, for they all occur less than 7% of the time and, according to the rule, require fewer than 600 samples.* Of course, all these arguments depend on the assumption that our 600 puzzles are a representative sample of all puzzles.

*For cognoscenti, the normal approximation to the binomial distribution gives

$$.95 = P(\ |N(0,1)| < 1.96\ ) = P\left(\frac{|x/n-p|}{\sqrt{pq/n}} < \frac{.02}{\sqrt{pq/n}} \right)$$

where x is the number of times a word appears in n puzzles, p is the probability of it occuring in a puzzle, and q is the probability of it not occuring. With p=.08, q=.92,

$$n = (1.96)^2 \times .08 \times .92 / (.02)^2 = 707.$$

A

Clue	Answer
Aardvark meal	ANTS
Abacus	ADDER
Abadan's country	IRAN
Abandoned	LEFT
Abate	LETUP
Abba of Israel	EBAN
Abdul the Bulbul's rival	IVAN
Abele or teil	TREE
Abet	INCITE
Abhor	HATE
Ability	TALENT
Ablative, for one	CASE
Abner	LIL
Abner's creator	CAPP
Abode	AERIE
Abominates	HATES
Abounds	TEEMS
About	ANENT,AROUND
About the ear	OTIC
About, in Spain	POR
About: Prefix	PERI
About 3.7 quarts	OMER
About, Up and	ARISEN
Above	ATOP
Aboveboard	OVERT
Above: Ger.	UBER
Abrade	RUB
Abrasive	EMERY
Abridge	ELIDE
Abrupt	CURT
Abrupt change	LEAP
Abrupt flexure	GENU
Abscond	DECAMP,ELOPE
Absconded	RAN
Absinthe flavoring	ANISE
Absolute	UTTER
Absorbed	RAPT
Abstain	SHUN
Abstract being	ENS
Abstract beings	ENTIA
Abukir's river	NILE
Abundance	STORE
Abundant	RICH,RIFE
Acapulco residence	CASA
Acapulco wave	OLA
Accelerate	SPEED
Accentuate	STRESS
Accept a challenge	CALL
Access	ENTREE
Accesses	GATES
Accessory for a kimono	OBI
Accessory, Golf	TEE
Access to a mine	ADIT
Access to a plane	RAMP
Acclaim	HAIL
Accolade	KUDOS
Accompanying	ALONG
Accomplishes	DOES
Accomplishment	DEED
According to	ALA
Account	TALE
Account, Long	ILIAD
Account of a sort	EPIC
Accrue to	ENURE
Accurate	TRUE
Accustomed	USED
Accustom: Var.	ENURE
Ace	CARD,ONER
Ace of tennis	ASHE
Ach!	ALAS
Achaea's neighbor	ELIS
Aches	PINES
Achieved	GOT
Aching	SORE,URGE
Acid	AMINO
Acid salt	ESTER
Acknowledge	ADMIT,OWN
Aconcagua's range	ANDES
Acquired (with "by")	CAME
Act	MOVE
Act, Formal	RITE
Act in "East Lynne"	EMOTE
Action	STEP
Action at Aqueduct	BET
Action by police	RAID
Action, Put into	EXERT
Action, Suffix denoting	URE
Active person	DOER
Activity	EVENT
Activity, Coast Guard	RESCUE
Activity for Scouts	DEED
Act, of a sort	RIOT
Actor Alan	ALDA
Actor Beerbohm	TREE
Actor Burl	IVES
Actor Erwin	STU
Actor Ladd	ALAN
Actor Lloyd	NOLAN
Actor Paul	MUNI
Actor Richard	EGAN
Actor's big day	DEBUT
Actor Sellers	PETER
Actor's part	LINES
Actor Walter	ABEL
Act peevishly	CARP
Actress Adams	EDIE
Actress Bayes	NORA
Actress Berger	SENTA
Actress Foch	NINA
Actress Hagen	UTA
Actress Sommer	ELKE
Actress Stevens	INGER
Actress Terry	ELLEN
Acts	DEEDS
Actual	VERY
Actual being	ESSE
Adage	SAW
Adam, for one	MALE
Adams	EDIE
Adam's-apples' opposites	NAPES
Adam's grandson	ENOS
Adam's rib	EVE
Adam's son	ABEL
Add	TOT
Added frosting	ICED
Addict	USER
Add interest to	COLOR
Addison's forte	ESSAY
Additional	MORE
Addition and all	MATH
Additions for buildings	ELLS
Addition to Carmel or Juan	ITA
Additive for a cocktail	OLIVE
Addlebrains	ASSES
Addled	ASEA
Addresses	APOS
Address for a king	SIRE
Address to English queen	MAAM
Adds spirits	LACES
Adduce	CITE
Adherents: Suffix	ITES
Adhere to	ABIDE
Adjective ending	ENT,IAL,ULAR
Adjective, French	SES

Adjective suffix ICAL,ILE
Adjunct, Golfer's TEE
Adjust ADAPT,ALIGN,ALINE,TUNE
Adjust to ORIENT
Adjutants AIDES
Ad men's concerns MEDIA
Administered DEALT
Admiral kind REAR
Admit, with "up" OWN
Admonish WARN
Admonition NONO
Ado STIR
Ad offerings SALES
Adolescent TEEN
Ado or Orphant ANNIE
Adorn DRESS
Adriatic SEA
Adriatic port TRIESTE
Adriatic seaport BARI
Adriatic wind BORA
Adroit NEAT
Adult insect IMAGO
Advance GAIN,PROMOTE
Advance, In AHEAD
Advantage AVAIL,EDGE,ODDS,STEAD
Advantages USES
Adventurous RASH
Adversary ENEMY
Advertised event SALE
Advocate URGE
Aerie ROOST
Aeries NESTS
Aesop, for one SLAVE
Aesop's home SAMOS
Affable, Be AGREE
Affair of 1797 XYZ
Affair, Social TEA
Affectations AIRS
Affected, in a way ARTY
Affect feeling EMOTE
Affectionate name MOM
Affirm ASSERT
Affirmative YEA,YES
Affirmative, French OUI
Affirms AVERS
Afflict TRY
Afflicted SORE
Affliction, Eye STY
Afforded LENT
Affords LENDS
Affront SLAP
Afghanistan neighbor IRAN
A flat, for one TONE
Aforementioned SAID
African animal OKAPI,ZEBRA
African antelope ELAND,GNU
African cat CIVET
African city CAIRO
African country CHAD
African foxes ASSES
African grass ALFA
African language BANTU
African lily plant ALOE
African plant IXIA
African port ORAN
African province NATAL
African range ATLAS
African region SUDAN
African republic MALI
African river ORANGE,UELE
African town STAD
African tree COLA,KOLA
African tribesman IBO
After avril MAI
After fa SOL
After: Fr. APRES
After Matthew MARK
After pi RHO
After: Prefix META
After printemps ETE
After quatre CINQ
Aftersong EPODE
After uno and due TRE
Afterward LATER
After a while ANON
Again ANEW
Again, Showed RERAN
Against ANTI
Against, Vote NAY
Agalloch ALOES
Age AEON
Agency of the 1930's NRA
Agency, Soviet TASS
Agency, Wartime OSS
Agenda, for short SKED
Agenda unit ITEM
Agent DOER,SPY
Agent, Antitoxic SERUM
Agent, Pickling BRINE
Agents TMEN
Age, Of an ERAL
Ages ERAS
Ages ago YORE
Ages and ages EONS
Agile SPRY
Agitate ROIL,STIR
Agnew SPIRO
Agog EAGER
Agora money OBOL
Ago: Scot. SYNE
Agreeable NICE
Agreed ATONE
Agreeing with PRO
Agreement ACCORD
Agreement, In ATONE
Agreement kind ORAL
Agreement word AMEN
Agreements PACTS
Agrees to ASSENTS
Ahead of time EARLY
"Ah, me!" ALAS
"Aida" OPERA
Aida or Salome ROLE
Aid, Gardening HOE
Aid, Golfer's TEE
Aid, Navigator's LORAN
Aid's companion ABET
Aids, Filing-card TABS
Aid, Shopper's LIST
Ailment AGUE
Ailment, Swelling EDEMA
Aim, Deviates from ERRS
Aims ENDS
Air MIEN,TUNE
Aircraft and trust prefix ANTI
Air or sea route LANE
Air-pollution factor SMOG
Airport gear RADAR
Airport, Paris ORLY
Airport runway STRIP
Air: Prefix ATMO
Akin AGNATE
Akron output TIRE
Aladdin's friend GENIE
Alan LADD
Alarm PANIC,SCARE
Alaskan cape NOME
Alaskan find OIL
Alaskan Indian DENE
Alaskan island ATTU
Alaskan native ALEUT
Albee's field DRAMA
Albert of Tennessee GORE
Albert or Carnegie HALL
Albion's neighbor ERIN
Al Capp's Old Man Mose SEER

Clue	Answer
Ardor	ELAN,FIRE
Area, African	NATAL
Area, Bowling	LANE
Area, Hurricane	EYE
Area, Land	ASIA
Area, Neck	NAPE
Area of Africa	SUDAN
Area of Europe	SAAR
Area of France	MIDI
Area of Lago Maggiore	ALPS
Area of pollution	AIR
Area, River	DELTA
Areas in the Seine	ILES
Areas, Garden	BEDS
Areas, Golf	TEES
Area, Sports	ARENA
Areas, Tech	LABS
Area, Theater	LOGE
Area, Vaulted church	APSE
Arena	RING,RINK
Arena figure	TORO
Arena material	SAND
Arena sounds	OLES
Argentine dictator	PERON
Argentine tune	GATO
Argot	SLANG
Aria	SOLO,SONG
Arid	SERE
Aries	RAM
Arikara	REE
Arithmetic, Does	ADDS
Arithmetic word	PLUS
Arizona city	MESA
Arizona Indian	HOPI,PIMA
Arizona river	GILA
Arizona sight	CANYON
Ark groupings	TWOS
Ark weather	RAIN
Arles, Summers in	ETES
Armadillo	APAR
"Armageddon", Author of	URIS
Arm bones	ULNAE
Armed merchant ship	RAIDER
Armenian river	ARAS
Arm: Fr.	BRAS
Arm of Black Sea	AZOV
Armor	MAIL
Armor plate	TASSE
Army destinations	APOS
Army for a sheriff	POSSE
Army group	UNIT
Army meal	MESS
Army member	WAC
Army station	BASE
Arno city	PISA
Aroma	ODOR,SCENT
Aromatic ointment	NARD
Aromatic plant	ANISE,HERB
Arrange compactly	STOW
Arranged	SET
Arrangements	DEALS
Arranges	SORTS
Arrayed	CLAD,ROBED
Arrest	STEM
Arrested	HELD
Arrests	NABS
Arrive	COME
Arrived	CAME
Arrow poison	INEE
Arry's place	OME
Arsenal contents, for short	AMMO
Art colony center	TAOS
Artemis's victim	ORION
Artery	AORTA
Art figure	NUDE
Art form	THEATER
Artful	SLY
Art gallery	SALON
Arthritis aid	ACTH
Arthur Hailey title	HOTEL
Arthur of tennis	ASHE
Arthur's middle name	ALAN
Arthurian lady	ELAINE
Arthurian wife	ENID
Article	ITEM,THE
Article of clothing	STOLE
Article, in Arles	UNE
Artificial	ERSATZ
Artist's medium	OILS
Artless	NAIVE
Art movement	DADA
Art style	GENRE
Ascend	CLIMB,SCALE
Ascends	RISES
Ascertain	LEARN,SEE
Ascetic, Ancient	ESSENE
Aseptic	STERILE
As a friend, in Amiens	ENAMI
Ashe's specialty	ACES
Ash or elm	TREE
Asia Minor, Mountain in	IDA
Asia Minor region	IONIA
Asian	TAI,THAI
Asian, Ancient	MEDE
Asian animals	ONAGERS
Asian border river	AMUR
Asian capital	HANOI,SEOUL
Asian deer	ROE
Asian evergreen	UPAS
Asian fiber	RAMIE
Asian finch	MORO
Asian garment	SARI
Asian holiday	TET
Asian land	INDIA,IRAN,JAPAN,LAOS
Asian land: Prefix	INDO
Asian land: Var.	IRAK
Asian locale	KOREA
Asian monk	LAMA
Asian ox	ANOA
Asian palm	ARECA,BETEL
Asian prefix	SINO
Asian range	ALAI,URAL
Asian river	ILI
Asian sea	ARAL
Asian shrub	THEA
Asian shrubs	TEAS
Asian V.I.P.	AMEER
Asian weight	TAEL
Aside	APART
Aside, Put	STORE
Ask earnestly	CRAVE
Askew	AGEE,ALOP
Asks for	BEGS
Asp.	URAEUS
Asparagus tidbit	SPEAR
Aspect	AURA,FACET,PHASE
Asperity	IRE
Aspiration	AIM
Aspire to	HOPE
Assam silkworm	ERIA
Assayer's concern	ORE
Assegai or trident	SPEAR
Assemble	MASS,MEET
Assembly room	HALL
Assent	AMEN,NOD
Assent, in Paris	OUI
Assents	YESES
Assert	AVER,STATE
Asserts	SAYS
Assets for no-trump	ACES
Assign	ALLOT
Assignment	POST
Assist	ABET
Assistant	AIDE
Assists	AIDS
Associate	ALLY

Clue	Answer
Associate of Andy	AMOS
Assuage	EASE
Assume	DON
Astaire	ADELE
Asteroid	EROS
As to	ANENT,INRE
Astonish	AMAZE
Astray, Go	ERR
Astringent	ALUM
Astrologers	SEERS
Astrological sign	ARIES
As well	ALSO
At all	ANY,EVER
At ease	IDLE
Atelier man	ARTIST
Athens sight	AGORA
Athens's rival	SPARTA
Athirst	AVID,EAGER
Athlete in Hall of Fame	OTT
Athlete of L.A.	RAM
Athletic equipment	MAT
Athletic events	MEETS
Athletic field	OVAL
Athos and Porthos	AMIS
Atlanta man	BRAVE
Atlantic cape	ANN
Atlantic fish	OPAH
Atlantic game fish	CERO
Atlantic island group	FAROE
Atlantic nation	ICELAND
Atlas name	RAND
Atmosphere	AURA
Atmosphere: Prefix	AER
Atmospheric hybrid	SMOG
Atoll component	ISLE
Atomic prefix	ISO
Atoms, Charged	IONS
Atop	UPON
A to Z	GAMUT
Attachments	TIES
Attack	RAID
Attacks	ONSETS
Attack zealously	CRUSADE
Attains	GETS
Attempt	STAB
Attempted	ESSAYED
Attempts	TRIES
Attend	HEAR
Attend to	HEED
Attention	CARE,EAR
Attention, At	ERECT
Attention-getter	AHEM
Attention-getters	PSTS
Attestation	OATH
Attila	HUN
Attire	DRESS
Attired	CLAD,ROBED
Attract	DRAW
Attracted	DREW
Attraction, Zoo	SEALS
Attractive	CUTE
At variance with	AJAR
Au courant	UPON
Auction-bidders' moves	NODS
Auctioneer's word	SOLD
Audibly	ALOUD
Audience	EAR
Auditing word	LOSS
Auditioned	HEARD
Auditor's entry	ASSET
Auditory	OTIC
Augie's other nickname	GUS
Augur	SEER
Auguries	OMENS
Aunt: Fr.	TANTE
Auntie of fame	MAME
Aunt: Sp.	TIA
Aura, Angelic	HALO
Aureoles	HALOS
Auricle	EAR
Auricular	OTIC
Auriculate	EARED
Aurora	EOS
Austen heroine	EMMA
Austere	STERN
Australian city	PERTH
Australian native, for short	ABO
Austrian town	ENNS
Authentic	REAL,TRUE
Authenticate	SEAL
Author, American Pulitzer	AGEE
Author, British	AMIS
Author Carmer	CARL
Author Deighton	LEN
Author: 1823-92, French	RENAN
Author, Fabled	AESOP
Author, First name for an	ERLE
Authoritative statements	DICTA
Authorize	CLEAR
Author linked with roast pig	ELIA
Author of "Mildred Pierce"	CAIN
Author of "Pygmalion"	SHAW
Author of "Topaz"	URIS
Author of sayings	MAO
Author Paton	ALAN
Author, Prolific	ANON
Author, U.S.	OHARA,POE
Author Vidal	GORE
Autocrat	TSAR
Auto, Early	REO
Auto gear	DRIVE
Autograph	SIGN
Automotive pioneer	OLDS
Auto need	OIL
Autonomous	SEPARATE
Auto outings	SPINS
Auto part	AXLE,TIRE
Auto that was	EDSEL
Autumn pear	BOSC
Avail	USE
Available	ONTAP
Average	NORM,SOSO
Aves	STS
Avid	EAGER
Avidity	GREED
Avoid	ELUDE,MISS,SHUN
Avoid wedding expenses	ELOPE
Awake	ALERT
Awaken, country style	ROUST
Award	MEDAL,OSCAR
Award, Theater	TONY
Aware of	ONTO
Away	OUT
Away, Eat	ERODE
Away from the wind	ALEE
Away, Run	FLEE
Away, Store	STASH
Awkward	INEPT
Awkward craft	ARKS
Awkward spot	HOLE
Awry	AGEE
Ax, Chop with an	HEW
Axe	TOOL
Azov, for one	SEA

B

Clue	Answer
Baba	ALI
Babbles	PRATES
Babe Ruth, once	ORIOLE
Baboon	APE
Baby carriage	PRAM
Babylonian god	ANU,BEL

Clue	Answer
Bacchanalian cry	EVOE
Bacchante	MAENAD
Back	FRO
Back-comb hair	TEASE
Backed	AIDED
Backers of 21st Amendment	WETS
Back, in France	DOS
Backslide	LAPSE
Back talk	SASS
Back up	ABET
Bacon order	CRISP
Bad	EVIL
Bad actors	HAMS
Baden or Evian	SPA
Badger	BAIT
Badgers	PESTERS
Badger's relative	OTTER
Badly	ILL
Bad: Prefix	DYS,MAL
Baffle	EVADE,STUMP
Bag attachment	STRAP
Bagel's partner	LOX
Baghdad's republic	IRAQ
Bagnold	ENID
Bags, Certain	TOTES
Bail	LADE
Bailiwick	AREA
Baits	LURES
Baker	OVEN
Baker's need	SIEVE
Baker Street word	ELEMENTARY
Bakery aid	ICER
Bakery item	BUN
Bakery items	PIES
Bakery work, Did	ICED
Baking ingredient	YEAST
Balanced	EVEN,LEVEL
Balanced, More	SANER
Balcony	LOGE
Balks, equine style	REARS
Ball club	METS
Ball or biscuit	TEA
Ball team	REDS
Ballads	LAYS
Ballerina's garb	TUTU
Ballet maneuver	SPIN
Balloon ingredient	GAS
Balmoral Castle's river	DEE
Baloney!	BOSH
Baltic gulf	RIGA
Baltic native	LETT
Baltic port	RIGA
Baltimorean	ORIOLE
Baltimore player	COLT
Bambi	DEER
Bancroft	ANNE
Band, Heraldic	ORLE
Band instrument	SAX,TUBA
Bandit brothers	JAMES
Band, Leather	STROP
Bandman Shaw	ARTIE
Band, Vestment	MANIPLE
Band, Waist	OBI
Bandy words	SPAR
Bangkok money	BAHT
Banish	EXILE,EXPEL
Bank customer	SAVER
Banker Kahn	OTTO
Bank fixture	SAFE
Bank job, Does a	LENDS
Bank on	RELY
Bankroll	WAD
Bankruptcy	RUIN
Bank worker	TELLER
Banned	TABU
Banner	FLAG
Banner maker	ROSS
Banquet	FEAST
Banquet man	EMCEE
Baptista's home	PADUA
Bar	SHUT
Bar figure	CLEF
Bar fruit	LIME
Bar I.O.U.	TAB
Bar order	ALE
Bar staple	OLIVE
Barbecue item	SPIT
Barbecue spot	PATIO
Barber's need	STROP
Barber's summons	NEXT
Barbershop chore	SHAVE
Barbershop item	RAZOR,TALC
Bard's nightfall	EEN
Bare	MERE
Barely	ONLY
Bare place on mountainside	SCAR
Bargain	DEAL
Bari, Money in	LIRE
Bark	YAP,YELP
Bark cloth	TAPA
Barley beards	AWNS
Barnacles and graylags	GEESE
Barnard concern	HEART
Barney of ring fame	ROSS
Barn or screech	OWL
Barnum's egress	EXIT
Barnyard areas	ROOSTS
Barnyard resident	HEN
Barnyard sound	MAA,MOO
Barnyard sounds	BAAS
Barometer	GLASS
Baronet's wife	DAME
Barrel	KEG
Barrelhead commodity	CASH
Barrel staves	LAGS
Barren	ARID,STERILE
Barriers	RAILS
Barrymore forbear	DREW
Bartender's need	ICE
Barter	TRADE
Barters	SWAPS
Barton	CLARA
Baseball brothers	ALOU
Baseball call	SAFE
Baseball deal	TRADE
Baseball gear	BAT
Baseball great	MAYS
Baseball hit	LINER
Baseball home	PLATE
Baseball statistic	ERROR
Baseball team	METS,NATS,NINE
Baseball term	ATBAT,OUT
Baseball thrill	HOMER
Baseball's Hank	AARON
Baseball's Man	STAN
Baseball's Pee Wee	REESE
Basement reading matter	METER
Base of some taxes	SALES
Bash	SWAT
Bashful	COY
Basic	ELEMENTARY
Basic part	CORE
Basic principles	ABCS
Basic thing	UNIT
Basis for a Scout badge	MERIT
Basketball-goal part	RIM
Basketball loop	CAGE
Basks	SUNS
Basra's country	IRAK
Bastes	SEWS
Batch	LOT
Bathe	LAVE
Bathing-suit parts	BRAS
Bathroom worker	TILER
Baths	SPAS
Bathsheba's husband	URIAH

Clue	Answer
Bath's river	AVON
Baton Rouge campus	LSU
Bator's partner	ULAN
Battery, Kind of	SOLAR
Battery pole	ANODE
Batting champ in 1964-5, A.L.	OLIVA
Batting-practice structure	CAGE
Battleground in France	STLO
"Battle Hymn" composer	HOWE
Battle site in 1776	TRENTON
Baubles	TOYS
Bauxite	ORE
Beach	SAND
Beach or bath	TOWEL
Beach sight	SURF
Beam	LASER,RAY
Beam of a certain shape	TBAR
Bean	LIMA,SOY
Beanery sign	EATS
Beanie	LID
Bean or dragon	SNAP
Bear	STAND,URSA
Bearcat	PANDA
Bearing	MIEN,POISE
Bearish time	SAG
Beast	ASS
Beasts of burden	OXEN
Beast, Woolly	LLAMA
Beat	PULSE
Beat it!	SCRAM
Beatle name	RINGO
Beatle's cry	HELP
Beatrice's friend	DANTE
Beautiful woman	HOURI
Beauty or charm	ASSET
Beauty parlor	SALON
Beauty-parlor job	WAVE
Because: Fr.	CAR
Bechamel, for one	SAUCE
Becloud	ROIL
Become active	ARISE
Become blurred	MIST
Become bored	TIRE
Become crusty	CAKE
Become fixed	ROOT
Become listless	MOPE
Become ready	RIPEN
Becomes dim	PALES
Become sunk in	BOG
Becomes weary	JADES
Bede	ADAM
Bedevil	HARASS
Bed frame	STEAD
Bed, in Paris	LIT
Bedouin	ARAB
Bedouin headband cord	AGAL
Bedouins' home	SAHARA
Beehive	SKEP
Bee: Prefix	API
Beer	BREW,SUDS
Beer container	KEG
Beer feature	FOAM
Beetle	DOR
Before	ERE,UNTIL
Before Columbia	HAIL
Before down	HOE
Before la	TRA
Before: Lat.	ANTE
Before one or body	ANY
Before: Prefix	PRE
Before twa	ANE
Before, verse style	ERE
Befriend	AID
Befuddle	ADDLE
Befuddled	ASEA
Beget	SIRE
Beginner	TIRO
Beginning	SEED

Clue	Answer
Beginning of a fairy tale	ONCE
Beginnings	ONSETS,ROOTS
Begins	OPENS
Begin to wake up	STIR
Begley and Sullivan	EDS
Begrudge	ENVY
Behave	ACT
Behind	AFTER
Behind the times	PASSE
Behold	ESPY,SEE
Behold!	ECCE
Beholden to, Be	OWE
Beige	ECRU
Be "in"	RATE
Being, Heavenly: Fr.	ANGE
Being, in Bordeaux	ETRE
Being: Lat.	ESSE
Being: Sp.	ENTE
Beldame	CRONE
Belem's other name	PARA
Belgian river	LYS,YSER
Belgrade name	TITO
Belief	CREDO
Beliefs	TENETS
Believe, old style	OPINE
Believer, Certain	DEIST
Belligerents	ENEMIES
Bell song	ARIA
Bell sound	RING,TING
Bell town	ADANO
Bellum prefix	ANTE
Belmont entry	MARE
Belmont transaction	BET
Beloved	DEAR
Below	UNDER
Belt	STRAP
Bemused	ATSEA
Ben Adhem	ABOU
Bench: Fr.	BANC
Benchwarmers	SUBS
Bend down	STOOP
Bends the elbow	TOPES
Beneath contempt	LOW
Benefit	AVAIL
Ben Jonson's plague	GOUT
Benumb	STUN
Ben William's middle name	AMES
Benzell	MIMI
Be off!	SCAT
Berg	FLOE
Berlin avenue	ALLEE
Berlin bonnet	EASTER
Berliner	HERR
Berliner's upper	OBER
Berlin housewife	FRAU
Berlin's forte	TUNE
Berlin sight	WALL
Bern's river	AAR,AARE
Bernadette and Jeanne	STES
Beseech	PRAY
Beset	ASSAIL,HARASS,TRY
Besets	PESTERS
Besides	ALSO,AND,ELSE,THEN
Best, Be	STAR
Best man's burden	RING
Best part	CREAM
Betelguese or Rigel	STAR
Betel palm	ARECA
Betimes	EARLY
Betrothal notice	BANNS
Bets	ANTES
Bets at dice	FADES
Betsy	ROSS
Better than never	LATE
Bettor's concern	ODDS
Between A.M. and P.M.	NOON
Between chicken and king	ALA
Between: Fr.	ENTRE

Between little and least LESS
Between once and a UPON
Between: Prefix INTER
Between ready and fire AIM
Beverage
ADE,ALE,BEER,CIDER,NOG,SODA,TEA
Beverage, in Lyons THE
Beverage nut COLA
Bewail MOAN
Bewilder STUN
Bewildered ASEA,ATSEA
Bex and Dax SPAS
Beyond PAST
Bible book PSALMS
Bible division VERSE
Biblical ancestor LEVI
Biblical animal lover NOAH
Biblical book ACTS
Biblical brother CAIN
Biblical character ARAN,ESAU
Biblical country ELAM
Biblical judge ELON
Biblical king AMON
Biblical kingdom MOAB
Biblical land NOD
Biblical measure OMER
Biblical mountain ARARAT
Biblical name
ADAM,ENOS,ERI,NER,OREN,SETH
Biblical preposition UNTO
Biblical priest ELI
Biblical pronoun THEE
Biblical symbol of power HORN
Biblical Syria ARAM
Biblical title ABBA
Biblical transit ARK
Biblical tribe LEVI
Biblical twin ESAU
Biblical underdog DAVID
Biblical verb ending ETH
Biblical victim ABEL
Biblical wall word MENE
Biblical weed TARE
Biblical well AIN
Biblical wife ESTHER
Biblical wise men MAGI
Biblical woman ADAH
Biblical word BEGAT
Bid for WOO
Bids, Manipulate RIG
Big bargain: Colloq. STEAL
Big bird EMU,RHEA,STORK
Big casino TEN
Big game ELKS
Big hit HOMER
Big-mouthed vessel EWER
Big name in Belgrade TITO
Bigoted NARROW
Big shot VIP
Big Ten member IOWA
Big Top TENT
Bigwig VIP
Bikini, for one ATOLL
Bikini part BRA
Bill DOLLAR,NOTE
Billboard SIGN
Billiard cushion BANK
Billiard stroke MASSE
Billing, Lead the STAR
Bill of fare MENU
Bill, Part of parrot's CERE
Bills ONES,TABS
Bills, Certain TENS
Bill's companion COO
Bill, Word on a REMIT
Billycocks HATS
Billy of show biz ROSE
Bin CRIB
Bind tightly, asea FRAP
Binet-Simon, for one TEST
Biography LIFE
Biologist's concern GENE
Birchbark CANOE
Birch of Indiana BAYH
Bird KITE,ORIOLE
Bird, Black ANI
Bird feature CRAW
Bird known for straight flight CROW
Bird: Lat. AVIS
Birdlike AVIAN
Bird, Marsh SORA
Bird of ballet SWAN
Bird of legend ROC
Bird on a quarter EAGLE
Bird, Plumed EGRET
Birds OWLS
Bird's abode AERIE
Bird's bill, Part of a CERE
Bird, Sea TERN
Birds in general AVES
Birds in the news DOVES
Bird sound COO,TRILL
Birds, Sea ERNES,ERNS
Birds, Silly GEESE
Birds, Wading RAILS
Bird, Wading HERON
Bird weapon CLAW
Birth-certificate item AGE
Birthplace of Eng and Chang SIAM
Bishopric SEE
Bishop's headdress MITER
Bit AUGER,IOTA
Bite, Had a ATE
Biting ACID,TART
Bit of poetry VERSE
Bit of time SPELL
Bit, Opera ARIA
Bits, Collect by GLEAN
Bitter brew ALE
Bitter drugs ALOES
Bivouac CAMP
Bizarre ODD,OUTRE
Bizet work OPERA
Blab TELL
Blabbermouth SIEVE
Blab to the D.A. SING
Black EBON,INKY
Blackbird OUSEL
Blackbirds ANIS,DAWS
Blackbirds' milieu PIE
Blackboard needs ERASERS
Black card SPADE
Black cat, for one OMEN
Blackens INKS
Black: Fr. NOIR
Black goldfish MOOR
Black Hawk's tribe SACS
Black, in Siena NERO
Blackjack player's word HIT
Black lacquer JAPAN
Blackmore girl LORNA
Blackmore heroine DOONE
Black one is best BELT
Black or Arrow SMITH
Black or White SEA
Black stuff SOOT
Blackthorn SLOE
Blacktops TARS
Blanc and neighbors ALPS
Blast TOOT
Blaster's need TNT
Blaze FLAME
Blazing AFIRE
Blazing light GLARE
Bleat BAA
Blind part SLAT

Clue	Answer
Bliss	PARADISE
Blithering one	IDIOT
Blithesome	GLAD
Bloated	OBESE
Blockhead	ASS,DOLT
Bloke	CHAP
Blond	FAIR
Blood ailment	ANEMIA
Bloodhound's forte	SCENT
Blood part	PLASMA
Blood: Prefix	HEMO
Blood vessel	AORTA
Blot	ABSORB
Blow	SLAP
Blow, Military	RAID
Blow one's horn	BRAG
Blue	NAVY
Blue flag	IRIS
Blue grass	POA
Blue-nose	PRIG
Blue or green shade	BICE
Blue or White	NILE
Blue-pencils	EDITS
Blueprint	PLAN
Blue Ridge sight	PINE
Blue shade	OPAL
Blunderbore	OGRE
Blunders	ERRS
Blunt	BALD,CURT
Board, Cleans the	ERASES
Board created in 1933	TVA
Boarding device	RAMP
Board's companion	BED
Boast	CROW
Boaster	BRAG
Boat	CANOE
Boat accessory	OAR
Boat feature	KEEL
Boating hazard	SNAG
Boating term	ALEE
Boat, Malayan	PROA
Boatswain's gear	PIPE
Bobbin	REEL
Bobby and safety	PINS
Bobby Orr's milieu	RINK
Bob of "The Rivals"	ACRES
Bock, for one	BEER
Bodily vigor	TONE
Body	TORSO
Body fluids	SERA
Body of principles	ETHIC
Body of water	POND
Body politic	STATE
Body politic, in France	ETAT
Body powder	TALC
Body style	SEDAN
Bog	MORASS
Bog down	MIRE
Boggy land	FEN
Bogus	SHAM
Bohea	TEA
Bohemian	ARTY
Bohemian river	ISER
Boisterous	AROAR
Boleyn	ANNE
Bolt's complement	NUT
Bombast	RANT
"Bonanza" figure	HOSS
Bond	KNOT,TIE
Bond et al.	AGENTS
Bondman	SERF
Bone, Arm	ULNA
Bone: Prefix	OSTE
Bones	OSSA
Bones, Feel in one's	SENSE
Bones, Hip	ILIA
Bonheur	ROSA
Bonneville Flats state	UTAH

Clue	Answer
Boobs	SAPS
Boodle	LOOT
Book binder	LACER
Bookbinding material	SIZE
Book, Church	ORDO
Book for an eleve	LIVRE
Book holders	ENDS
Bookies' entries	BETS
Bookmaker's concern	ODDS
Bookmark for some	DOGEAR
Book, Nabokov	ADA
Book of Bible	ESTHER
Book of O.T.	AMOS
Book of the Bible	ACTS
Books, Writer of boys'	ALGER
Boom	SPAR
Boone or O'Brien	PAT
Boor	CLOD,LOUT
Boorish	CRASS,RUDE
Booth	LOGE
Booty	SWAG
Booty, Hide	STASH
Bordeaux seasons	ETES
Border	RIM
Border in heraldry	ORLE
Border lake	ONTARIO
Border: Lat.	ORA
Border on	ABUT
Border river of Asia	AMUR
Borders	EDGES
Bored	BLASE
Bore out	REAM
Borer	AUGER
Bore, Tidal	EAGRE
Borge or Anderson	DANE
Boring tool	AUGER
Born	NEE
Borscht ingredient	BEET
Bosh!	ROT
Bosom bauble	STUD
Boss of a feudal manor	REEVE
Bot	STAIN
Botanist Gray	ASA
Botch	MESS
Bothers	AILS
Bothers: Colloq.	EATS
Bottleneck	JAM
Bottomless pit	ABYSS
Bounce	DASH,ELAN
Boundary	END
Bounder	CAD
Bouquet	AROMA,ODOR
Bourbon St. Feature	CAFE
Bovine name	ELSIE
Bovines	OXEN
Bovine's booth	CRIB
Bow expert	TELL
Bower	ARBOR
Bowlers' milieu	LANES
Bowler's place	ALLEY
Bowling number	TEN
Bowling term	RESET
Bows	ARCS
Bowsprit angle	STEEVE
Box	LOGE
Boxed	CASED
Boxer	DOG
Boxes	SPARS
Boxing maneuvers	JABS
Boxoffice quest	SEAT
Boys	LADS,MALES
Boy Scout founder	BEARD
Boy's name	EMIL,OREN
Boy's pistol fodder	CAPS
B.P.O.E.	ELKS
Brace	PAIR,STAY
Braces	TWOS
Bracing	CRISP

Clue	Answer
Brad	NAIL
Bradley	OMAR
Brahman, for one	CASTE
Braid	PLAT
Brain passage	ITER
Brainstorm	IDEA
Brake	SLOW
Brake part	SHOE
Branch angle	AXIL
Branches	ARMS,RAMI
Branch of math	TRIG
Brand	SEAR
Brand of fig	ELEMI
Brants	GEESE
Brass, for one	ALLOY
Brass member	TUBA
Bravo or Grande	RIO
Bravos	OLES
Brazilian macaws	ARAS
Brazilian palm	ASSAI
Brazilian port	NATAL
Brazilian state	ACRE
Breach	RENT
Breaches of the peace	RIOTS
Bread, Crisp	RUSK
Breaded: Fr.	PANE
Bread necessity	YEAST
Bread roll	BUN
Breadwinners	PAPAS
Break bread	DINE
Break a commandment	SIN
Break down a sentence	PARSE
Breakfast fare	CEREAL
Breakfast item	EGG,OMELET
Break off	CEASE
Break out	ERUPT
Break suddenly	SNAP
Breakwaters	MOLES
Breathe heavily	PANT
Breathe life into	RENEW
Breather	REST
Breathing sound	SNORE
Breath strengthener	ONION
Bred	REARED
Breed of hog	DUROC
Breed's or Bunker	HILL
Breezy	AIRY
Brew	BEER,STEEP
Brewer's need	MALT
Brews	ALES
Bribe	SOP
Bricklayer's need	HOD
Bridal word	NEE
Bride, Take a	ELOPE
Bridewise, Born	NEE
Bridge	SPAN
Bridge bid	SLAM
Bridge call	BID,PASS,RAISE
Bridge card	HONOR
Bridge contestants	PAIRS
Bridge contract	SLAM
Bridge groups	FOURS
Bridge kind	LOW
Bridge positions	EASTS
Bridge seat	WEST
Bridge term	SET
Bridle part	REIN
Brief	TERSE
Brief attempt	STAB
Brigham Young's destination	UTAH
Bright	STELLAR
Brightened	LIT
Brightening star	NOVA
Brightest point	NOON
Bright light	NEON
Brightly colored fish	OPAH
Bright saying	MOT
Brilliance	ECLAT
Brilliant	GEM,STELLAR
Brim	LIP
Brim over	TEEM
Bring into existence	CREATE
Brings under control	TAMES
Brings up	REARS
Bring to bay	TREE
Bring together	AMASS,UNITE
Bring to light	BARE
Bring to perfection	RIPEN
Bring to ruin	UNDO
Bring up-to-date	RENEW
Brinker	HANS
Brisk	ALERT
Bristle	AWN,SETA
Bristles	SETAE
Britain, for one	ISLE
British bar	PUB
British composer	ARNE
British court wear	WIG
Britisher	SCOT
Britisher's sovereign	QUID
British essayist	LAMB
British lockup	GAOL
British Navy girl	WREN
British noble	PEER
British novelist	AMIS,READE
British ordnance	STEN
British party	TORY
British P.M.	EDEN
British queen	ANNE
British sand hill	DENE
British school	ETON
British statesman	PEEL
British symbol	LION
British title	EARL
British trolley	TRAM
Broadcast	STREW
Broadcasts	AIRS
Broadway award	TONY
Broadway hit, informally	SMASH
Broadway musical	MAME
Broadway offering	DRAMA,REVUE
Broadway role	ABIE
Broadway's Alan	ALDA
Broadway signs	SROS
Brogan	SHOE
Broke bread	ATE
Broken tooth	SNAG
Broker's advice	SELL
Broke a traffic law	SPED
Bronc	HOSS
Bronx or East	RIVER
Bronze	AES
Bronze and golden	AGES
Bronze, for one	ALLOY
Bronzes	TANS
Bronze Star	MEDAL
Brood	MOPE
Brood of pheasants	NIDE
Brook	RILL
Brother, Biblical	ABEL
Brother of Jacob	ESAU
Brother of Moses	AARON
Brothers	MEN
Brought into line	TAMED
Brought to court	SUED
Brought up	REARED
Brouhaha	MELEE,TODO
Brown	TAN
Brown dye tree	IPIL
Browning device	TOASTER
Brown print	SEPIA
Brown quickly	SEAR
Bruckner or Chekhov	ANTON
Brusque	CURT
Brutal	FERAL
Brute	BEAST

Bryce or Chaco CANYON
Bryophyte MOSS
Buchwald ART
Buck DOLLAR,STAG
Buckeyes' home OHIO
Bucolic sound MOO
Buddenbrooks' creator MANN
Buddhist language PALI
Buddhist sacred mountain OMEI
Buddhist shrines TOPES
Buddy PAL
Buddy, out West PARD
Budget item RENT
Buffalo of India ARNEE
Buffalo's relative ANOA
Buffalo's waterfront ERIE
Bufo TOAD
Bug-eyed AGOG
Bugle call TAPS
Bugs GNATS
Builder of London churches WREN
Building beam IBAR
Building parts ELLS
Building pier ANTA
Building recess APSE
Building, Wing of ELL
Built MADE
Bulb LAMP,ONION
Bulbs for planting SETS
Bulb's relative SEED
Bulgar SLAV
Bulgarian coin LEV
Bulging jars OLLAS
Bulk MASS
Bulldog YALE
Bullfight-arena section SOL
Bullfight cry OLE
Bullish time RISE
Bullish times UPS
Bull-ring cries OLES
Bull: Sp. TORO
Bulrush TULE
Bumbling INEPT
Bumpkin LOUT,OAF
Bundled BALED
Bunker, for one HILL
Buoyant movement LILT
Burberry COAT
Burden LADE,LOAD,ONUS
Burden, Beasts of ASSES
Burl IVES,KNAR
Burma and others ROADS
Burn CHAR,SEAR
Burned out SERE
Burning AFIRE
Burns and others POETS
Burns, for one SCOT
Burr or brogue ACCENT
Burrow HOLE
Burrows ABE
Burst of energy BANG
Burst of laughter GALE
Burst of thunder CLAP
Business TRADE
Business end of a fork TINE
Business expense RENTAL
Business: Suffix ERY
Bus or potent prefix OMNI
Bus rider FARE
Bustle TODO
Bustles ADOS
Busy INUSE
Busy creatures BEES
Busy fellow ANT
Busy man on April 18, 1775 REVERE
Busy place HIVE
Butcher-shop item VEAL
Butt END
Butterfly SATYR
Button on a phone HOLD
Buttons et al. REDS
Button source NACRE
Butts RAMS
B'way group ANTA
By and by LATER
By any chance EVER
Bygone AGO,PAST
Bygone times YORE
By hand: Prefix MANU
Byron poem LARA
By: Sp. POR
Byway ALLEY,LANE
By word ORAL
Byzantine art work ICON
Byzantine empress IRENE

C

Cabal PLOT
Caballero's weapon BOLA
Cabbage KALE
Cabinet maker, for one ARTISAN
Cabinet wood EBONY,OAK
Cable LINE,ROPE
Cab, Took a RODE
Cache STORE
Caddoan Indian REE
Cadence BEAT
Cadiz cheer OLE
Caen's river ORNE
Caesar, for one SALAD
Caesar's bane IDES
Caesar's Behold ECCE
Caesar's words ETTU
Caesura REST
Cafe bill TAB
Cafe card MENU
Cafe patron EATER
Cafeteria gear TRAY
Caffeine-producing nut COLA
Cake TORTE
Cake base BATTER
Cakes' companion ALE
Cakes, Tea SCONES
Cake unit LAYER
Calaboose STIR
Calais cup TASSE
Calamus REED
Calcutta had one HOLE
Calendar, Church ORDO
California base ORD
California city LODI
California grape center NAPA
Calif. sea specialty ABALONE
Calif. town IONE
Calif. valley NAPA
Caliph ALI,IMAM
Caliph's name OMAR
Call HAIL
Calla lily ARUM
Call, Barber's NEXT
Called RANG
Called it a day ENDED
Callers GUESTS
Call for ASK
Call for attention AHEM
Call, Golf FORE
Calling CAREER
Call a number DIAL
Call of sorts SOS
Calloway CAB
Call, Phone RING

Clue	Answer
Calls, Ump's	OUTS
Call to Fido	HERE
Call, Ump's	SAFE
Call up	EVOKE
Calor	HEAT
Calorie project	DIET
Cambodian or Chinese	ASIAN
Cambridge tutor	DON
Came down	ALIT
Came into play	AROSE
Camel's cousin	LLAMA
Camel's-hair robe	ABA
Cameo stone	ONYX
Camera part	LENS
Came secretly, with "in"	STOLE
Came to rest	ALIT
Came up	AROSE
Campbell or Cove	GLEN
Campbells, for one	CLAN
Campers' aids	AXES
Camper's gear	COT
Camper's home	TENT
Camp item	TENT
Campus ordeal	EXAM
Campus vine	IVY
Campus, Western	UCLA
Canadian Indian	CREE
Canal	ERIE
Canape item	ROE
Canary food	SEED
Cancel	UNDO
Cancel, as a space launch	SCRUB
Candy	SWEET
Canea's island	CRETE
Canny man	SCOT
Canoe, Malaysian	PROA
Canonical hours	NONES
Canopus, e.g.	STAR
Cans	TINS
Cant	LIST
Cantaloupe	MELON
Canticle	ODE
Cantina fare	TACO
Canton of the Jungfrau	BERNE
Cants	LEANS
Canvas canopy	TILT
Canvas holder	EASEL
Canzone	SONG
Cap	BERET,TAM
Capability: Suffix	ILE
Capable	UPTO
Capable, More	ABLER
Capacious	LARGE
Cape	COD,NESS
Cape Horn natives	ONAS
Cape near Boston	ANN
Cape, Papal	ORALE
Caper	ANTIC,DANCE
Cape Verde island	SAL
Capital city	OSLO
Capital, Moroccan	RABAT
Capital of Italia	ROMA
Capital of Manche	STLO
Capital of the Ukraine	KIEV
Capital of Western Samoa	APIA
Capital of Yemen	SANA
Capitol Hill frequenter	SENATOR
Capitol Hill output	LAWS
Capone feature	SCAR
Capote	COAT
Capp creation	ABNER
Capricorn	GOAT
Capri or Wight	ISLE
Capri's neighbor	ITALY
Capri, to Spaniards	ISLA
Caps	TAMS
Capsule	PILL
Captain of fiction	NEMO
Captain of the Pequod	AHAB
Captive of Hercules	IOLE
Car	SEDAN
Caravansaries	INNS
Caravansary	SERAI
Card	SPADE
Card, as wool	TEASE
Card, Certain	SPADE
Card game	SKAT
Card, Honor	ACE
Cardiff citizens	WELSH
Card, Mystic	TAROT
Card round	DEAL
Cards	ACES
Careen	LIST
Care, Freedom from	EASE
Carefully move	EASE
Carefully study	PORE
Careless	LAX
Cargo	LOAD
Caribbean	SEA
Car, Mine	TRAM
Carnegie	DALE
Carney and Buchwald	ARTS
Carnival attractions	RIDES
Carob	TREE
Car of the '20s	REO
Carol	NOEL
Caroline island	YAP
Carousal	ORGY,SPREE
Carouse	REVEL
Carp	CAVIL
Car part	AXLE,TANK
Carping remark	BARB
Carriage	MIEN,PRAM
Carriers of water	HOSES
Carroll or Josephine	BAKER
Carry burdens	BEAR
Carry the football	RUSH
Carry on	RANT,RAVE
Carson	KIT
Carson's predecessor	PAAR
Cartographer's concern	MAP,SCALE
Cartoon character	POGO
Cartoonist	ARNO,NAST
Cartoonist Al	CAPP
Cartwright	HOSS
Caruso, for one	TENOR
Carved gem	CAMEO
Casaba	MELON
Casa division	SALA
Cascade peak	BAKER
Casca's blow	STAB
Case, Small	ETUI
Cash in Turin	LIRAS
Casino furniture	TABLE
Cask	TUN
Caspian, Sea near	ARAL
Caspian tributary	URAL
Cassia shrub	SENNA
Cassini	OLEG
Cassio's slanderer	IAGO
Cast	THROW
Cast, Heads the	STARS
Castile	SOAP
Castle	IRENE
Castor and Pollux	STARS
Castor's mother	LEDA
Cat	CIVET
Catawba, for one	WINE
Catch	ENTRAP,TRAP
Catch in a slip	TRIP
Catch one's breath	GASP
Catch sight	ESPY
Catch sight of	SPOT
Catchy tune	LILT
Categorize	CLASS
Category	GENRE,KIND

Clue	Answer
Cater to	ATTEND
Cathedral city on the Ouse	ELY
Cathedral feature	APSE
Cathode's partner	ANODE
Catlike	FELINE
Cat's-paw	TOOL
Cat: Sp.	GATO
Cattail	REED
Cattle	STEERS
Caucasian	OSSET
Caucho trees	ULES
Caught up in	RAPT
Cauldron	VAT
Caused to go	SENT
Cause of yawn	BORE
Caustics	LYES
Caustic stuff	ACID
Caution	WARN
Cavalry weapon	SABRE
Caviar	ROE
Cayce or Poe	EDGAR
Cayuse	HOSS
Ceaseless	ETERNAL
Cede	GRANT
Cede or date prefix	ANTE
Celebrated	FETED
Celebration	FETE
Celebrations	GALAS
Celebrity	LION
Celeste	HOLM
Celestial being: Fr.	ANGE
Celestial bodies	SUNS
Celestial handle	ANSA
Cells, Egg	OVA
Celt	ERSE,GAEL
Celtic sea god	LER
Censure (with "with")	TAX
Centavo's senior	PESO
Center	CORE
Centerboard	KEEL
Center for health	SPA
Center for trade	MART
Center of activity	HEART
Center of worship	ALTAR
Centers of storms	EYES
Central American Indian	RAMA
Central American tree	EBO,EBOE
Central European river	AAR
Central Florida city	OCALA
Central point	NODE
Central state	IOWA
Centuries	AGES
Century plant	ALOE
Ceramic material	FRIT
Cereal	BRAN,OAT,OATS
Cereal bristles	AWNS
Cereal grasses	RYES
Cereal plant disease	ERGOT
Ceremonial	RITE
Ceremonial staff	MACE
Ceremonial word	OBEY
Ceremonial words	IDO
Ceremonies	RITES
Certain intervals, At	HORAL
Certain node	ADAMSAPPLE
Certain noise	SNORE
Certain word	NOUN
Cetaceans	ORCS
Ceylon sandstone	PAAR
Cha	TEA
Chaff of grain	BRAN
Chagall	MARC
Chagrin	SHAME
Chair back	SPLAT
Chairman's call	ORDER
Chairman's concern	AGENDA
Chairman's place	DAIS
Chair stuffing	HAIR

Clue	Answer
Chalcedony	SARD
Chalcopyrites	ORES
Chalice	GRAIL
Chalk's partner	ERASER
Chalky mineral	TALC
Challenged	DARED
Chamber, Harem	ODA
Champs of 1969	METS
Chance	RISK
Chaney	LON
Change	ALTER,DIMES,REDO
Change from a yen	SEN
Channel	DRAIN
Channel, Brain	ITER
Channels	GATS
Chaotic, as type	PIED
Chaplain	PADRE
Chaplin	OONA
Chaps	LADS
Character	TONE
Character, Dickens	HEEP,NELL
Character, Dogpatch	ABNER
Character, "Exodus"	ARI
Character, Genesis	ESAU
Character, Ibsen	NORA
Character in "Ivanhoe"	ROWENA
Character in "Lear"	FOOL
Character in "Quo Vadis"	NERO
Character in "Ring" operas	WOTAN
Character, Irving	RIP
Characteristic	TRAIT
Characterization	ROLE
Characterless	INANE
Character, Melville	AHAB,OMOO
Character, Nabokov	ADA
Character, Nichols	ABIE
Character, Novel	NANA
Character, Opera	TOSCA
Character, "Peer Gynt"	ASE
Character, Racetrack	TOUT
Character, Shakespeare	IAGO
Character, Shakespearean	LEAR
Character, Verne	NEMO
Character, Wagner	SENTA
Character, "Zhivago"	LARA
Charge	ONSET
Charged particles	IONS
Charges	RATES
Charge with gas	AERATE
Chariot route	ITER
Charity	ALMS
Charity effort	DRIVE
Charles or George	LAKE
Charleston campus	CITADEL
Charming or Valiant	PRINCE
Charon's purlieu	STYX
Charter	HIRE
Charybdis feature	EDDY
Chase, as flies	SHAG
Chaser	SODA
Chasm	ABYSS
Chastise in a way	CANE
Chat	COZE
Chateaubriand title	RENE
Chateau room	SALLE
Chatter	CHIN,YAP
Chatters	PRATES
Chaw	QUID
Cheap cigar	ROPE
Check	REIN,STAY,STEM
Check, Restaurant	TAB
Check sharply	NIP
Cheer	ELATE,RAH
Cheer, Arena	OLE
Cheer finale	TIGER
Cheerful: Fr.	GAI
Cheerful tune	LILT
Cheerless	DREAR

Cheers RAHS,ROOTS
Cheese BRIE
Cheesecake LEG
Cheese covering RIND
Cheese-eaters MICE
Cheese, Like some AGED
Cheese residue SERUM
Cheeses EDAMS
Chef's concern MENU,SAUCE
Chela CLAW
Chemical ending ENOL
Chemical endings INES
Chemical prefix AMID
Chemical suffix ASE,OLE,OSE
Chemical suffixes ATES,ENES,IDES
Chemicals ESTERS
Chemist's vessel VIAL
Chem. suffixes ANES
Cherished DEAR
Cherry and ruby REDS
Cherub AMOR
Chess-game ending DRAW
Chess piece KING,ROOK
Chess pieces MEN
Chest ARCA
Chesterfield SOFA
Chevalier song MIMI
Chew EAT
Chewer EATER
Chew on GNAW
Chianti country ITALY
Chicago airport OHARE
Chicago team BEARS
Chicago-New Orleans product JAZZ
Chic end of London WEST
Chick GAL
Chicken bone WISH
Chicken, for one BIPED
Chicken-out word SHOO
Chided RATED
Chief ARCH
Chihuahua DOG
Child BABE,TOT
Child, at times BRAT
Child in painting AMOR
"Child of the sun" INCA
Children's game TAG
Children's poet MOORE
Children's zoo favorite LLAMA
Chilean cape HORN
Chilean export NITER
Chill AGUE,ICE,NIP
Chimed RANG
Chimney lining SOOT
Chimps APES
Chinese dynasty HAN,HSIA,MING,TANG
Chinese great MAO
Chinese peak OMEI
Chinese: Prefix SINO
Chinese tea CHA
Chinese weight LAN,TAEL
Chip FLAKE
Chipped in GAVE
Chit of a sort IOU
Chkalov's river URAL
Choice ELITE
Choler IRE
Choleric IRATE
Choose ELECT
Chooses OPTS
Choosy eater SPRAT
Chop down FELL
Chopin work OPUS
Chop off LOP
Chopped HEWED
Choppers AXES
Chop up MINCE
Choral compositions CANTATAS
Choreographer's concern STEP
Chorus, Certain ANVIL
Chorus voice ALTO
Chose TOOK
Christen NAME
Christian, Eastern UNIAT
Christian, for one ERA
Christian Science name EDDY
Christie, O'Neill's ANNA
Christmas decoration TREE
Christmas or Easter item SEAL
Christmas trio MAGI
Chum PAL
Church area AISLE,ALTAR,NAVE
Church booklet ORDO
Church court ROTA
Churchill symbol VEE
Churchill's successor EDEN
Church leader ELDER
Churchman PRELATE
Churchman's cap BIRETTA
Church member, Eastern UNIAT
Church plate PATEN
Church recess APSE
Church song MOTET
Church title FRA
Cicatrix SCAR
Cicero's knee GENU
Cicero's tongue LATIN
Cider girl IDA
Cinch SNAP
Cinched ONICE
Cincinnati team REDS
Cinderella's destination BALL
Cinderella's garb RAGS
Cinders ELLA,LAVA,SLAG
Cinnabar ORE
Circa 1,000 B.C. IRONAGE
Circle HALO,RING
Circle, Kind of INNER
Circuit, Electrical GRID
Circus employee FLEA
Circus feature TENT
Cites QUOTES
Citizen of Tabriz IRANI
Citrus fruit LIME
City air problem SMOG
City, Alaskan NOME
City, Algerian ORAN
City, Asian HANOI
City, Dutch EDE
City, English ELY
City, Florida MIAMI
City founded by Pizarro LIMA
City, German EMDEN,ESSEN
City Hall tenant MAYOR
City, Hawaiian HILO
City in Arizona MESA
City in Georgia MACON,ROME
City in Hoover Dam's state RENO
City in Iraq AMARA
City in N.W. Greece ARTA
City in need of a bell ADANO
City in New Jersey ORANGE
City in Sicily ENNA
City in the Keystone State ERIE
City in Vermont BARRE
City in Yemen SANA
City, Irish SLIGO
City, Italian ESTE,PARMA
City known for biased view PISA
City: Lat. URBS
City near Milan LODI
City near Silver Springs OCALA
City near Tel Aviv GAZA
City, North African TUNIS
City north of Des Moines AMES
City of India AGRA

Clue	Answer
City of Kansas	IOLA
City of Okinawa	NAHA
City of purple	TYRE
City of Spain	AVILA
City of styles	PARIS
City of Syria, to French	ALEP
City of the Circo Massimo	ROMA
City of the Storting	OSLO
City, Okinawa	NAHA
City, Oklahoma	ENID
City on Lake Michigan	GARY
City on S.F. Bay	ALAMEDA
City on the Aar	BERNE
City on the Alleghany	OLEAN
City on the Delaware	TRENTON
City on the Dnieper	KIEV
City on the Meuse	SEDAN
City on the Missouri	OMAHA
City on the Orne	CAEN
City on the Rhone	ARLES
City on the Seyhan	ADANA
City on the Willamette	SALEM
City, Scottish	PERTH
City trains	ELS
City, Turkish	ANKARA
City 200 miles south of Moscow	OREL
City, W.W.II battle	STLO
Civil Defense condition	ALERT
Civil or Crimean	WAR
Civil War general	GRANT
Civil War soldier	REB
Civil wrong	TORT
Clad	ROBED
Claim	AVER,AVOW
Claim on property	LIEN
Claire and others	INAS
Clamor	DIN,NOISE,ROAR
Clan	SEPT
Clangor	DIN
Clarinet, for one	REED
Clarinets' cousins	OBOES
Clashing	AJAR
Class	ILK,KIND,ORDER
Class comprising the birds	AVES
Classed matter	MAIL
Class, First	AONE
Classic of 1819	IVANHOE
Classic, Prefix for	NEO
Classifieds	ADS
Classifies	RATES
Classify	SORT
Classroom needs	ERASERS
Class, Top	ELITE
Claw	TALON
Clay, Western	ADOBE
Clean a blackboard	ERASE
Cleanse	RINSE
Cleans floors	MOPS
Cleansing agent	BORAX
Clean up	SCRUB
Clear	OPEN,RID
Clear the blackboard	ERASE
Clears	NETS
Clear sky	ETHER
Cleave	RIVE
Clemens	TWAIN
Cleo's attendant	IRAS
Cleo's quietus	ASP
Clergyman's cap	BIRETTA
Clerical arm scarf	MANIPLE
Clerical title	ABBE
Cleveland suburb	PARMA
Cleveland's waterfront	ERIE
Clever remark	MOT
Cliff	SCAR
Cliff edge	BROW
Cliffhanger of silents	SERIAL
Cliff, Steep	CRAG
Climb, in a way	SHIN
Climbing pepper	BETEL
Climbing plant	PEA
Climbing vine	LIANA,LIANE
Clip	TRIM
Clique	SET
Cloak	HIDE,WRAP
Cloak, Arab's	ABA
Cloak, Spaniard's	CAPA
Clock fame, Thomas of	SETH
Clock symbol	III
Clog	SABOT
"Cloister and Hearth" author	READE
Close	SHUT
Close by, in poems	ANEAR
Close-fisted	NEAR
Closes	ENDS
Close tightly	SEAL
Closet menace	MOTH
Closing, Musical	CODA
Closing word	AMEN
Cloth	LAME
Cloth, Arabian	ABA
Cloth design	PLAID
Clothe	ENDUE
Clothes rack	TREE
Clothing	TOGS
Clothing size	LARGE
Cloth measures	ELLS
Cloth, Mulberry	TAPA
Clotho	FATE
Cloud nine	BLISS
Cloverleaf crossings, to some	MAZE
Clover yield	HONEY
Clowns	APERS
Cloy	PALL
Club	BAT,MACE
Club, Golf	IRON
Club income	DUES
Club secretary's concern	AGENDA
Club, Service	USO
Clue	HINT,KEY
Clumsy	INEPT
Clumsy craft	ARKS
Clumsy fellow	OAF
Clung to	STUCK
Coach	CAR
Coachman or herl	FLY
Coal bed	SEAM
Coalition	BLOC
Coal-mine car	TRAM
Coarse	CRUDE
Coarse cloth	TAPA
Coarse corn	SAMP
Coast campus	UCLA
Coasted	SLID
Coasters	SLEDS
Coast Guard girl	SPAR
Coast Guard role	RESCUE
Coat	REEFER
Coated iron	TERNE
Coat fur	LAPIN
Coating	RIND
Coat kind	RAIN
Coat piece	LAPEL
Coat, Seed	ARIL
Coat thinly	WASH
Cob, Corn on the	EAR
Cobra	ASP
Cobra or crab	KING
Cobra's cousin	KRAIT
Cobweb	GOSSAMER
Cochineal	DYE
Cockatoo	ARARA
Cockney's 50 per cent	ARF
Cockney's headgear	ATS
Cockney's pad	OME
Cocktail additive	ONION

Clue	Answer
Cocktail fruit	OLIVE
Cocktail variety	SOUR
Coconut meat	COPRA
Cod catcher	NET
Code word for "A"	ALFA
Code word for A	ABLE
Coded region	AREA
Cod's cousin	HAKE
Cody event	RODEO
Coeds	GALS
Coed's pride	PIN
Coffee	JAVA
Coffee beans	NIBS
Coffee break	REST
Coffee cake	BABA
Coffeemakers	URNS
Cognate	AKIN
Cognizant	AWARE
Coiffure gadget	RAT
Coil	TWINE
Coil: Prefix	SPIRO
Coin	CENT,SPECIE
Coin, Bronze	AES
Coincide	AGREE
Coin of Bulgaria	LEV
Coin of Iran	RIAL
Coin of Norway	ORE
Coin of old Greece	OBOL
Coin of Peru	SOL
Coin openings	SLOTS
Coin or salad activity	TOSS
Coins	DIMES
Coin, Word on a	UNUM
Cold Adriatic wind	BORA
Cold, cold sea	ROSS
Cold forecast	ZERO
Cold sheet of sorts	FLOE
Collapsed	GAVE
Collar prop	STAY
Collars	ETONS,NABS
Collation	MEAL
Colleague	ALLY
Collect	AMASS,GLEAN
Collected	COOL
Collections	SETS
Collections, Literary	ANAS
Collector's book	ALBUM
Colleen's land	EIRE
College degrees	ABS,BAS
College event	PROM
College in Iowa	COE
College in Michigan	ALMA
College in North Carolina	ELON
College in N.Y.C.	PACE
College in Ohio	HIRAM
College official	DEAN
College sport	CREW
College study	ARTS
College town	AMES
Colloq. coffee	JAVA
Colloq. gossip	DIRT
Colloq. looks over	CASES
Colloq. opposed to	AGIN
Colloq. seizes	NABS
Colloq. silly	GAGA
Colloq. think	OPINE
Colloq. willing	GAME
Collude with	ABET
Cologne water	EAU
Colombian people	ICA
Colon and dinar	MONEY
Colonial patriot	OTIS
Colonizer of Greenland	ERIC
Color	AQUA, GREEN,ROSE,RUST,SEPIA,TAUPE,TINT
Colorado tributary	GILA
Color, Blue or green	BICE
Color, Dark	EBON
Colorful fish	OPAH
Color, Horse	ROAN
Color, Light	TAN
Color, Lose	FADE
Color, Pale	ECRU
Colors	DYES,HUES,REDS
Colosseum, for one	ARENA
Colt	FOAL
Columbus's birthplace	GENOA
Columned walk	STOA
Columnist Pearson	DREW
Column trims	TORI
Comb in a way	TEASE
Combo member	SAX
Comb's target	HAIR
Comedian Bert	LAHR
Comedian Bob	HOPE
Comedian Fred	ALLEN
Comedian Wheeler	BERT
Come forth	EMANATE,EMERGE
Comes up	RISES
Come into being	ARISE
Come into view	LOOM
Comely, in Cannes	JOLIE
Come out	DEBUT,ERUPT
Come to agreement	ARRANGE
Come to a peak	CREST
Comforted	EASED
Comforts	EASES
Comic	MIME,OPERA
Comic's specialty	ADLIB
Comic strip character	LULU
Comic-strip sound	WHAM
Command	BEHEST,EDICT
Commander in Revolution	ASHE
Command, in days past	HEST
Commandment number	TEN
Commandos' job	RAID
Command to a dog	STAY
Command to Pussy	SCAT
Commencement V.I.P.'s	GRADS
Commend	LAUD
Commends	CITES
Commercials	ADS
Commit a crime	STEAL
Commit a holdup	ROB
Committed a faux pas	ERRED
Common adverb	THERE,WHERE
Common art figure	NUDE
Common choice in an exam	TRUE
Common contraction	ARENT,DONT,ISNT,IVE
Common correlative	NOR
Common fish	PERCH
Common footnote	IDEM
Common French verb	ETRE
Common, in Hawaii	NOA
Common Latin notation	ETAL
Common Latin verb	AMAT,AMO,ERAT,ESSE
Common noun ending	ENCE
Common possessive	OURS
Common prefix	PRE
Common response	ISEE
Common skink	ADDA
Common suffix	ING,LESS
Common suffixes	ETTES
Common verb	ARE,BEEN,WAS
Common vetch	TARE
Common vulgarism	AINT
Common word	AND,NOT
Commotion	TODO
Communal insects	ANTS
Commune in Iowa	AMANA
Communications word	MEDIA
Communities	TOWNS
Community, Greek	DEME
Community, Iowa	AMANA

Commutes RIDES
Como, for one LAGO
Compacts, e.g. CARS
Companion of alpha OMEGA
Companion of beast MAN
Companion of cry HUE
Companion of hither YON
Companion of means ENDS
Companion of pitch TOSS
Companion of radius ULNA
Companion of scotch SODA
Companion of shine RISE
Companion on the range PARD
Companions of starts FITS
Companion to now HERE
Company GUESTS
Company of lions PRIDE
Comparative ending IER
Compared with THAN
Compass mark NNE
Compass point ENE
Compass reading ESE,SSE
Compatible AKIN
Compete VIE
Competent ABLE,UPTO
Competition RACE
Competitor RIVAL
Competitors, Bridge PAIRS
Compiegne's river OISE
Complain AIL,CARP
Complete ENTIRE,UTTER
Completed DONE,OVER
Completely QUITE
Complete turns LAPS
Complication NODE
Comply OBEY
Component of a joint TENON
Component of Westerns POSSE
Composed CALM,SEDATE
Composer BACH
Composer Charles IVES
Composer of "Good-bye" TOSTI
Composer Orff CARL
Composer Rorem NED
Composer Vogler ABT
Composition OPUS
Composure POISE
Compound, Acid-alcohol ESTER
Compound, Chemical ENOL
Comprehend SEE
Comprehending words ISEE
Comprehends, informally GETS
Computer controls DIALS
Computer fodder DATA
Computer parts MEMORIES
Comstock, for one LODE
Conceal VEIL
Concealed danger PIT
Concede ADMIT
Conceit EGO
Conceited VAIN
Conception prefix IDEO
Concepts IDEAS
Conceptual beings ENTIA
Concern, Actor's LINES
Concerned CARING
Concern, Farmer's CROPS
Concern, Golfer's LIE
Concerning ABOUT,ANENT,ASTO,INRE
Concern of a certain maid METER
Concern of editors MSS
Concern of O.T.B. BETS
Concern of public figures IMAGE
Concern, Renter's LEASE
Concerns, Students' TESTS
Concern, Student's EXAM
Concert hall ODEUM
Concert passage ARIA
Concise TERSE
Conclude ENDUP
Concludes ENDS
Conclusion FINIS
Conclusions ENDS
Concoction BREW
Concorde, for example SST
Concrete piece SLAB
Concur AGREE
Concurs ASSENTS
Condensed files TAPES
Condescend STOOP
Condition CASE,SHAPE,STATE
Condition of a sale ASIS
Conduit MAIN
Coney or Midway ISLAND
Confederate ALLY
Confederates UNITES
Confess ADMIT,AVOW
Confess: Slang SING
Confidence HOPE
Confidence in, Have RELY
Confined LOCAL,PENT,TIED
Confines PENS
Conflict, in literature AGON
Conform ADAPT
Conforming SAME
Confound ADDLE,STUMP
Confronted FACED
Confronts MEETS
Confuse ADDLE
Confused ASEA,ATSEA
Confusion MAZE
Congealed dew RIME
Congers EELS
Conglomeration OLIO
Congolese river UELE
Congo native HIPPO
Conifer PINE
Conjunction AND,NOR,THAN
Conjunctions ORS
Conjunctive NOR
Conjuration SEANCE
Conjuror, old style MAGE
Connecting land NECK
Connective NOR
Connectives ORS
Connelly MARC
Connery SEAN
Connotation SENSE
Consanguineous AGNATE
Conscious AWARE
Consecrate BLESS
Conservative TORY
Consider ENTERTAIN
Consigned SENT
Consonant, Unaspirated LENE
Consort of Siva DEVI
Constantly EVER
Constellation ARA,ARGO,ARIES,LEO,ORION,URSA
Constellation Lepus HARE
Consternate AMAZE
Constituent UNIT
Constituents of modern jam CARS
Constitutional Convention figure YATES
Construction piece IBAR
Consume EAT
Consumed ATE,EATEN
Consumer USER
Consumes USES
Contained HELD
Container BIN,CAN,CASK,PAIL,TUN,VAT,VIAL
Container, Certain TEAPOT
Containers CASES,POTS,TINS
Containers, Coffee URNS

Contaminate TAINT
Contemporary of Thackeray YATES
Contempt SCORN
Content GLAD
Contents of a Shakespearean purse TRASH
Contest DUEL,MATCH,RACE
Contestant ENTRY
Continent ASIA
Continuously EVER
Contour feather PENNA
Contra ANTI
Contract LEASE
Contraction ISNT
Contraction in Shakespeare title ALLS
Contraction of sorts, Common AINT
Contraction, Poetic EER,OER,TIS
Contrary one MARY
Contributes in a way ANTES
Contrite SORRY
Control REIN,RULE
Control board PANEL
Control, Brought under TAMED
Contumely SCORN
Convenes SITS
Convention, Russian RADA
Conversation CHAT
Conversational phrase ISEE
Convex molding OVOLO
Convex moldings TORI
Convey TOTE
Conveyance BUS,CART
Convinced: Colloq. SOLD
Cookie SNAP
Cooking aid LARD
Cooking direction BASTE,STIR
Cooking fat OLEO
Cooking herbs SAGES
Cooking word, French ROTI
Cookout ROAST
Cooks STEAMS
Cooks, maids, etc. HELP
Cool ICE
Cool drinks ADES
Cooling equipment ICER
Cooper character SPY
Cooperstown name MEL
Copied APED
Copland AARON
Copper, Gold or METAL
"Copperfield" character HEEP
Copy IMITATE
Copycats APERS
Copy, for short STAT
Copy, Work on EDIT
Coquette TEASE
Coquettish COY
Coral formation REEF
Cordage TWINE
Cordage fiber SISAL
Corday victim MARAT
Corded fabrics REPS
Cordial flavoring ANISE
Cores ESSENCES
C or G CLEF
Cork's land EIRE,ERIN
Corkwood BALSA
Corn SALT
Corn bread PONE
Corn leaving COB
Corn lily IXIA
Corncob PIPE
Corncrake RAIL
Corned-beef hash HASH
Corners TREES
Corn-oil product OLEO
Corn on the cob EARS
Corny TRITE
Corolla segment PETAL
Coronets TIARAS
Corpulent OBESE
Correct TRUE
Corrects EMENDS
Correlative NOR
Correlatives ORS
Corrida performer TORO
Corrida plaudits OLES
Corrode EAT
Corrodes RUSTS
Corruption EVIL
Corso money LIRA
Corundum EMERY
Costae RIBS
Costly DEAR
Cot BED
Cote mothers EWES
Coteries SETS
Cote sound COO
Cotton or linen cloth TOILE
Cotton fabric LENO,PIMA
Cotton state ALABAMA
Cotton thread LISLE
Cottonwood ALAMO
Coty RENE
Cougar PUMA
Counterfeit FALSE,IMITATE,SHAM
Counterman's call NEXT
Counterpart IMAGE
Countertenors ALTOS
Count on RELY
Country ITALY
Country, Arabian YEMEN
Country, Asian KOREA
Country, Bible ELAM
Country in Asia IRAQ
Country, Island EIRE
Country on the Caspian IRAN
County in N.C. ASHE
Couple, as oxen YOKE
Couples PAIRS
Courage GRIT,HEART
Course CAREER,PATH,ROAD
Court WOO
Court champ ASHE
Court cry OYEZ
Court decree ARRET
Court-game starter TAP
Court hearing OYER
Court proceedings ACTA
Courtroom story ALIBI
Courtyard PATIO
Cousin of Arroyo WADI
Cousin of stout ALE
Cousin of the bay ROAN
Cousin of the cuckoo ANI
Couturier's concern HEMS
Cove INLET
Covenant PACT
Covent Garden offering OPERA
Cover LID
Covered CLAD
Covering HAT,WRAP
Coverlet THROW
Cover of a kind SHAM
Cover, Seed ARIL
Cover up HIDE
Cover-up name ALIAS
Covet ENVY
Coveted figurine OSCAR
Cow DAUNT
Cowboy ROPER
Cowboy gear REATA
Cowboy's equipment RIATA
Cowboy's place RANCH
Cowboy wear SPUR
Cow-headed goddess ISIS

Clue	Answer
Cozy spot	NEST
Cracow man	POLE
Cradle locale	TREE
Craft	ART,BOAT
Craft, Malayan	PROA
Craftmanship	ART
Craft of sorts	UFO
Craftsman	ARTISAN
Craggy hill	TOR
Cranberries' home	BOG
Craving	YEN
Craze	MANIA
Creator of an Alice	ALBEE
Creator of Lefty	ODETS
Creator of marionettes	SARG
Creator of the schmoo	CAPP
Creature, heavenly: Fr.	ANGE
Creature of the forest	DOE
Creche figures	MAGI
Credit of a kind	KUDOS
Credits	ASSETS
Credulous	NAIVE
Creek: Fr.	ANSE
Creep	INCH
Creepy	WEIRD
Creme de la creme	ELITE
Cremona family	AMATI
Crescent	ARC
Cretan mountain	IDA
Crew	MEN
Cribbage card	NOB
Cricket sides	ONS
Cries	SOBS
Cries, Corrida	OLES
Crimean city	YALTA
Crime, Commit a	ROB
Criminals' hangout	LAIR
Crimson Tide	ALABAMA
Crine prefix	ENDO
Crispbread	RUSK
Criterion	RULE
Critical remark	BARB
Critic of a sort	CENSOR
Crooked	ALOP
Crop	CRAW
Cropped up	AROSE
Crossing, Rural	STILE
Crossing sign	STOP
Crossing sound	TOOT
Cross out	DELE
Cross over	SPAN
Crosspiece	RUNG
Crow	BRAG
Crowlike bird	DAW
Crown	DIADEM
Crowns	TIARAS
Crow's cousin	ROOK
Crucifix	ROOD
Cruise port	RIO
Cruising	ASEA
Crumbs	ORTS
Crushed-fruit drink	SMASH
Crusoe's creator	DEFOE
Cry	SHOUT,SOB
Cry, Bacchanals'	EVOE
Cry, Bird's	CROW
Cry from the fold	MAA
Cry, Golf-links	FORE
Cry of disgust	BAH,UGH
Crystal gazer	SEER
Crystal-gazer's first words	ISEE
Crystalline mineral	SPAR
Crystallized snow	NEVE
Cuban money	PESO
Cubic meter	STERE
Cubs and Cards	NINES
Cub Scout unit	DEN
Cuchalainn's wife	EMER
Cuckoopint	ARUM
Cuckoos, Black	ANIS
Cucumber	PEPO
Cud chewer	DEER
Cuddle	NESTLE
Cuddle in	NEST
Cudgel	DRUB
Culet	FACET
Culinary aid	TIMER
Culinary direction	GRATE,STIR
Culinary item	HERB
Culmination	ACME,END
Cult	SECT
Cultivate	RAISE
Cultivates	HOES
Culture medium	AGAR
Cummerbund	SASH
Cunning	SLY
Cup: Fr.	TASSE
Cupid	AMOR,EROS
Cupidity	GREED
Curiosity Shop girl	NELL
Curious one	GAPER
Current	EDDY
Current events	NEWS
Current playwright	ALBEE
Current unit, for short	AMP
Currier's partner	IVES
Curtain material	LENO
Curved line	ARC
Curved moldings	OGEES
Curve, Road	ESS
Cushioned	PADDED
Custard pastry	FLAN
Customary practice	RITE
Customers	USERS
Customer, Slippery	EEL
Customs	USES
Cut	HEWED,MOW,SLIT,SNIP
Cut down	FELL,PRUNE
Cute	SLY
Cut grain	REAP
Cutlet material	VEAL
Cut of meat	LOIN
Cut of veal	CHOP
Cut, old style	SNEE
Cuts	AXES
Cuts close	CROPS
Cuts in, at a dance	TAGS
Cuts of meat	RIBS
Cuts off	LOPS
Cut: Suffix	SECT
Cutter of leaves	ANT
Cutters	SLEDS
Cutting device	DIE
Cutting instrument	RAZOR
Cutting instrument: Suffix	TOME
Cutting part	EDGE
Cuttlefish	SEPIA
Cycle for a washer	RINSE
Cygnet's sire	COB
Cygnus	SWAN
Cypress feature	KNEE
Cyprinoid fish	IDE
Cyrano's worry	NOSE
Czar's name	IVAN
Czar's say-so	UKASE
Czech	SLAV
Czech river to Elbe	ISER

D

Clue	Answer
Dab	DROPINTHEBUCKET
Daffy or Dizzy	DEAN
Dagger	DIRK
Dagger, Malay	KRIS
Daily grind	ROTE
Dainty	DELICATE
Dairy surrogate	OLEO
Dais personality	EMCEE
Daisy Mae's son	ABE
Dali watch, Like a	LIMP
Dallas school	SMU
Dallies	TOYS
Dally	LAG
Dame Edith	EVANS
"Damn Yankees" girl	LOLA
Dance	BALL,BOLERO,HULA,PROM,REEL
Dance extra	STAG
Dance: Fr.	BAL
Dance kind	TOE
Dance of sorts	TAP
Dance step	PAS
Dandy	BEAU,FINE
Dangerous ice	THIN
Danish coin	ORE
Danish counties	AMTS
Danny Kaye role	NOAH
Dante's gal	BEA
Danube tributary	ENNS,ISAR
Dark	EBON,INKY
Dark-room event	SEANCE
Dark soil	LOAM
Dark wood	EBONY
Darlings	DEARS
Dart	FLIT
Dartmoor, e.g.	GAOL
Dash	ELAN
Dashboard items	DIALS
Dashes	DARTS
Dashes with spirits	LACES
Dashiell's contemporary	ERLE
Dash's partner	DOT
Da's opposite	NYET
"Das Rheingold" role	ERDA
Data, Collection of	ANA
Data, Scoreboard	RUNS
Dated	OLD
Date in the Forum	IDES
Date or party	LINE
Date-producing country: Var.	IRAK
Daughter of Cadmus	INO
Daughter of Chaos	GAEA
David, for one	CAMP
David's specialties	PSALMS
Da Vinci, for one	ARTIST
Davis's domain	CSA
Davy Jones' home	DEEP
Dawn	SUNUP
Dawn goddess	EOS
Day for trees	ARBOR
Days of yore	OLDEN
Day time	NOON
Dazzling light	GLARE
D.D.E.	IKE
Deacon's vehicle	SHAY
Deadlocked	TIED
Dead or Black	SEA
Dead Sea feature	SALT
Deal	SALE
Dealer in hot goods	FENCE
Dealers	TRADERS
Deal in scarce tickets	SCALP
Deal or deed prefix	MIS
Dealt	METED
Dealt with	TRADED
Dean of a group	ELDEST

Clue	Answer
Dear me!	ALAS
Dear one	LAMB
Death Valley product	BORAX
Debacles	ROUTS
Debatable	MOOT
Debating side	NEGATIVE
Debauchee	ROUE
Debris, Certain	LAVA
Debt chits	IOUS
Decades	TENS
Decamp	FLEE
Decamped	FLED
Decays	ROTS
Deceitful one	LIAR
Deceive	DUPE
December song	NOEL
Decides	OPTS
Deck officer	MATE
Deck wood	TEAK
Declaim	RANT
Declare	ASSERT,STATE
Declare openly	AVOW
Declares	AVERS
Declare verboten	BAN
Decline	SAG
Declined	EBBED
Declines	EBBS
Decorate	PAINT,TRIM
Decorate again	REDO
Decorated metal work	NIELLO
Decoration	MEDAL
Decorative brass	ORMOLU
Decorative wear	SASH
Decorator of sorts	ICER
Decor, Campus	IVY
Decor, Handbag	INITIAL
Decorticate	SKIN
Decrease	ABATE
Decree	EDICT,ENACT,UKASE
Decrees	ACTS
Dec. 31, for one	EVE
Dedicate	ALLOT
Dedicated	AVID
Deductible item	LOSS
Deed, in France	ACTE
Deep blue and others	SEAS
Deep in thought	RAPT
Deep pink	CORAL
Deep-red pigment	LAKE
Deep sleep	SOPOR
Deer	ROES,STAG
Deer, Female	DOES
Deer, Large	ELKS
"Deer Park" author	MAILER
Deer tracks	SLOTS
Deface	MAR
Defeat	BEST,LOSS,ROUT,STOP,WORST
Defeated narrowly	EDGED
Defeat, One headed for	GONER
Defeats at bridge	SETS
Defect, Blood	ANEMIA
Defect, Speech	LISP
Defendant's action	PLEA
Defendant's plea	NOLO
Defense arm	NAVY
Defense, Legal	ALIBI
Defensive structure	REDAN
Defiant one	REBEL
Deficient	POOR
Defied	FACED
Defiles	TARS
Definite refusal	NONO
Deft	AGILE
Defunct car	EDSEL,REO
Degree	NTH

Degree, In any	ATALL
Deities	LARES
Deity, Egyptian	AMON,PTAH
Deity, Hindu	RAMA
Deity, Norse	ODIN
Deity, Teutonic	NORN
Delaware, New York, etc.	EAST
Delay	STAY
Delayed	LATE
Deles	ERASES
Dele's opposite	STET
Delft, for one	WARE
Delicacy, Mexican	TACO
Delicate color	TINT
Delicatessen item	LOX
Delighted: Slang	SENT
Delineate	ETCH
Deliver	SEND
Deliverance	RESCUE
Deliver a discourse	SPEAK
Delivered	DEALT,SENT
Della	REESE
Delusion's partner	SNARE
Demand	CALL
Demands	NEEDS
Demeanor	MIEN
Demolish	RAZE,RUIN
Demon, Arabian	GENIE
Demonstration	RIOT
Demo or auto suffix	CRAT
Demure	COY
Den	LAIR
Denial	NAY
Denial, Scotsman's	NAE
Denomination	SECT
Denouement	END
Denounce (with "at")	RAIL
Dense one	IDIOT
Dental concern	MOLAR
Dental degree	DDS
Dentists' concerns	BITES
Dentist's gear	BURR
Denver building	MINT
Depart	QUIT
Departed	GONE
Departing wedding gift	RICE
Depart in haste	DECAMP
Department in France	ORNE
Department of France	NORD
Dependable	SAFE
Depend on	RELY
Deplorable	SAD
Deposit	STORE
Deposit, Mineral	LODE
Deposits containing gold	PLACERS
Depressed	GLUM
Depression	DENT
Depression agency	CCC
Derby, for one	RACE
Derby winner, 1955	SWAPS
Derby winner, 1935	OMAHA
Dereliction	NEGLECT
Deride	SNEER
Derrick part	MAST
Descartes	RENE
Descendant of Mohammed	EMIR
Descended	ALIT
Describe	RELATE
Describe, in a way	PARSE
Describing Latin or Sanskrit	DEAD
Describing an otary	EARED
Desert coat	ABA
Deserters	RATS
Desertlike	ARID
Desert-like	SERE
Desert lizard	GILA
Deserve	EARN
Deserve: Colloq.	RATE
Desiccated	DRIED,SERE
Design	CREATE
Designate, in a way	TAB
Designates	NAMES
Designer of St. Paul's	WREN
Design transfer	DECAL
Desire	HOPE,ITCH,URGE,WISH
Desk for Picasso	EASEL
Desk item	CALENDAR,LAMP
Desperate	DIRE
Despicable one	RAT
Despise	ABHOR,SCORN
Despot	TSAR
Dessert	BABA,PIE
Dessert, Frozen	ICE
Destination for Hansel	OVEN
Destiny	LOT
Destitute	POOR
Destroy	RAZE,RUIN
Destroy by fire	GUT
Destroyed	SLEW
Destroy slowly	ERODE
Destructive fishes	GARS
Detached	SEPARATE
Details	ITEMS
Detect	ESPY
Detection medium	SONAR
Detective-fiction name	NERO
Deteriorate	ERODE
Deteriorates	ROTS
Determinate amount	UNIT
Determination	GRIT
Determined	SET
Detest	HATE
Detroit player	TIGER
Detroit players	LIONS
Detroit product	AUTO
Develop	ENSUE,RIPEN
Deviate	ERR
Device, Detection	SONAR
Device, Fastening	HASP
Device, Metal	TNUT
Device, Navigational	LORAN
Devil	SATAN
Devilfish	MANTA
Devilish	EVIL
Devise	SHAPE
Devonian and Permian	AGES
Devotee	FAN
Devour	EAT
Devoured	ATE
Dexterous	AGILE
D.F.C., for one	MEDAL
Diadem	TIARA
Diagonal	BIAS
Diagram	MAP
Diamond lady	LIL
Diamonds, etc.	STONES
Diamond slip	ERROR
Diamonds, to Lorelei	ICE
Diary of a sort	LOG
Dick Button's milieu	ICE
Dickens character	TIM
Dickens girl and others	NELLS
Dickens's Fagin, for one	FENCE
Dickens villain	HEEP
Dickinson and Whittier	POETS
Dictate, Czar's	UKASE
Dictation	NOTES
Did a bank job	LENT
Did a base-running job	STOLE
Did a cake job	ICED
Did a card chore	DEALT
Did the crawl	SWAM
Did mending	SEWED
Dido	ANTIC
Did the same	APED
Did work at Belmont	RODE

Dies down	EBBS
Diet	FARE
Dieter's lunch	SALAD
Diet for aardvarks	ANTS
Dietrich feature	LEGS
Different	OTHER
Differently	ELSE
Difficulties	SNAGS
Difficulty	RUB,STRAIT
Difficulty, In	ATSEA
Dig	SPADE
Digit	ONE
Digits	TOES
Dignified	SEDATE
Digs	ROOTS
Dijon donkey	ANE
Dilatory	SLOW,TARDY
Dilettante	ARTY
Dill	ANET
Diluted	WEAK
Diminish	ABATE
Diminished by	LESS
Diminutive of Antoinette	TONI
Diminutive suffix	KIN,ULE
Diminutive suffixes	ETTES
Dimmed	FADED
Dimple	DENT
Dined	ATE
Diner drink	JAVA
Dinero	MONEY
Diner's sign	EATS
Dines	EATS
Dinesen and Andersen	DANES
Dinette appliance	TOASTER
Dinghy	BOAT
Dinner check	TAB
Dinner course	ROAST
Dinner of a kind	MESS
Din or pal suffix	ETTE
Dinsmore	ELSIE
Diplomacy	TACT
Direct	LEAD
Directed	BADE,SENT,STEERED
Direction	EAST,ENE,ESE,NNE,SSE,WAY
Direction, General	TENOR
Direction, in Paris	NORD
Direction, Printing	STET
Directions, Rx.	DOSES
Direction to a horse	GEE
Director Kazan	ELIA
Direct to a target	HOME
Disagreeable one	PILL
Disappeared	GONE
Disarray	MESS
Disaster, Automotive	EDSEL
Disburden	EASE
Disburse	DOLE,SPEND
Discard	SCRAP,SHED
Discharge	EMIT,FIRE
Discharge, informally	AXE
Disclaim noisily	RANT
Disconcert	ABASH
Discord goddess	ERIS
Discordant	AJAR,SOUR
Discount word	AGIO
Discover	ESPY,LEARN
Discussion group	PANEL
Disdain	SCORN
Disdaining one	SNOB
Disease: Suffix	ITIS
Disease, Swelling	EDEMA
Disentangle	UNTIE
Disfigure	MAR
Disgrace	SHAME
Disgust, Exclamation of	PHEW
Dish	TUREEN
Dish, Breakfast	CEREAL
Dish for Kamehameha	POI
Dish: Fr.	PLAT
Dish, Seafood	CRAB
Disinclined	AVERSE
Disintegrate	MELT,ROT
Disk, Solar	ATEN
Dislodge	EVICT
Dismal, in verse	DREAR
Dismay	DAUNT
Dismissed	SENT
Dismisses	OUSTS
Dismiss: Slang	BOOT
Dismounted	ALIT
Disney character	CLEO
Disney's Donald to purists	DRAKE
Disown	DENY
Disparages	SLURS
Dispatch	HASTE,SEND
Dispatch boat	AVISO
Dispatched	SENT
Dispels	ROUTS
Dispensation	DOLE
Disperse	ROUT
Display	PRESENT
Display frame	EASEL
Display lighting	NEON
Displeasure	ANGER
Disposed	APT
Dispossess	OUST
Disquiet	ROIL
Disreputable place	DIVE
Disseminates	SOWS
Dissolute one	RAKE,ROUE
Dissolve	MELT
Distaff rabbit	DOE
Distance runner	MILER
Distant	AFAR
Distant: Prefix	TELE
Distillery item	VAT
Distinct	OTHER
Distinction	NOTE,STYLE
Distinctive	RARE
Distinctive person	ONER
Distinctive quality	AURA
Distress	AIL,PAIN
Distribute	ALLOT
Distributed	DOLED
District	AREA
District of Asia Minor, Old	IONIA
Distrustful	SHY
Disturb	STIR
Disturbances	RIOTS
Disturbed	IRATE
Ditto	SAME
Ditto: Lat.	IDEM
Ditty	AIR
Divagate	ROVE
Diva Lucine	AMARA
Divas' highlights	ARIAS
Dive or song	SWAN
Divide	REND
Divine food	MANNA
Diving-bell inventor	EADS
Diving bird	LOON
Diving duck	SMEW
Divisible by two	EVEN
Division of Greece	DEME
Division, Religious	SECT
Division word	INTO
Divulges	BARES
Dixie river	ALABAMA
Dizzy	DEAN
Do art work	ETCH
Do better than	TOP
Do a cartographer's job	REMAP
Docile	TAME
Doctor's frequent advice	REST
Doctor's group	AMA
Doctrinal group	SECT

Doctrine TENET
Doctrines ISMS
Document PAPER
Document, Legal DEED
Do damage SCAR
Dodge EVADE
Do a dressmaker's job ALTER
Doer ACTOR
Doer: Suffix IST
Does a banking job LENDS
Does business DEALS
Does editing EMENDS
Does a field job TEDS
Does a hair job DYES
Does martinis STIRS
Does mending SEWS
Does a metermaid's job TAGS
Does a number job ADDS
Does ushering SEATS
Do fancywork TAT
Do a farmer's job SOW
Doff SHED
Do a fish-cleaning job SCALE
Do the floors SAND
Do, for one NOTE
Dog CHOW
Do a garden task WEED
Dogie CALF
Dog, in heraldry ALAN
Dog in "Peter Pan" NANA
Dog, Movie ASTA
Dog, Name for a ROVER
Dog or Hamlet DANE
Dog or North STAR
Dogpatch hero ABNER
Do the Gretna Green bit ELOPE
Dog's word in a comic strip ARF
Do a gymnastic exercise CHIN
Do a host's job GREET
Do housework CLEAN,IRON
Doing UPTO
Doing, Social TEA
Do a judge's task TRY
Do a kitchen chore PUREE
Do lawn work RAKE
Doleful DREAR
Dole out METE
Dollar bill, Word on a UNUM
Dollar: Slang CLAM
Doll's cry MAMA
Dolly of "Hello Dolly" LEVI
Dolt CLOD
Do, Make EKE
Dome of note TEAPOT
Domestic slave, Old ESNE
Domineer BOSS
Dominion EMPIRE
Don TUTOR
Donations ALMS
Done OVER
Done for, informally SHOT
Do newsroom work EDIT
Donizetti work OPERA
Don Juan's mother INEZ
Donkey, in France ANE
Donnybrook MELEE
Donovan's group OSS
Doone LORNA
Door fastener HASP
Door opener KEY
Door part KNOB
Door parts SILLS
Door sign ENTER,EXIT
Do penance ATONE
Do a pocket job PICK
Do a political chore ORATE
Do a printing chore RESET
Do public relations work PROMOTE
Doris and others DAYS
Do a rodeo job ROPE
Dorothy's dog TOTO
Do a shoe chore LACE
Dossier FILE
Do a stable job SHOE
Dostoevski novel, with "The" IDIOT
Do tailoring SEW
Dote on LOVE
Dotted cube DIE
Dotted with stars, in heraldry SEME
Double agent SPY
Double curves OGEES
Double helix DNA
Double is one HIT
Double-reed OBOE
Doublet VEST
Double-talker LIAR
Doublet's partner HOSE
Douceur SOP
Douceurs TIPS
Douglas, for one FIR
Dour GRIM
Do ushering SEAT
Dovetailing piece TENON
Down EIDER
Down at the heels SEEDY
Down East or Southern ACCENT
Downed ATE
Down in the dumps, Be MOPE
Downright RANK
Downwind ALEE
Down with: Fr. ABAS
Downy coat NAP
Do without MISS
Dowry DOT
Dozes NAPS
Drab color OLIVE
Draft animals OXEN
Draft classification ONEA
Draft HQ SSS
Drag LUG
Drama, King of LEAR
Dramatic conflict AGON
Dramatis personae CAST
Dramatist Connelly MARC
Draped garment SARI
Drat! DARN
Draw LIMN,TIE
Draw back SHY
Drawing PLAN
Drawing room SALON
Draw near COME
Draw off TAP
Draw the wrong straw LOSE
Drayman's need CART
Dread AWE,FEAR
Dreadful DIRE
Dream, in Paris REVE
Dregs LEES
Dresden housewife FRAU
Dress adornment PANEL
Dress alterations DARTS
Dress detail PLEAT
Dressed CLAD
Dress feature SASH
Dress goods PIQUE
Dressing tool ADZE
Dress insert GORE
Dress length MIDI
Dressler MARIE
Dress material LAME,ORLON,SATIN
Dress of rank ROBE
Dress panel INSET
Dress part YOKE
Dress-shirt feature STUD
Dreyfus defender ZOLA
Dried coconut COPRA

Dried orchid tubers	SALEP
Drift	TREND
Drill	AUGER,BORE
Drink	BEER,CIDER,NOG,TEA
Drink, as of rum	TOT
Drinkers' rocks	ICE
Drink flavor	COLA,LIME
Drink heavily	TOPE
Drinking counter	BAR
Drink-maker	TEAPOT
Drink of redeye	SNORT
Drink, Pub	ALE
Drinks, Fountain	SODAS
Drink slowly	SIP
Drink, Small	DRAM
Drinks, Summer	ADES
Drip	WEEP
Dripping	ASOP
Drive, Baseball	LINER
Drive off	SHOO
Drivers' game	GOLF
Driver's help	MAP
Drives into	RAMS
Drives slantingly	TOES
Drizzle	MIST
Drizzles	WETS
Droll fellow, familiarly	CARD
Drome prefix	AERO
Drone	BEE,IDLER
Drooping	ALOP
Droops	LOPS,SAGS
Droplets	DEW
Dropsy	EDEMA
Dross	SLAG
Drowse	NOD
Drudge	PEON,PLOD,SLAVE
Drug-yielding plant	ALOE
Drum	BONGO
Drum sound	ROLL
Drunkard	SOT
Drury, for one	LANE
Dry	ARID,PARCH,SEC
Drying chambers: Var.	OSTS
Dry periods	SERES
Dry riverbed of West	WASH
Dry's opposite	SWEET
Dry, Spreads to	TEDS
D.S.C. winner	HERO
Dub	NAME
Duchess of Alva painter	GOYA
Duck	EIDER,EVADE,TEAL
Duck!	FORE
Duck genus	ANAS
Duck, in Germany	ENTE
Duckling, Certain	UGLY
Ducks, Pintail	SMEES
Dud	LEMON
Dudes' place	RANCH
Duke, Spanish	ALBA
Dull	ARID,TAME
Dull finish	MATTE
Dulling influence	OPIATE
Dull person	CLOD
Dullwitted one	DODO
Dumb one	DORA
Dumfound	AMAZE
Dunce	DOLT
Dundee man	SCOT
Dunderhead	DOLT,IDIOT
Dungeon	KEEP
Dunk	SOP
Dunne or Castle	IRENE
Dupe	CATSPAW
Dupes	TOOLS
Duplicate	SAME
Dupre's instrument	ORGAN
Durable wood	OAK
During	AMID
Durocher	LEO
Dust Bowl migrant	OKIE
Duster	RAG
Dutch commune	EDE
Dutch export	EDAM
Dutch or brick	OVEN
Dutch or front	DOOR
Dutch painter	HALS
Dutch skater's name	HANS
Dutch uncles	EMES
Dutch weight	ONS
Duty	CHORE
Duty officer's list	ROSTER
Duty turn	TOUR
Dvorak	ANTON
Dwarf	STUNT
Dwelling	ABODE
Dye	ANIL,TINT
Dyeing apparatus	AGER
Dye mixture	STAIN
Dynamics, Prefix for	AERO

E

Each	PER
Eager	AGOG
Eagerly awaiting	ATIP
Eagerness	ELAN
Eagerness plus	ZEAL
Eagle	ERNE
Eagle feature	TALON
Eagle, Sea	ERN
Eagle's retreat	AERIE
Earl of Avon	EDEN
Early	SOON
Early age	IRON,STONE
Early Archbishop of Canterbury	ANSELM
Early ascetics	ESSENES
Early Asian	MEDE
Early astronaut	GLENN
Early car	REO
Early Coloradans	UTES
Early explorer	ERIC
Early Irishman	AIRE
Early Japanese	AINU
Early laborer	ESNE
Early Mongolian	HUN
Early motor man	OLDS
Early patriot	OTIS
Early Peruvian	INCA
Early Tuileries resident	ROI
Early western name	EARP
Early word on TV repair cost	ESTIMATE
Earn	MERIT
Earnest	EAGER
Earnest: Prefix	SERIO
Ear parts	TRAGI
Ear shell	ABALONE
Earth	SOD
Earthbound bird	EMU
Earthen jars	OLLAS
Earth goddess	CERES,GAEA
Earth's constant companion	MOON
Earth, Volcanic	TRASS
Ease off	LETUP
Easily handled, as a ship	YARE
Eastern alliance	SEATO
Eastern area	ASIA
Eastern astrologers	MAGI
Eastern campus	YALE
Eastern capital	TRENTON
Eastern chieftain	EMEER
Eastern-church title	ABBA
Eastern collegian	ELI

Clue	Answer
Eastern countries	ORIENT
Eastern country	LAOS
Easterner, Middle	IRAQI
Eastern faith	ISLAM
Eastern Indians	ERIES
Eastern inn	SERAI
Eastern ketch	SAIC
Eastern language	URDU
Eastern league	IVY
Eastern name	ABOU,ALI,OMAR
Eastern notable	AMEER
Eastern nurses	AMAHS
Eastern pepper plant	BETEL
Eastern prince	AMIR,RAJA,RAJAH
Eastern-rite Christian	UNIAT
Eastern title	AGHA,EMIR,TUAN
Eastern U.S. river	TIOGA
Eastern V.I.P.	AGA,RANI
Eastern woman	RANEE
East Indian shrub	SOLA
East, in Naples	EST
Easy	SOFT
Easy and one-way	STREETS
Easy job	SNAP
Easy mark	DUPE
Easy, Take it	REST
Eat	DINE,ERODE
Eat greedily	CRAM
Eat, in Berlin	ESSEN
Eban	ABBA
Ebbets Field name	REESE
Ebbing and flowing	TIDAL
Ecclesiastic	PRELATE
Ecclesiastical court	ROTA
Echoes	APES
Eciton	ANT
Eclipse kind	SOLAR
Ecological communities	SERES
Economical one	SAVER
Ecuadorean province	ORO
Edge	TRIM
Edge of a hill	BROW
Edging	LACE
Edging, Do	TAT
Edible root	TARO
Edict	UKASE
Edison's middle name	ALVA
Edit	EMEND
Editor, Famous	DANA
Editor's mark	CARET
Edna of stage	BEST
Edsel, for one	LOSER
Ed the singer	AMES
Education officials	REGENTS
Efface	ERASE
Effacement	ERASURE
Effectively, Reach	GETAT
Effect's trigger	CAUSE
Effort: Colloq.	STAB
Effortless	EASY
Effrontery	GALL
Egad or drat	OATH
Egg: Prefix	OVI,OVO
Eggs	ROE
Egg-shaped	OVATE
Eggs: Lat.	OVA
Eggs on	ABETS
E.g., Kwajalein	ATOLL
Ego	SELF
Egos' sources	IDS
E.g., Wight	ISLE
Egyptian charmer	CLEO
Egyptian deity	AMEN
Egyptian god	AMON,ATON,PTAH
Egyptian goddess	BAST,ISIS,SATI
Egyptian sacred bull	APIS
Egyptian tongue	ARABIC
Egyptologist's quest	RELIC

Clue	Answer
1898 naval casualty	MAINE
1870 surrender site	SEDAN
1836 locale	ALAMO
1825, Canal finished in	ERIE
Eight: Lat.	OCTO
E. Indian tree	SAL
Eisteddfod item	SONG
Eject	EMIT
Ejects	OUSTS
Ekberg	ANITA
Elanet	KITE
El Bahr	NILE
Elbe, River to the	EGER
Elder	DAD
Elder or alder	TREE
Eldritch	WEIRD
Elected ones	INS
Electioneer	STUMP
Electrical hookup	GRID
Electrical unit	REL,WATT
Electric force	ELOD
Electric or slippery	EEL
Electrified particle	ION
Electrode	ANODE
Electron stream	RAY
Electron tube	DIODE
Elegance	TONE
Elegant	FINE
Elemental	RUDE
Element, Gaseous	NEON
Elephant-eating bird	ROC
Elevate the spirits	ELATE
Elevator	LIFT
Elevator buttons	UPS
Elevator sign	INUSE
11:30 P.M., to some	LATE
Elfin creature	PERI
Eli	YALE
Elia	LAMB
Eliot hero	BEDE
Elizabethan drama king	LEAR
Elizabethan and Christian	ERAS
Elizabeth 2, e.g.	LINER
Elliot	NESS
Elliptical	OVAL,OVATE
Ellis Parker Butler subject	PIGS
Elm or ash	TREE
Elm's forte	SHADE
Else: Scot.	ENSE
Elusive fellow	EEL
Elysiums	EDENS
Emanation	AURA
Emanations	AURAE
Embarks	SAILS
Embarrass	ABASH
Embellishes an expense account	PADS
Embezzled	STOLE
Emerge	RISE
Emergency call	SOS
Eminent	NOTED
Emit vapor	REEK
Emmys	AWARDS
Emollient	BALM
Emoters	HAMS
Emotion	IRE
Emotional sounds	SOBS
Emotions	HATES
Emperor	NERO,TSAR
Emperor of 10th century	OTTO
Emphasis	ACCENT
Emphasize	STRESS
Emphatic denial	NEVER
Emphatic negative	NONO,OHNO
Employees' goal	RAISE
Employers	USERS
Employs	HIRES,USES
Emptiness	AIR
Empty	BARE,IDLE,INANE,VOID

Empty talk BLAH,BOSH
Ems and Baden SPAS
Emulate Bryan ORATE
Emulate a girl-watcher OGLE
Emulate Socrates ASK
Emulate thespians EMOTE
Emulate a willow WEEP
Emulator RIVAL
Enameled metalware TOLE
Enchanting MAGIC
Encircle RING
Enclosure PALE
Enclosure, in Scotland REE
Enclosures PENS
Encomium ELOGE
Encompass SPAN
Encompassed by AMID
Encore! BIS
Encounter MEET
Encouragement, Corrida OLES
Encourages ABETS
End, The OMEGA
Endeavor TRY
Ended DONE,OVER
Ending AMEN,OMEGA
Ending, Feminine ETTE
Ending meaning small ETTE
Endings, Chemical ENES
Endings, Superlative ESTS
Ending with block or stock ADE
Ending with cup and pay OLA
Ending with gyro or thermo STAT
Endless ETERNAL
End of washing RINSE
Endorse SIGN
End to, Puts an QUASHES
Endure STAND
Endured STOOD
Endures LASTS
Endure use WEAR
Energy kind SOLAR
Energy unit ERG
Enervate SAP
Enervates JADES
Engage HIRE
Engage in seamy work SEW
Engage in a sport SKI
Engine puff PANT
English actor TREE
English admiral DRAKE
English aviators RAF
English cathedral city ELY
English colonist SMITH
English composer ARNE
English gallery TATE
English gun STEN
English manor court LEET
"Englishmen, Drink of" ALE
English money, Old ORA
English novelist READE
English novelist and scientist SNOW
English novelist of 1800's YATES
English painter OPIE
English poet DONNE,POPE
English queen ANNE
English repast TEA
English river ARUN,AVON,OUSE,TYNE,URE
English sand hill DENE
English town ETON
English track ASCOT
English writer AMIS,LAMB
Engrave ETCH
Engrossed RAPT
Eng. title BART
Enigmatic one SPHINX
Enjoy a book READ
Enjoyed the surf SWAM
Enjoy a repast DINE
Enlisted men GIS
Enliven ANIMATE,STIR
Enoch, Tennyson's ARDEN
Enrich LARD
Enroll ENTER
Ensign FLAG
Ensuing NEXT
Entanglement WEB
Entente PACT
Enter ENROL
Entertainer EMCEE
Entertainment FETE
Enthusiasm ARDOR,ELAN,ZEST
Enthusiastic KEEN
Entirely ALL
Entire range GAMUT
Entrance GATE
Entrance, Mine ADIT
Entreat PRAY
Entreaty PLEA
Entree CHOP
Entree order VEAL
Entries ITEMS
Entry, Scoreboard GOAL
Enunciates SAYS
Environs AREA
Enzyme ending ASE
Epic poem ILIAD
Epic writer HOMER
Episcopacy SEE
Epithet used in politics LIAR
Epochal ERAL
Epochs ERAS
Equable EVEN
Equal EVEN,MATCH,PEER,SAME
Equal: Fr. EGAL
Equality PAR
Equal: Prefix ISO
Equals PEERS,TIES
Equator LINE
Equine of a kind HOSS
Equine parent DAM
Equipment GEAR,RIG
Equipment, Baking OVEN
Equipment, Baseball BATS
Equipment for Tell ARROW
Equipment, Playground SEESAW
Equipment, Rowing OAR
Equipment, Ski-slope TBAR
Equipment, Sporting SKIS
Equitable EVEN
Equivalent of a miss AMILE
Erase DELE
Erect REAR
Ericson, for one NORSE
Erie Canal city ROME
Ermines STOATS
Erode EAT,WEAR
Eroded EATEN
Err GOOF,SIN,SLIP
Erroneous AMISS
Error LAPSE
Erudition LORE
Escapade CAPER
Escape FLEE
Escaped FLED
Escape slowly OOZE
Eschew AVOID
Escort ATTEND
Escritoire DESK
Eskimo ALEUT
Eskimo craft UMIAK
Eskimo settlement ETAH
Espies SEES
Espionage name HARI
Espouse PROMOTE
Essayist ELIA,LAMB
"Essay on Man" author POPE

Essays TRIES
Essence ATTAR
Essences ODORS
Essential NEED,NEEDED,VITAL
Essential being ESSE
Essential oil ATTAR
Essential part CORE
Establish BASE
Establishes SEATS
Estaminet patron EATER
Estate ACRES
Estate kind REAL
Ester, Certain OLEATE
Estuary RIA
Et al., Hemingway PAPAS
Et al., Saratoga SPAS
Eternally EVER
Eternities EONS
Ethereal AIRY
Ethiopian lake TANA
Etruscan title LARS
Etymon ROOT
Eucharistic plate PATEN
Euphoria BLISS
Eurasian river URAL
European SLAV
European basin SAAR
European capital
BERN,BERNE,OSLO,ROMA,ROME
European, Certain CELT
European food fish IDE
European head of state TITO
European language NORSE
European measure KILO
European money FRANC
European region ALPS,RUHR
European river LOIRE,ODER,RHONE,YSER
Europeans LETTS
European thrush: Var. OUSEL
Europe's neighbor ASIA
Evade SHUN
Evaluate ASSAY
Evangelist Roberts ORAL
Evans or Robertson DALE
Evening: Fr. SOIR
Evening, in Naples SERA
Evens TIES
Event, Athletic MEET
Event for Cinderella BALL
Event, School PROM
Event, Track DASH
Event, Western RODEO
Eve, originally RIB
Evergreen genus THEA
Everlasting ETERNAL
Every 60 minutes HORAL
Evian SPA
Evidence CLUE
Evidence of anger GLARE
Evidence of S.R.O. QUEUE
Evident CLEAR
Evil spiris DEMON
Evoke CALL
Ewes, Like OVINE
Exacerbated IRED
Exacerbates IRES
Exact NICE
Exacting RIGID
Exactly PAT
Exactly suited NEAT
Exact satisfaction for AVENGE
Exaggerated PADDED
Exalt ELEVATE
Exam ORAL
Exam-cheater's aid CRIB,TROT
Examination TEST
Examine closely SIFT
Examiner CENSOR
Example, Perfect IDEAL
Exams ORALS
Exasperate TRY
Exasperate: Colloq. RILE
Exasperates TIRES
Ex-Card Slaughter ENOS
Excavation MINE
Exceed TOP
Excellent AONE
Except SAVE
Exceptional RARE
Excessive OVER
Excessively TOO
Excessively dry ARID
Exchange SWAP
Exchange fee AGIO
Excitable ones HENS
Excite ELATE,STIR
Excite curiosity PIQUE
Excited AGOG
Excited state STEW
Exclamation
ALAS,GEE,OHO,OHOH,PHEW,RATS,TUT
Exclamation in Bonn ACH
Exclamation, Old EGAD
Exclamations AHAS
Exclamation, Scrooge's BAH
Exclude SHUT
Exclusive ONLY
Exclusively ALONE
Excuse ALIBI
Execrate ABHOR
Executes DOES
Exempt FREE
Exercises USES
Exercise vigorously EXERT
Ex-Giant star MAYS
Exhaust DRAIN,SAP,TIRE
Exhausted SPENT
Exhibit STAGE
Exhort URGE
Exigency NEED
Ex-isle? ELBA
Exist ARE
Exist, in France ETRE
Existed WAS
Existence ESSE
Existence of sorts RUT
Existing ALIVE
Exit word SCAT
"Exodus" hero ARI
Exorbitant STEEP
Expand needlessly PAD
Expectant AGOG,ATIP
Expectation HOPE
Expedited SPED
Expedition TREK
Expeditiously APACE
Expel EJECT
Expels OUSTS,ROUTS
Expense-account item TIPS
Expensive DEAR
Experienced HAD,SEEN
Experimental places LABS
Experiments TESTS
Expert ONER
Experts ACES
Expiate ATONE
Expiation PENANCE
Explode ERUPT
Exploit GESTE
Exploits DEEDS
Explorer ERIC
Explosive TNT
Expose BARE
Express AIR
Express an idea OPINE
Expression TERM

Clue	Answer
Expression of relief	ATLAST
Express scorn	SNORT
Ex-senator Fong of Hawaii	HIRAM
Extemporise	ADLIB
Extended	LONG
Extends	LIES
Extensive	VAST
Extent	AREA,SIZE
Exterior	OUTER
External: Prefix	ECTO
Extinct bird	MOA
Extinct birds	DODOS
Extinguish	DOUSE
Extra	OVER
Extraordinary person	ONER
Extra special	CHOICE
Extra to a Highlander	ORRA
Extreme	UTTER
Extreme in opinion	RABID
Extremely	TOO,ULTRA
Extremities	ARMS
Extrinsic	ALIEN
Exude moisture	OOZE
Exude slowly	WEEP
Exultant	ELATED
Exultant song	PAEAN
Ex-V.P. Agnew	SPIRO
Ex-Yankee slugger	MARIS
Eye	OGLE
Eye ailments	STIES
Eye brightener	SMILE
Eyebrow shape	ARC
Eye cosmetic	LINER
Eye: Fr.	OEIL
Eye part	IRIS,LASH,LENS
Eye product	TEAR
Eye section	UVEA

F

Clue	Answer
Fabled mountain	OSSA
Fable man	AESOP
Fabric	LACE,LINEN,MOIRE,ORLON,PILE,SATIN
Fabrication	LIE
Fabric, Camel's-hair	ABA
Fabric fluff	LINT
Fabrics	NETS
Fabric surface	NAP
Fabulist	AESOP,ESOP,LIAR
Fabulous bird	ROC
Faced the dawn	AROSE
Faces, Certain	DIALS
Face shape	OVAL
Facet	PANE
Face with courage	BRAVE
Facial feature	BROW
Facial pair	LIDS
Facing a glacier's path	STOSS
Facts	DATA
Facts, Collection of	ANA
Fad	MANIA,RAGE
Fading star	NOVA
"Faerie Queen" maiden	UNA
Fail	MISS
Fail to do	NEGLECT,OMIT
Fail to take action	SITON
Failure	DUD
Fair	SOSO
Fair-haired boy	BLOND
Fair site in '70	OSAKA
Fairy, Persian	PERI
Fairy-tale character	GNOME
Fairy-tale figure	OGRE
Fairy-tale word	UPON
Fallacious	UNTRUE
Fall behind	LAG
Fall forecast	COOL
Fall guy	GOAT,SAP
Falling-out	SPAT
Fall in power	WANE
Falls behind	LAGS
False	UNTRUE
False alarm	SCARE
False god	BAAL
Fame	ECLAT
Famed cartoonist	CAPP
Famed chorus	ANVIL
Famed couturier	DIOR
Famed explorer	ERIC
Famed fountain	TREVI
Famed Hollywood Mountie	EDDY
Famed lion	LAHR
Famed lioness	ELSA
Famed name of French stage	SARAH
Famed pianist	IGNACE
Famed puppeteer	SARG
Famed sculptor	RODIN
Famed showman	COHAN
Famed statuette	OSCAR
Famed U.S. editor	DANA
Familiarize	ORIENT
Familiar negative	ARENT,NOPE
Familiar palindrome	MADAM
Familiar pen name	ELIA
Familiar protest	NYET
Familiar sight in London	PUB
Familiar sign	EXIT
Familiar solecism	AINT
Familiar with	ONTO
Family	CLAN
Family, Anthony's	EDENS
Family, Baseball	ALOU
Family member	AUNT, DAD,MAMA,MOM,NIECE,SIS,SON,UNCLE
Family member, familiarly	GRAMP
Family member, French	MARI
Family member, in Caen	TANTE
Family member, in Soho	MATER
Family members	PAPAS
Family-room unit	HIFI
Famous	EMINENT
Famous Athenian	SOLON
Famous Auntie	MAME
Famous duelist	BURR
Famous explorer	ERIC
Famous fan dancer	RAND
Famous friend	DAMON
Famous Italian	AMATI
Famous Knick	REED
Famous last words	ETTU
Famous lover	ROMEO
Famous marquis	SADE
Famous middle name	ALVA
Famous name in comedy	ALLEN
Famous Norwegian	LIE
Famous one	LION
Famous papers	XYZ
Famous Persian	OMAR
Famous pilgrim	ALDEN
Famous publisher	OCHS
Famous rider	REVERE
Famous river	NILE
Famous Roman	CATO
Famous Russian	LENIN
Famous seven	SEAS
Famous shrine	ALAMO
Famous Uncle	SAM
Famous U.S. editor	DANA
Famous West Point dropout	POE
Fanatical	RABID

Fanfare	ECLAT
Fanon	ORALE
Fare	DIET
Fared	DID
Fare for the gander	SAUCE
Farewell	ADIEU
Farewell for Ovid	VALE
Farewell or greeting	ALOHA
Fare with tea	SCONE
Farm animal	CALF,LAMB,RAM
Farm animals	EWES,OXEN,SOWS
Farm basket	SKEP
Farm building	SILO
Farm chore, Do a	SOW
Farmer kind	DIRT
Farmer of India	RYOT
Farmer's hangout	DELL
Farmer's necessity	LAND
Farmers' reward	CROP
Farmer's tool	HOE
Farm implements	PLOWS
Farm sound	MOO
Farm sounds	BAAS
Farm structure	BARN,CRIB
Farm structures	STIES
Farm unit	ACRE
Far out	ULTRA
Far: Prefix	TEL,TELE
Far removed	ALIEN
Farrow	MIA
Farsighted one	SEER
Farthest from hole, in golf	AWAY
Fashion	MODE,STYLE
Fashionable	SMART
Fashion creator	DIOR
Fashioned	MADE
Fashion name	FATH
Fast	RAPID
Fasten	LASH,NAIL,SEAL,SECURE
Fastener	HASP,TIER
Fasteners	PINS
Fasten, in a way	RIVET
Fastidious	NICE
Fast moving	DART
Fast plane	SST
Fat	LARD,SUET
Fate	LOT
Father, French	PERE
Father, in Spain	PADRE
Father of Goneril	LEAR
Father of Kish	NER
Father of Leif	ERIC
Father of the Pleiades	ATLAS
Fathers	SIRES
Fatigue	WEAR
Fat product	SOAP
Fatuous	INANE
Fatuous, Be	DOTE
Fat-yielding tree	SHEA
Faucet	TAP
Faucet position	SHUT
Faucet word	HOT
Fault, Find	CARP
Faux pas	SLIP
Favoring	FOR,PRO
Favorite	IDOL,PET
Favorite ones	SONS
F.D.R.'s mother	SARA
Fearsome one	OGRE
Feather	PENNA
Feathered missile	DART
Feather holder of a sort	TAR
Feathery pieces	BOAS
Feat of skill	STUNT
Feature, Angel	HALO
Feature, Beach	SURF
Feature, Dress	DART
Feature, Farm	SILO

Feature, Highway	LANE
Feature, Kitchen	OVEN
Feature of "Arabian Nights"	ROC
Feature of Lake Mead	DAM
Feature of N.E. Australia	REEF
Feature of Rome	HILL
Feature of some used cars	DENT
Feature of Utah flats	SALT
Feature, Opera	ARIA
Feature, Rug	PILE
Feature, Skirt	GORE
Features of horses	MANES
Feature, TV	NEWS
Feb. 22 event	SALE
Federal agency	USIA
Fedora	HAT
Fee	TOLL
Feeble	WAN
Feeds the kitty	ANTES
Feel	SENSE
Feel inclined	LIKE
Feeling	SENSE
Feeling responsible	CARING
Feel pity for	ACHE
Fees	DUES
Feet of some animals	PADS
Feign	SEEM,SHAM
Feigns	ACTS
Fell	HEW
Fell gradually	EBBED
Fellow	CHAP
Fellow, Unusual	ONER
Felt or straw	HAT
Female animals	DOES
Feminine ending	ESS
Feminine name	EDNA,ENID,SARA
Feminine suffix	TRESS
Feminine suffixes	ETTES,INES
Femme fatale	SIREN
Fenced in	PALED,PENNED
Fence parts	RAILS
Fencing weapons	EPEES
Fender damage	DENT
Ferber	EDNA
Fermented drink	MEAD
Ferments	STEWS
Fervor	HEAT,ZEAL
Festival, Passover	SEDER
Festivals	GALAS
Festivals, Certain	ALES
Festive time	YULE
Fetch	GET
Fete	GALA
Fetish	OBEAH
Fetters	IRONS
Feuchtwanger	LION
Fewer	LESS
F.F.V. name	LEE
Fiasco	DUD
Fibber	LIAR
Fiber	BAST,RAMIE
Fiber cloth	TOILE
Fiber cluster	NEP
Fiber shrub	RAMIE
Fibs	LIES
Fiction	TALE
Fictional bird	ROC
Fictional captain	NEMO
Fictional gumshoe	MOTO
Fictional heroine	TESS
Fiction, Girl of	TESS
Fictitious name	ALIAS
Fiddler	CRAB
Fidel's late cohort	CHE
Fido's friend	ROVER
Field flies, in batting practice	SHAG
Field for Cicero	AGER
Field of operation	THEATER

Field of snow NEVE
Fields AREAS,LEAS
Field's co-star WEST
Field, Study ARTS
Fieldwork with two faces REDAN
Fiend DEMON,SATAN
15th-century caravel NINA
Fight DUEL
Fighter's maneuvers JABS
Fighting equipment ARMS
Fight this with itself FIRE
Figure, Civil War REB
Figure, French Revolution MARAT
Figure, Genesis ABEL
Figure, Geometric CONE
Figure in Hindu myth RAMA
Figure, June BRIDE
Figure on a quarter EAGLE
Figure, Race-track TOUT
Figure, Sigmoidal ESS
Figure, Star-shaped ETOILE
Figure, Steinbeck OKIE
Filches STEALS
File RASP
Filed material DATA
File marker TAB
Fill SATE
Fill the bill SUIT
Filler for bird feeder SUET
Fill with pride ELATE
Fill with resolution STEEL
Filly's relative MARE
Film part REEL
Film produced by oxidation PATINA
Filmy GOSSAMER
Final NET
Finale END,OMEGA
Finally ALDER,ATLAST
Final word AMEN
Financier Kahn OTTO
Find LOCATE
Find agreeable LIKE
Find fault CAVIL
Find fault pettily CARP
Find a new place for RESET
Fine chap PRINCE
Fine cloth PINA
Fine fettle, In HALE
Fine-grained rock SHALE
Fine vase MING
Finials, Roof EPIS
Finicky NICE
Finis, Cleopatra's ASP
Finish END
Finished DONE,OVER
Finished, in verse OER
Finishes second LOSES
Finish, Fabric MOIRE
Finish an "i" DOT
Finishing tool REAMER
Finnish lake ENARE
Finnish port ABO
Fiord of Norway OSLO
Fired SHOT
Fire escape, e.g. EXIT
Fireplace GRATE
Fireplace area HOB
Fireworks ingredient NITER
Firmly fixed FAST
Firm-name ending SONS
Firm up SET
First asteroid CERES
First-born ELDEST
First Governor of Alaska EGAN
First home EDEN
First lady EVE
First Lady BESS
First man, in Nordic myth ASK
First name in baseball lore TRIS
First name in detective fiction ERLE
First name in Louvre MONA
First name in spying MATA
First name in stage lore OTIS
First name in U.S. fiction EDGAR
First name of Mrs. F.D.R. ANNA
First name of noted basso EZIO
First-rate AONE
First, second, etc. BASES
First woman M.P. ASTOR
First word in Vergil work ARMA
First word of a letter DEAR
First word of Mass. motto ENSE
First word of N.C. motto ESSE
Fiscal and leap YEARS
Fish EELS, PERCH,SHAD,SKATE,SMELT,TROLL,TUNA
Fish, Bright OPAH
Fish dish SOLE
Fish-eating bird ERN
Fished EELED
Fish eggs ROE
Fisherman EELER
Fisherman of Galilee PETER
Fishermen hope for a full one CREEL
Fish, European IDE
Fish, Freshwater DACE
Fish garnish ASPIC
Fishgig SPEAR
Fishhook part BARB
Fishing adjunct LURE
Fishing gear RODS
Fishing maneuver CAST
Fishing net SEINE
Fishline leader SNELL
Fish, Mackerel-like CERO
Fish, Predatory GAR
Fish sauce ALEC
Fissile rock SHALE
Fissure RENT
Fit ABLE
Fit together easily NEST
Fitzgerald ELLA
506 DVI
Fix MEND,REDO
Fix again RESET
Fix a chair CANE
Fix closely RIVET
Fix martinis STIR
Fix over ALTER
Fixed SET
Fixed charge RATE
Fixed potatoes RICED
Fixed practice RUT
Fixed a squeaky wheel OILED
Fizzle DUD
Flabbergast AMAZE,STUN
Flaccid LIMP
Flag IRIS
Flagrant GROSS,RANK
Flamboyance BLARE
Flanders river YSER
Flap TAB
Flaring star NOVA
Flash GLEAM
Flat LEVEL,STALE
Flat-bottomed boat SCOW
Flatcar, Empty IDLER
Flat, Cockney's OME
Flatfoot COP
Flat plinth ORLO
Flat sides PANES
Flat surface AREA
Flat-topped hill MESA
Flavor LIME,SAPOR
Flavorful TANGY

Flavoring ANISE,DILL
Flavoring plant HERB
Flavorsome TANGY
Flaw HOLE
Flaxen BLOND
Flax, Soak, as RET
Fled RAN
Fleeting EVANESCENT
Fleming IAN
Flemish river LYS
Fleshy fruit PEAR
Flexible sheepskin ROAN
Flexible shoot BINE
Flier KITE
Flightless bird EMU
Flight: Prefix AERO
Flinch WINCE
Fling TOSS
Flint product CAR
Flippered sea creature MANATEE
Flirts EYES
Flock belles EWES
Flood deposit SILT
Flood, in a way GLUT
Flood stage CREST
Floor STORY
Flooring TILE
Floor, in Paris ETAGE
Floors, Clean SCRUB
Flop LEMON
Flop, Ford EDSEL
Floral leaf PETAL
Florence's river ARNO
Florid RED
Florida city OCALA
Florida hub MIAMI
Florida product LEMON
Flossy ARTY
Flow RUN
Flow along LAVE
Flower ASTER,IRIS,POSY,ROSE
Flower bearer STEM
Flower, for short GLAD
Flowering shrub ELDER
Flower or fish STAR
Flower part PETAL,SEPAL,STEM
Flower places BEDS
Flowers' forte AROMA
Flower stalk SCAPE
Flower, Western SEGO
Flowing hairdos MANES
Flow out EMANATE
Flow, Tidal EAGRE
Fluffy stuff LINT
Fluid SERUM
Fluid rock LAVA
Fluids INKS,SERA
Flunky of old ESNE
Flurries ADOS
Flushed RED
Fly SOAR
Fly chaser of sorts TAIL
Fly, for one PEST
Flying prefix AERO
Foal COLT
Focusing device LENS
Fodder FEED,SILAGE
Fog MIST
Foil, Fencing EPEE
Fokker's foe SPAD
Fold PLEAT,WRAP
Folding money TENS
Folio LEAF
Folk singer IVES
Folksinger Joan BAEZ
Follow ENSUE,TAIL
Follow closely DOG
Follower of a belief DEIST
Follower of Cancer LEO
Follower of fa SOL
Follower of Joel AMOS
Follower of Zeno STOIC
Followers: Suffix ITES
Following blindly APISH
Follow orders HEED
Follow slavishly APE
Fond of, Be ADORE
Food ALIMENT
Food acid AMINO
Food fish CARP,HAKE,IDE,SHAD,SMELT
Food fragment ORT
Food, Hawaiian POI
Food, Hog MAST,SLOP
Food, Mexican TACO
Food, Spiritual MANNA
Food staple RICE
Foofaraw TODO
Fool IDIOT,OAF
Foolish GAGA
Foolish one SAP
Fools ASSES
Fool's gold, Bauxite and ORES
Foot ailment GOUT
Footballer, L.A. RAM
Football kick SPIRAL
Football player END
Football scores TDS
Football setback LOSS
Football's Tarkenton FRAN
Football team minus two NINE
Football throw SPIRAL
Football yardage GAIN
Footfall STEP
Footing for Eliza ICE
Footless APOD
Footlike part PES
Foot model LAST
Footnote word IDEM
Foot: Prefix PED
Foot soldier, in India PEON
Foot: Suffix PEDE
Footwear BOOT,SANDAL,SPATS
Footwear of a sort SKI
Forage crop RAPE
Foray RAID
Forbid BAN,VETO
Forbidden TABU
Forbidding GRIM
Forbode OMEN
Force, as payment EXACT
Forcefully AMAIN
Ford EDSEL,ERNIE,WADE
Fordhamite RAM
For each PER
Forearm bone ULNA
Foreboding OMEN
Foreign: Prefix XENO
Fore's partner AFT
Forest animal BOAR,DEER
Forest denizen DOE
Forest god PAN
Forest of "As You Like It" ARDEN
Foretoken BODE,OMEN,PROMISE
For example, Iliad EPIC
For example, "I wasn't there" ALIBI
For fear that LEST
Forgive REMIT
For, Hanker CRAVE
Form SHAPE
Formal dance: Fr. BAL
Formalities RITES
Former actor Erwin STU
Former Alaskan governor EGAN
Former alliance SEATO
Former Archbishop of Canterbury ANSELM

Former Broadway star	COHAN	Foundations	BASES
Former Chief Justice	CHASE	Found a line	SIRE
Former dancer Castle	IRENE	Fountain drink	COLA
Former dictator	PERON	Fountainhead	ROOT
Former diva	ALDA	Fountain items	SODAS
Former Downing St. name	EDEN	Fountain items, in Rome	COINS
Former French President	COTY	Fountain of note	TREVI
Former Knick star	REED	Fountain order, for short	MALT
Former Met star	PONS	Four-bagger	HOMER
Former movie star	LADD	Four gills	PINT
Former Mrs.	MISS	Four-handed exercise	DUET
Former ruler	TSAR	Four Hundred, The	ELITE
Former slugger	MARIS	Four-in-hand	TIE
Former Spanish queen	ENA	Fourth, Henry's	ANNE
Former spouses	EXES	Fowl	HENS
Former U.N. name	LIE	Fox's pride	TAIL
Former V.P.	AGNEW	Foxy	SLY
Formerly	ERST,ONCE	Fra	MONK
Formerly Castrogiovanni	ENNA	Fraction	TENTH
Formerly Christiania	OSLO	Fractional prefix	SEMI
Formerly, old style	ERST	Fraction, for one	RATIO
Formicidae	ANTS	Fragment	ORT
Form, Music	JAZZ	Fragments	ENDS
Form of address	SIR	Fragments, Literary	ANAS
Form of amo	AMAT	Fragrance	AROMA,SCENT
Form of decoration	ICING	Fragrances	ODORS
Form of Esperanto	IDO	Fragrant	OLENT,SWEET
Form of fuel	GAS	Fragrant resin	ELEMI
Form of to be: Fr.	SONT	Fragrant wood	CEDAR
Form of verse	ODE	Frame	EASEL
Forms an opinion	IDEATES	France, Coty of	RENE
For the nonce	PROTEM	France, River in	ISERE,MARNE
For one, Ash	TREE	France, River of	ORNE,RHONE
For one, Canopus	STAR	France's Corse, for one	ILE
For one, Clotho	FATE	Frank	OPEN
For one, Forsyte	SAGA	Franklin	BEN
For one, Fra	MONK	Franklin device	KITE
For one, Frost	POET	Fraternal doorkeeper	TILER
For one, Henna	RINSE	Fraternal one	ELK
For one, Hoover	DAM	Frat man's wear	PIN
For one, Hot Springs	SPA	Fratricide	CAIN
For one, Indian	OCEAN	Frau's consort	HERR
For one, Maggiore	LAGO	Fred Astaire prop	CANE
For one, Napoleon	EXILE	Fred or Lewis	STONE
For one, Nicholas	TSAR	Fred or Woody	ALLEN
For one, Not guilty	PLEA	Free	UNTIE
For one, Othello	MOOR	Free and clear	NET
For one, Phosgene	GAS	Freedom from worry	EASE
For one, Robert E.	ALEE	Free-for-all	MELEE
For one, Sheik	ARAB	Free from tension	RELAX
For one, Siamese	CAT	Free of	RID
For one, Smuts	BOER	Free of taboo, in Hawaii	NOA
For one, Swan	DIVE	Freighter area	HOLD
For one, Tweed	BOSS	French arm	BRAS
For one, "Un bel di"	ARIA	French article	LES,UNE
For short, Summary	RECAP	French artist	MATISSE
For: Sp.	POR	French as a friend	ENAMI
Forsyte's account	SAGA	French at last	ENFIN
Forte of former Met star Pons	ARIA	French author	ZOLA
Forte, Pindar's	ODE	French battle site	MARNE
Fortes, Inventors'	IDEAS	French beverage	THE
Forth, Call	EVOKE	French body of water	MER
Forth, Sends	EMITS	French born	NEE
Forth, Sound	ORATE	French brainstorm	IDEE
Fortification	REDAN	French bread	PAIN
Fort near Monterey	ORD	French byway	ALLEE
Fortress	CITADEL	French cake	BABA
Fortune teller	SEER	French city	ARLES
Fortune-teller's words	ISEE	French clergyman	ABBE
Fortune-telling pack	TAROT	French composer	LALO
45 inches	ELL	French cup	TASSE
49ers' quests	LODES	French dance	BAL
49th, The	ALASKA	French denial	NON
Forty-weekday period	LENT	French direction	NORD
Forum garb	TOGA	French donkey	ANE
Forum tongue	LATIN	French dream	REVE
Forward	SEND	French drink	EAU
Foster	ABET	French empress	MARIE

Clue	Answer
French eye	OEIL
French family man	PERE
French floor	ETAGE
French friend	AMI,AMIE
French handle	ANSE
French head	TETE
French here	ICI
French historian	RENAN
French husband	MARI
French impressionist	DEGAS,MONET
French infinitive	ETRE
French king	ROI
French land area	ILE
French laugh	RIRE
French lifeline	SEINE
Frenchman's name	RENE
French measure	METRE
French menu entry	ROTI
French merry	GAI
French milk	LAIT
French mine	AMOI
French money	FRANC
French month	MAI
French nobleman	DUC
French nothing	RIEN
French novelist	GIDE
French numeral	CINQ
French passion	AMOUR
French pastry	TARTE
French political unit	ETAT
French port	BREST,CAEN
French possessive	MON,SES
French president	COTY
French priest	CURE
French pronoun	MOI,NOTRE,NOUS
French pronouns	ELLES
French reading matter	LIVRE
French relative	MERE,TANTE
French reply	OUI
French resort	NICE
French revenue	RENTE
French revolutionist	MARAT
French river	AISNE,EURE,ISERE, LOIRE,MEUSE,OISE,ORNE,SAONE,YSER
French salt	SEL
French school	ECOLE
French scream	CRI
French sculptor	RODIN
French seasons	ETES
French soldier	POILU
French spa	EVIAN
French spirit	AME
French stars	ETOILES
French, Syrian city, to	ALEP
French their	LEUR
French then	ALORS
French titles	MMES
French toast	SANTE
French town	STLO
French verb	SONT
French very	TRES
French waterway	RHONE
French wave	ONDE
French weapon	ARME
French with	AVEC
French without	SANS
French writer	ANET
French yesterday	HIER
Frenziedly	AMOK
Frequently	OFTEN
Fresh	NEW,SASSY
Fresh gossip	LATEST
Freshen	RENEW
Freshly	ANEW
Freshness, Lost	FADED
Freshwater clam	MUSSEL
Freshwater duck	TEAL
Freshwater fish	IDE
Fresh-water fish	DACE
Frets	STEWS
Freuchen subject	SEA
Freudian terms	IDS
Freudian topic	EGO
Friars Club event	ROAST
Friend	AMIGO
Friend, Dante's, for short	BEA
Friend: Fr.	AMI
Friend, in Lille	AMIE
Friend, in Sonora	AMIGO
Friendly chat	COZE
Friend of Narcissus	ECHO
Friend, out west	PARD
Friend, Servicemen's	USO
Friendship	AMITY
Friends, in Paris	AMIS
Friends, Scottish	EMES
Friend William	PENN
Frigg's spouse	ODIN
Frighten	ALARM
Frightening	EERIE
Frightens	AWES
Frightful fellow	OGRE
Frivolous	IDLE
Frolic	PLAY
From a distance	AFAR
From, Draw	TAP
From, Free	RID
From, in Germany	AUS
Front	PROW
Front-page boxes	EARS
Front: Prefix	PRE
Frost	RIME
Frosted	ICED
Frost et al.	POETS
Frowning	GLUM
Frozen	ICED
Fruit	APPLE,DATE,LIME,PEAR
Fruit drink	ADE
Fruit for Bacchus	GRAPE
Fruiting spike	EAR
Fruit parts	CORES,STONES
Fruity part of the neck	ADAMSAPPLE
Frying-pan item	LARD
Fuegians	ONAS
Fuel	GAS,OIL,PEAT
Fugue master	BACH
Full of calories	RICH
Full of life	SPRY
Full of: Suffix	OSE
Full speed, old style	AMAIN
Fully paid	EVEN
Fully satisfied	SATED
Fume	REEK
Functions	ACTS,ROLES,USES
Fundamental	BASAL
Fundamentals	ABCS
Fundy, for one	BAY
Funeral oration	ELOGE
Fur	LAPIN,OTTER
Fur bearer, for short	COON
Fur-bearing animal	OTTER
Furlough	LEAVE
Furnace	OAST
Furnish	LEND
Furniture style	ADAM
Furniture wood	TEAK
Furrow	PLOW
Furrows	RUTS
Further	AID
Furthermore	ALSO
Furtive	SLY
Fury	RAGE
Furze	GORSE
Fuse	UNITE
Fuse by heat	FRIT

Fuss	TODO	Futile call on a rainy day	TAXI
Fusses	ADOS	Future, for one	TENSE
Fussy	NICE	Future racer	FOAL
Futile	VAIN	Fuzz	LINT

G

Gab at length	JAW	Garment for a quaestor	TOGA
Gable or Mansard	ROOF	Garment, Indian	SARI
Gabor	EVA	Garment, Roman	TOGA
Gad	ROAM,ROVE	Garments, Priest's	ALBS
Gaelic	ERSE	Garner	REAP
Gaelic god	LER	Garnish	ASPIC,CAPER
Gaelic name	IAN	Gary Cooper word	NOPE
Gaggle components	GEESE	Gas	NEON
Gaiety	MIRTH	Gases, Like some	INERT,RARE
Gain	EARN,NET	Gasman's reading matter	METER
Gain altitude	CLIMB	Gas: Prefix	AER,AERO
Gainer	DIVE	Gas, Thin, as	RARE
Gains	GETS,WINS	Gas users	CARS
Gainsay	DENY	Gateway to Russia in W.W.II	BASRA
Gait	STEP,TROT	Gather	AMASS,GLEAN,MASS
Gaiters	SPATS	Gather in	REAP
Galahad's quest	GRAIL	Gatherings of sorts	BEES
Galena	ORE	Gaucho item	RIATA
Galileo's birthplace	PISA	Gaucho weapon	BOLA
Gall	NERVE	Gave audience to	HEARD
Gallery	TIER	Gave a hand	AIDED
Gallery hanging	NUDE	Gavel-wielder's word	ORDER
Galley notation	STET	Gave sparingly	DOLED
Gallic friend	AMIE	Gay	RIANT
Gallic name	RENE	Gay blade	RAKE
Gallic season	ETE	Gay place	PAREE
Gallic soul	AME	Gaze	STARE
Gallivant	ROAM	Gazelle	ARIEL
Galls	IRKS	Gazelle of Tibet	GOA
Gals	DAMES	Gear, Cowboy	SPURS
Galway Bay islands	ARAN	Gear, Detection	SONAR
Galway's land	EIRE	Gear, Fencing	EPEES
Gambler's concern	ODDS	Gear, Fishing	CREEL
Gambler's headaches	IOUS	Gear for a horse thief	NOOSE
Gambling milieu	RENO	Gear, Scull	OARS
Gambrel or Mansard	ROOF	Gear, Sports	SKIS
Game	DEER	Gear, Stereo	HIFI
Game, Child's	TAG	Gear, Vaquero	REATA
Game divided into chukkers	POLO	Gear, Waiter's	TRAY
Game fish	CERO	Geisha garb	OBIS
Game piece	TILE	Gelling agent	AGAR
Game pieces	MEN	Gem stone	ONYX
Game place	ARENA	Gemstone	OPAL
Game, Pub	DARTS	Gen. Bradley	OMAR
Game scores	TDS	Gender	SEX
Games in a sweep	ALL	General character	TONE
Game, Stake in a	ANTE	General idea	TENOR
Game, Started off a	TEED	General in Michigan	MOTORS
Gamma or beta	RAY	General, Revolutionary	GATES
Gang	CREW	Generous	OPENHANDED
Ganges garb	SARIS	Generous piece of bread	SLAB
Ganges sight	GHAT	Genesis figure	ADAM,ESAU,LEVI
Gangster's money	KALE	Genesis man	ENOS
Gantry	ELMER	Genesis name	SHEM
Garb, Cinderella	RAGS	Genesis victim	ABEL
Garb, G.I.'s	ODS	Geneva's river	RHONE
Garden chore, Do a	WEED	Genitive or ablative	CASE
Gardener's box	FLAT	Genoa, Money in	LIRE
Garden green	KALE	Genre	ILK
Garden implement	RAKE	Gentlemen, Gypsy	RYES
Garden occupant	ADAM	Gentleman of Acapulco	SENOR
Garden pest	APHID	Gentle or Big	BEN
Garden plot	BED	Genu	KNEE
Gardens	EDENS	Genus of geese	ANSER
Garden tools	HOES	Genus of maples	ACER
Gardner	AVA,ERLE	Genus of trees	OLEA
Garishness	GLARE	Genus, Willow	ITEA
Garlands	LEIS	Geographical feature	RIVER
Garment	BRA,ROBE,STOLE,WRAP	Geography word	AREA
Garment addition	INSET	Geological formation	IONE
Garment, Arab	ABA	Geological times	EONS

Geologic period, Of a ERIAN
Geologic periods AGES
Geologic times ERAS
Geologist's term STOSS
Geometric line ARC
Geometric shape CONE
George Eliot's real name EVANS
George M. COHAN
George W. confessed to him DAD
Georgia city MACON
Georgian no NYET
Geraint's love ENID
Germ SEED
German admiral SPEE
German article DAS,DER,EIN,EINE
German composer ABT
German craft UBOAT
German exclamation ACH
German export BEER
German king OTTO
German nyet NEIN
German over UBER
German port EMDEN,ESSEN
German preposition AUS
German pronoun SIE
German region SAAR
German river EDER,ELBE,EMS,ODER,WESER
German river to Elbe EGER
German's never NIE
German state HESSE
German title HERR
German wife FRAU
Gershwin IRA
Gershwin heroine BESS
Gest DEED
Get along AGREE,COME
Get around EVADE
Get away from ELUDE
Get feline revenge SCRATCH
Get the hard way EARN
Get in good graces ENDEAR
Get off START
Get a result REAP
Get rid of EJECT
Gets 40 winks NAPS
Gets hot under the collar STEAMS
Gets on AGES
Getter of attention AHEM
Getters of attention PSTS
Get together MEET
Get-togethers TEAS
Get under one's skin RILE
Get up ARISE,RISE
Get wind of HEAR
Ghastly ASHY
Ghost SHADE
Giant among Giants OTT
Giant killer DAVID
Giants' old grounds POLO
Gibbons APES
Gibe at DERIDE
Gibson ingredient ONION
Gielgud vehicle DRAMA
Gift for 35th anniversary CORAL
Gift recipient DONEE
Gifts for men TIES
Gifts for the poor ALMS
Giggle TEHEE
Ginsberg, for one POET
Giraffe's cousin OKAPI
Giraffe's pride NECK
Girl LASS
Girl, Dumb DORA
Girl, Fictional TESS
Girl Friday's role AIDE
Girl in "Gone With the Wind" MELANIE
Girl in Afton song MARY
Girl, Little NELL
Girl of song AMY,LOLA,MIMI,NOLA,SUE
Girl, Orphan ANNIE
Girl, "Pompeii" IONE
Girl's name ADA,ADAH, ADELA,ADELE,AMANDA,ANNE,AVA,AVIS, CORA,ELLA,ELLEN,ELSA,ENA,INEZ, IRMA,ISABEL,LAURA,NORA,OLGA,RAE
Girl's nickname BEA,ETTA,MEG,PAM,TONI
Girls' nicknames NANS
Girl, Stowe EVA
Girl's toy DOLL
Girl, "Zhivago" LARA
G.I.'s food CHOW
Give aid to ABET
Give ear HEED
Give heed ATTEND
Give off fumes REEK
Give orders BOSS
Give out METE
Gives a hard time TRIES
Give the slip to EVADE
Gives the nod LETS
Gives out EMITS
Gives up CEDES
Give a wide berth to SHUN
G.I. wear ODS
Giza's river NILE
Glacial ridges OSAR
Glacial snow NEVE
Glaciology term STOSS
Gladden ELATE
Glade: Prefix NEMO
Glance over SCAN
Glaring light FLARE
Glasgow negative NAE
Glass PANE
Glass vessel VIAL
Gleamed SHONE
Glean REAP
Glengarry man SCOT
Glide high SOAR
Glip PAT
Global area ASIA,EAST
Globes ORBS
Gloomy aura PALL
Gloomy Dean INGE
Glossy paint ENAMEL
Glossy varnish JAPAN
Gloves, in away MATES
Glowing AFIRE
Glowing, as a coal LIVE
Glue on ATTACH
Gluts SATES
Glutten SATED
G-man AGENT
Gnat MIDGE
Gnat or rat PEST
Gnawed EATEN
Gnaws EATS
Goad INCITE,URGE
Goads PRODS,SPURS
Go after a fly SWAT
Go ahead LEAD
Go-aheads YESES
Goal AIM,END,IDEAL
Goat KID
Go away! SHOO
"Go away!" SCAT
Gob TAR
Go bad SOUR
Gobi, Like the ARID
God, A LER,AMOR
Goddesses of the seasons HORAE
Goddess, in Rome DEA
Goddess in Wagner's "Ring" ERDA
Goddess of dawn EOS
Goddess of destiny NORN

Clue	Answer
Goddess of discord	ERIS
Goddess of infatuation	ATE
Goddess of peace	IRENE
Goddess of vengeance	ARA
Goddess of Victory	NIKE
Goddess of youth	HEBE
Go-devils	SLEDS
God, in old Rome	DEUS
God of love	EROS
God of Memphis	PTAH
God, Olympian	ARES
Gods led by Odin	AESIR
God's Little and others	ACRES
Goes bad	ROTS
Goes for a spin	MOTORS
Goes gaga over	DOTES
Goes limp	SAGS
Goes to the plate	BATS
Goes wrong	ERRS
Going-steady symbol	PIN
Go in the red	OWE
Golconda	MINE
Gold-bearing deposits	PLACERS
Golddigger's target	HEIR
Golden and Iron	AGES
Golden Fleece ship	ARGO
Golden or general	RULE
Golden Rule word	UNTO
Gold, for instance	METAL
Gold, Spanish	ORO
Gold vein	LODE
Gold, Weight in	CARATS
Golf area for an astronaut	MOON
Golf ball position	LIE
Golf club parts	TOES
Golf-club parts	SOLES
Golf clubs	IRONS
Golfer Sarazen	GENE
Golfer's last act	PUTT
Golfer's target	PIN
Golfer's thrill	ACE
Golfer's word	FORE
Golfing area	TEE
Golfing feat	EAGLE
Golfing great	SNEAD
Golfing unit	HOLE
Golf nickname	ARNIE
Golf score	PAR
Golf shot	DRIVE
Golf tourney, Certain	OPEN
Go motoring	DRIVE
Gone	AWAY,LEFT
Goneril's father	LEAR
Good advice	TRY
Good buy: Colloq.	STEAL
"Good-bye" composer	TOSTI
Good citizen	VOTER
"Good Earth" heroine	OLAN
Good exercise	HIKE
Good Feeling et al.	ERAS
Good guy	HERO
Good guys, The	POSSE
Goodman or Jane	ACE
"Goodnight" girl	IRENE
Goods	WARE
Good sense	REASON
Good shape, In	HALE
Good times	UPS
Goodwill	AMITY
Good wood for rafts	BALSA
Goofed	ERRED
Go off on the q.t.	ELOPE
Gook or muck	OOZE
Go on	RANT
Go one better	CAP
Go onstage	ENTER
Goose egg	ZERO
Goose genus	ANSER
Gooseneck, e.g.	LAMP
Go over again	ITERATE
Go over briefly	RECAP
Go places	TOUR
Gore	INSET
Gorge	CHASM
Gorges	SATES
Gossamer	WEB
Gossip	CHAT,DIRT,SIEVE
Got the fire going again	RELIT
Gothic or classic, Prefix for	NEO
Go through a sieve	SEEP
Got off	ALIT
Got on	FARED
Go to ruin	ROT
Got saddle sores	RODE
Got wind of	HEARD
Goulash	STEW
Gould's railroad	ERIE
Gourmand's reading	MENU
Govern	RULE
Government agency	USIA
Gov't. agents	TMEN
Gown	DRESS
Gown material	LAME
Graceful birds	SWANS
Graceful rhythm	LILT
Grace herb	RUE
Grackle	DAW
Grade of admiral	REAR
Grade of meat	CHOICE
Grade of seaman	ABLE
Gradually move	EDGE
Grafted, in heraldry	ENTE
Grain	OATS
Grain appendage	AWN
Grain exchanges	PITS
Grain product	BRAN,MALT
Grains	RYES
Grammatical term	NOUN
Gram or dynamics prefix	AERO
Gram or meter prefix	DIA
Gram or sode prefix	EPI
Gram prefix	TELE
Grampuses	ORCS
Grand Canyon area	RIM
Grand duke of Muscovy	IVAN
Grande or Rita	RIO
Grand, for one	HOTEL
Grandiloquize	ORATE
Grandparental	AVAL
Grand slam, at times	HOMER
Granite center	BARRE
Granny	KNOT
Grant	ADMIT,CEDE
Grape	UVA
Grape juice	SAPA,STUM
Grape: Lat.	UVA
Grape refuse	MARC
Graph or crat word	AUTO
Graph or vision prefix	TELE
Grasp	SEE,SENSE
Grass	ALFA
Grass, Cereal	OAT
Grass, Kentucky	POA
Grasslands	LEAS
Grassy plain	LLANO
Gratified	SATED
Gratify	FEED
Gravelly ridges	OSAR
Gravy hazards	SPOTS
Gravy holder	BOAT
Gray	ASHEN
Gray color	TAUPE
Graylags	GEESE
Gray wolf	LOBO
Grazed	FED
Grazing area	LEA

Great EPIC
Great amount REAM
Great amounts TONS
Great Asian river AMUR
Greater MORE
Great, Ivan the TSAR
Great Lake ONTARIO
Great Lake city ERIE
Greatly like, informally ADORE
Great name in art GOYA
Great number, informally SLEW
Great or Terrible IVAN
Great throng HORDE
Great, to the younger set NEAT
Greedy AVID
Greedy gulp SWIG
Greedy ones PIGS
Greek clan division OBE
Greek coin OBOL
Greek colonnade STOA
Greek commune DEME
Greek contest AGON
Greek god ARES,EROS,PAN
Greek goddess ATHENA,EOS,ERIS,HERA,IRENE,NIKE
Greek goddesses HORAE
Greek island CRETE,SAMOS
Greek letter CHI,DELTA,IOTA,PHI,RHO,TAU
Greek letters BETAS,ETAS,OMEGAS,PSIS
Greek nickname ARI
Greek peak OSSA
Greek Pluto DIS
Greek poet HOMER
Greek theater, Old ODEUM
Greek theaters ODEA
Greeley, for one EDITOR
Green RAW
Greenhouse decor GLASS
Greenish blue TEAL
Green isle ERIN
Greenland base ETAH
Greenland colonizer ERIC
Greenland vehicles SLEDS
Green light OKAY,YES
Green plums GAGES
Green rust on old bronze PATINA
Green shade NILE
Green stones JADES
Greet HAIL
Greeting ALOHA
Greeting for a villain HISS
Gregorian or Julian CALENDAR
Grenoble item SKI
Greta Garbo word ALONE
Grew ashen PALED
Gridiron thrill PASS
Grid successes TDS
Grieg character ASE
Grievous SORE
Grill device SPIT
Grim STERN
Grimace MOUE
Grimm bad man OGRE
Grit SAND
Grizzly, for one BEAR
Grocery item OLEO
Grommet EYELET
Groom COMB
Groove in a wall DADO
Grooves RUTS
Grouch CRAB
Ground LOT
Ground corn SAMP
Groundless IDLE
Groundwork BASE
Group, Family CLAN
Group, Fraternal ELKS
Group, Jurors' PANEL
Group, Matched SET
Group, Moonlighting NASA
Group of fitted objects NEST
Group of pheasants NIDE
Group organized in 1890 DAR
Group, Secret KLAN
Group serving servicemen USO
Group, Social CASTE
Group: Suffix OME
Group, W.W.II AXIS
Group, Western OAS
Growing out ENATE
Growing trend WAVE
Growl SNARL
Grow less early LATEN
Growls GNARS
Grownup ADULT
Grub CHOW,LARVA
Gruesome threesome FATES
Guadeloupe, Here, in ICI
Guantanamo and others BASES
Guarantee SEAL
Guaranteed SURE
Guardhouse BRIG
Gudrun's spouse ATLI
Guest's bed, at times COT
Guffaws YAKS
Guggenheim offering ART
Guide LEAD,REIN
Guide, Mariner's STAR
Guides STEERS
Guinea pigs' home LAB
Guinness ALEC
Guinness or Raleigh SIR
Guitar-player's term BARRE
Guitar's ancestor LUTE
Gulf of Ionian Sea ARTA
Gulf of Mideast ADEN
Gull DUPE,TERN
Gulls MEWS
Gully WADI
Gulp SWIG
Gumbo OKRA
Gum resins ELEMIS
Gumshoe TEC
Gun, British STEN
Gunlock catch SEAR
Gunpowder ingredient NITER
Gush forth SPEW
Guthrie ARLO
Guy CHAP
Guy Fawkes specialty PLOT
Guys' friends GALS
Gym equipment MAT
Gym shoes SNEAKERS
Gypsum GESSO
Gypsy ROM
Gypsy men RYES
Gyrate SPIN

H

Haberdashery item BELT
Habit USAGE
Habitation ABODE
Habituate ENURE,INURE
Hacienda material ADOBE
Hack TAXI
Hackneyed TIRED
Hacks CABS
Had brunch ATE
Hades, River of LETHE
Had occasion for NEEDED
Hag CRONE

Hagen UTA
Haggard heroine SHE
Hail AVE,GREET
Hair TRESS
Hair fabric ABA
Hair, Horse MANE
Hair line PART
Hairnet SNOOD
Hairpieces RATS
Hair style AFRO,BUN
Hair tint RINSE
Halfback's vulnerable spot KNEE
Half a fifth TENTH
Half a fly TSE
Half a musical title IDO
Half of N.B. NOTA
Half: Prefix DEMI,SEMI
Half a prison SING
Halfway smile GRIN
Haliotis ABALONE
Hall, Army MESS
Hall, in Paris SALLE
Hallmark of the good HALO
Hall of Famer OTT
Halloween apparel SHEET
Halloween word BOO
Halt, Called a ENDED
Halter REIN
Halting place REST
Ham-act EMOTE
Hamburg's river ELBE
Hamilton, for short ALEX
Hamlet DANE,DORP
Hamlet, for one ROLE
Hammer part CLAW
Hammer's target NAIL
Hammers and saws TOOLS
Hamper CLOG,CRAMP
Ham's click DOT
Ham's field RADIO
Handbags, Certain TOTES
Hand, Bridge EAST
Handcuffs IRONS
Handel work LARGO
Handkerchief cloth PINA
Handkerchief extra INITIAL
Handle SEETO
Handle a bobsled STEER
Handled USED
Handle, in France ANSE
Handle: Lat. ANSA
Handles, as a shrew TAMES
Handle-with-care material TNT
Hand or boot word FREE
Hand over CEDE
Hand, Provides a LENDS
Hands on hips AKIMBO
Handwork, Do TAT
Handy ONTAP
Handy hints TIPS
Handy, to poets ANEAR
Hanger-on PEST
Hang on, in poker STAY
Hangs back LAGS
Hangs down LOPS
Hanker CRAVE,LONG
Hankering URGE
Hankerings YENS
Hansoms CABS
Haphazard attempt STAB
Hapless one GONER
Hap or nomer prefix MIS
Happening EVENT
Happy sounds HAHAS
Harangue ORATE
Harass BAIT,BESET
Harbinger OMEN
Harbor craft SCOW
Harbored HELD
Harbor of Guam APRA
Hard STONY
Harden SEAR,STEEL
Hard-hit baseball LINER
Harding of films ANN
Hard look STARE
Hardly 'eaven ELL
Hard to believe TALL
Hard to find RARE
Hard to understand DEEP
Hardware item NAIL
Hardwood TEAK
Hard wood ELM
Hardwood tree OAK
Hardy heroine TESS
Hardy plant of Europe GORSE
Harem rooms ODAS
Hari MATA
Harmful EVIL
Harmful agent BANE
Harmonize AGREE
Harmonized TONED
Harmony ACCORD
Harness-race event PACE
Harness unit HAME
Harold of old comics TEEN
Harp on ITERATE
Harries PESTERS
Harriman, to friends AVE
Harry, Light-horse LEE
Harsh STERN
Hart MOSS
Harte BRET
Harvest REAP
Harvest in India RABI
Harvests CROPS
Has a bite EATS
Has debts OWES
Has it made RATES
Hasten SPEED
Hasty RASH
Hat, Bishop's MITER
Hats: Colloq. LIDS
Hatteras or Horn CAPE
Haul TOTE,TOW
Hautboy OBOE
Have it made RATE
Havelock ELLIS
Have-nots NEEDY
Havens ARKS
Have reference RELATE
Have sway RULE
Have trust in RELY
Have a yen for CRAVE
Having auricles EARED
Having a dull surface MATTE
Having fewer bright moments TAMER
Having had it, with "up" FED
Having musical quality TONAL
Having no feet APOD
Having a will TESTATE
Haw's partner HEM
Hawaiian beach feature SURF
Hawaiian cliff PALI
Hawaiian dish POI
Hawaiian gifts LEIS
Hawaiian island OAHU
Hawaiian loincloth MALO
Hawaiian port HILO
Hawaiian royalty ALII
Hawaiian veranda LANAI
Hawaiian yam HOI
Hawk KITE
Hawkeyes' home IOWA
Hawser ROPE
Hay and oats FEED
Hayden of Arizona CARL

Clue	Answer
Haymarket and others	RIOTS
Hay, Spreads	TEDS
Hayworth	RITA
Hazard	PERIL
Hazards, Road	ESSES
Hazlitt's contemporary	ELIA
Headband, Bedouin	AGAL
Head decor	WIG
Headdress	MITER,TIARA
Head, French	TETE
Headgear	BERET,TAM,TAMS
Headgear, Angelic	HALO
Headland	NESS
Headlight word	DIM
Headliners	STARS
Head part	PATE
Headpieces	TIARAS
Headquarters	SEAT
Headwear	SNOOD,TAM
Head woes	ACHES
Heal	MEND
Healing agency	BALM
Health clubs	SPAS
Health: Fr.	SANTE
Healthy in Spain	SANO
Healthy look	TAN
Heap	PILE
Hearing aids	EARS
Hearing, for one	SENSE
Hearing of a deed in court	OYER
Heart	CORE
Hearty dish	STEW
Hearty's companion	HALE
Hear ye!	OYEZ
Heaters	ETNAS
Heath genus	ERICA
Heathen	PAGAN
Heating device	LAMP
Heaven	PARADISE
Heavenly body	ORB
Heavenly spirit: Fr.	ANGE
Heavens	ETHER
"Heavens!"	EGAD
Heaven: Sp.	CIELO
Heavily walked	TROD
Heavy cloth	SHAG
Heavy hair	MANE
Heavy jacket	REEFER
Heavy reading matter	TOMES
Heavy shoe	SABOT
Heavyweight name	ALI
Heavy wood	EBONY
Hebrew judge	ELI
Hebrew letter	ALEF,MEM
Hebrew letters	NUNS
Hebrew measure	OMER
Hebrew month	ADAR,ELUL
Hebrew precept	TORAH
Hebrew prophet	AMOS
Hebrew zither	ASOR
Hebrides island	IONA
Heckle	BOO
Hector's home	TROY
Heed	EAR
Heep	URIAH
Heidelberg memento	SCAR
Height	ACME
Height: Prefix	ACRO
Heir	SON
He is: Lat.	EST
Held	ANNA
Held court	SAT
Held the reins	LED
Helen's milieu	TROY
Helical	SPIRAL
Helicon	TUBA
Hellenic mountain	OSSA
Hellespont girl	HERO

Clue	Answer
Hello, Spaniard's	HOLA
Helm position	ALEE
Helms's outfit	CIA
Helot	SERF
Helot's home	SPARTA
Help	AID
"Help!"	SOS
Helped	AIDED
Helper	AIDE
Help in a way	ABET
Hem	BASTE
Hemingway	PAPA
Hemisphere group	OAS
Hemp fiber	BAST
Hence	ERGO
Henhouse area	ROOST
Henhouse unit	NEST
Henley sights	OARS
Henna	RINSE
Henna, rose and cherry	REDS
Henry VIII's second	ANNE
Henry VIII's sixth	PARR
Hep	ONTO
Hepburn	KATE
Heraldic bearing	ORLE
Heraldry, Dog in	ALAN
Heraldry, Dotted, in	SEME
Heraldry, Grafted in	ENTE
Herb	RUE
Herbage	GRASS
Herb, Dill	ANET
Herb, East Indian	SOLA
Herb, Flavoring	DILL
Herb, Flavorsome	ANISE
Herb, Forage	RAPE
Herb of West	SEGO
Herbs	SAGES
Herb's predecessor	CAL
Hercules's captive	IOLE
Here, in Brest	ICI
Hereditary factor	GENE
Here's companion	NOW
Herman or Ruth	BABE
Hermit, for one	CRAB
Hero	IDOL,STAR
Hero, Broadway	ABIE
Heroic	EPIC
Heroine, Biblical	ESTHER
Heroine, Dickens	NELL
Heroine of "Private Lives"	AMANDA
Heroine, Wagnerian	ERDA
Heroine, "Zhivago"	LARA
Heron	EGRET
Hero of Western film	SHANE
Hero, Tennyson	ARDEN
Hero, Uris	ARI
Hero, Verne	NEMO
Hero-worship subject	IDOL
Hersey town	ADANO
Hesitates	HEMS
Hesitations	ERS
He sold his birthright	ESAU
He's overboard	MAN
He took a bath	MARAT
Hew	FELL
He was, in Rome	ERAT
Hewer	AXE
Hex	CURSE
Heyerdahl	THOR
H.H. Munro	SAKI
Hiatus	LULL
Hiawatha's craft	CANOE
Hibernated	SLEPT
Hickam Field's island	OAHU
Hidden explosive	MINE
Hide	STASH
Hideout	DEN,LAIR
Hiding place	CACHE

Hied SPED
Hi-fi gear STEREO
High action DRAMA
Highborn REGAL
Highbrow SNOB
High crag TOR
High dwelling AERIE
Higher, in Berlin OBER
Highest note ELA
Highest point ACME,CREST,NOON
High flier KITE
Highland group CLAN
Highland hillside BRAE
High-low card signal ECHO
High: Mus. ALT
High nest: Var. AERY
High: Prefix ALTI
High-priced DEAR
High priest ELI
High rank ESTATE
High-school subject LATIN
High silk hat TILE
High spirits GLEE
High-strung TAUT
High waves SEAS
Highway ROAD
Highway sign EATS
Highway stops MOTELS
Highway unit LANE
Hike TRAMP
Hilarity MIRTH
Hill RISE
Hill dweller ANT
Hill in S.F. NOB
Hill of sand, in England DENE
Hill, Scottish BRAE
Hill slope SIDE
Hilo greeting ALOHA
Hinder DETER
Hinder growth STUNT
Hindmost REAR
Hindu epic hero RAMA
Hindu garment SARI
Hindu goddess DEVI
Hindu monastery MATH
Hindu month ASIN
Hindu pundit GURU
Hindu queen RANI
Hindu reign RAJ
Hindu title SRI
Hindu weights SERS
Hint CLUE,CUE,ODOR,TIP
Hipbones ILIA
Hippie's home PAD
Hippy feature HAIR
Hire LEASE
Hirsute HAIRY
His: Fr. ALUI,SES,SON
His or Hers TOWEL
Historian and theologian BEDE
Historic French river AISNE
Historic island ELBA,LEYTE
Historic periods ERAS
Historic ship MAINE
Historic vessel NINA
Historic waterway NILE
History, Muse of CLIO
Hitch SNAG
Hitchcock's game POLO
Hit hard: Slang PASTE
Hither HERE
Hither's partner YON
Hit in a way TAMP
Hitler's love EVA
Hit sharply SLAP
Hit sign SRO
H.M.S. Pinafore's fleet NAVEE
Hoard STORE
Hoarfrost RIME
Hock PAWN
Hockey equipment SKATE
Hockey-puck maneuver ICING
Hodgepodge MESS,OLIO
Hoffmann's forte TALES
Hog feed MAST,SLOP
Hogshead VAT
Hogs' housing STIES
Hoist LIFT
Hokinson or Hayes HELEN
Hokkaido indigene AINU
Hokkaido port OTARU
Hokum BLAH
Holbrook HAL
Hold back STAY
Hold dear ADORE
Holder for small items ETUI
Holder, Fishhook SNELL
Holder, Wheel AXLE
Hold in REIN
Holding arms a la Puck AKIMBO
Hold kind TOE
Hold, Legal LIEN
Hold on LAST
Holds a session SITS
Hold sway RULE
Hole PIT
Hole-in-one ACE
Holiday FETE
Holiday season NOEL
Holiday time YULE
Holiday times EVES
Holiday, Vietnam TET
Holly ILEX
Hollywood area LOT
Hollywood man AGENT
Hollywood memento OSCAR
Holm ISLET
Holmes OLIVER
Holmesian word ELEMENTARY
Holm oak ILEX
Holms AITS
Holy image ICON
Holy Roman Emperor OTTO
Holzman or Grange RED
Home, Bulldog's YALE
Home for a jinni LAMP
Home for a queen HIVE
Home for two billion or so ASIA
Home, Hippie PAD
Home, in Veracruz CASA
Home, Incas' PERU
Homely UGLY
Home, Mets' SHEA
Home of Chang and Eng SIAM
Home of the Incas ANDES
Home of Irish kings TARA
Home of Krupp ESSEN
Home, of sorts TEPEE
Home of Wilson Dam ALABAMA
Homer opus ILIAD
Homers, e.g. HITS
Home-run star MARIS
Homes for fledglings NESTS
Honduran port TELA
Hone STROP,WHET
Honey MEL
Honeybee genus APIS
Honey factory HIVE
Honey hunter BEAR
Hong Kong skirt feature SLIT
Honkers GEESE
Honolulu greeting ALOHA
Honor LAUD
Honor card KING,TEN
Honor cards ACES
Honored FETED

Clue	Answer
Honshu volcano	ASAMA
Hood	ROBIN
Hoof it	LEG
Hook together	YOKE
Hoople oath	EGAD
Hoosier poet	RILEY
Hooter	OWL
Hoover and others	DAMS
Horace or Thomas	MANN
Horatian, for one	ODE
Horatio	ALGER
Horizontal	LEVEL
Hormone substance	ACTH
Horne	LENA
Horn kind	ALTO
Horn or May	CAPE
Horse	ARAB,ROAN,STEED
Horse color	BAY
Horse driver's command	GEE
Horse food	OATS
Horsehair	MANE
Horse opera	OATER
Horse play	POLO
Horse race	TROT
Horses	MARES
Horseshoe wedge	CALK
Horse show, Certain	RODEO
Horse's predecessor, in saying	CART
Horse, Western	PINTO
Horsey sound	SNORT
Hosiery mishaps	SNAGS
Hosiery shade	TAN
Hospital department	XRAY
Hospital ship	HOPE
Hoss-thief chasers	POSSE
Hoss thief's neckpiece	NOOSE
Host	ARMY
Hostelries	INNS,MOTELS
Hostile one	ENEMY
Hostilities	WAR
Hostility	ANIMUS
Host, Valhalla	ODIN
Hot and Warm Springs	SPAS
Hot coal	EMBER
Hotel tariff	RATE
Hot fiddler	NERO
Hot or driver's	SEAT
Hot places	OVENS
Hot rock	LAVA
Hot time	SPREE
Hot time in Nice	ETE
Hounds' quarry	HARE
Hour, Canonical	NONES
Hourglass, e.g.	TIMER
Hourglass part	SAND
Hour: It.	ORA
Hourly	HORAL
Hour, A scholar's	TEN
Housatonic	RIVER
House areas	DENS
House for senors	CASA
Household figure	MOM
Household god, Roman	LAR
Household gods	LARES
House, in Mexico	CASA
House part	EAVE
House pets	CATS
Housewife in Munich	FRAU
House wing	ELL
Houston player	ASTRO,OILER
Hover	POISE
Howe	ELIAS
However	ONLY
Hubbub	DIN
Hubs	NAVES
Hudson, for one	RIVER
Hue	COLOR,TINT
Hue of blue or green	BICE
Hues	TONES
Hue's companion	CRY
Huey or Russell	LONG
Huge amount	SEA
Hula wear	LEI
Hullabaloo	NOISE
Hum	SING
Human	BEING,MAN
Human race progenitor	ADAM
Hume contemporary	KANT
Humorist	ADE
Humorist Bill	NYE
Humorous poet	NASH
Humpty Dumpty	EGG
Hunch	IDEA
Hunk	SLAB
Hun of legend	ATLI
Hunt bargains	SHOP
Hunted animal	BOAR,PREY
Hunter of the sky	ORION
Hunting cry	SOHO
Huntley	CHET
Huntsman's quarry	STAG
Hurdles	LEAPS
Hurdy-gurdy	ROTA
Hurling or curling	GAME
Hurricane areas	EYES
Hurried	RAN,SPED
Hurried home, in baseball	SLID
Hurry	HIE,RACE
Hurt	ACHE,ACHED
Husband, Gudrun's	ATLI
Husband, Gypsy	ROM
Husband, in Lyon	MARI
Husband, Reine's	ROI
Husk, Seed	ARIL
Hussar's gear	SABRE
Hussein subject	ARAB
Hustled	SPED
Hyde Park sight	PRAM
Hymn	PSALM
Hymn of praise	PAEAN
Hymn sung a capella	MOTET
Hyson and others	TEAS

I

Clue	Answer
I am unwilling: Lat.	NOLO
Iberian river	EBRO
Ibsen character	ASE
Ibsen heroine	NORA
Ibsen output	DRAMA
ICBM	ATLAS
Ice mass	FLOE
Icon	IMAGE
Icy crust	RIME
Icy look	GLARE,STARE
Identifies	NAMES
Idiot	DOLT
Idler	DRONE
I do	YES
Idol	BAAL
Idolizes	ADORES
Id's master	EGO
"Idylls" heroine	ENID
I.e., in full	IDEST
If ever	ONCE
If not	ELSE
"I get you," radio style	ROGER
Ignominy	SHAME
Ignore	OMIT
I, in Latin	EGO
Iliad	SAGA
"Iliad," for one	EPIC
Ill-fated date	IDES

Illiberal	NARROW
Illimitable	VAST
Illinois city	CAIRO
Illinois Indian	SAC
Illuminated	LIT
Illusory	FALSE
Illustrated	DREW
Ill-wishers	ENEMIES
I love: Lat.	AMO
Image	IDOL
Image, Sacred	ICON
Imitate	ECHO
Imitate the Cheshire cat	GRIN
Imitation	SHAM
Imitation fabric: Suffix	EEN
Imitative	APISH
Imitator	APER,MIME
Immediately	ATONCE,NOW,UPON
Immense	VAST
Immerse	DOUSE
Immunological items	SERA
Immutable	ETERNAL
Impact	SLAM
Impair	MAR
Impaired: Prefix	DYS
Imparted	LENT
Imparts	LENDS
Impassive	STOIC
Impediment	BAR
Impersonates	ACTS,APES
Impertinence	LIP,SASS
Impertinent	SASSY
Impertinent one	SNIP
Impetuosity	ELAN
Impetuous	RASH
Implant firmly	ETCH
Implants	ROOTS,SOWS
Implement, Farm	PLOW
Implements	HOES
Implied	TACIT
Implore	PRAY
Important age	TEEN
Important, be: Colloq.	RATE
Important French river	SEINE
Important nights	EVES
Important range	ANDES
Importune	PRAY,URGE
Impose	LEVY
Impost	LEVY
Impresario's favorite sign	SRO
Impress clearly	ETCH
Impressed	AWED
Impression	IDEA
Impressively great	EPIC
Improbable	TALL
Improper	UNFIT
Improve	AMEND
Improvise	ADLIB
Imprudent	RASH
Impudence	GALL
Impudent	SASSY
Impulses	URGES
Inactive	ASLEEP,IDLE
Inactivity	SLEEP
In addition	ELSE,YET
In the altogether	NUDE
In any way	EVER
In attendance	PRESENT
Inattentive, Be	NOD
In the back	REAR
Incantation	SPELL
Incarnadine	ROSY
Incarnation of Vishnu	RAMA
Incas' land	PERU
Incensed	IRATE
Incenses	IRES
In the center	AMID
Incentive	SPUR
Incessantly	EVER
Inchcape or Plymouth	ROCK
Incident	EVENT
Incipient	INITIAL
Incisor's neighbor	MOLAR
Incite	ABET,EGG
Incites	PRODS
In the clear	SAFE
Incline	RAMP,TEND
Inclined	ATILT
Inclines	LEANS
Inclusive word	ALL
Income, Certain	RENTAL
Income, French	RENTE
Incompetent	UNFIT
Incompletely: Prefix	SEMI
Incongruity	IRONY
Incorrect, Be	ERR
Increase	GAIN
Increased	ADDED
Increases	ADDS
Incubators	HENS
Incubator sound	PEEP
Incumbents	INS
Indebted, Be	OWE
Indefinite degree	NTH
Indefinite word	ANY
Indelicate	CRASS
Independently	APART
Independent one	LONER
Indexed	ONFILE
Indian	HOPI,INCA,OTOE
Indiana city	GARY
Indian, Algonquian	CREE
Indiana's Birch	BAYH
Indian buffalo	ARNEE
Indian clarinet	BEEN
Indian cymbals	TAL
Indian, e.g.	OCEAN
Indian flour	ATTA
Indian garments	SARIS
Indian hominy	SAMP
Indian lute	SITAR
Indian money	LAC
Indian nurse	AMAH
Indian Ocean vessel	DHOW
Indian or Lake	HURON
Indian peasant	RYOT
Indian queen	RANI
Indian ruler	RAJA
Indian, Siouan	OSAGE,OTO
Indians of Tierra del Fuego	ONAS
Indian, Sonoran	SERI
Indians or Braves	NINE
Indian sovereignty	RAJ
Indian state	ASSAM
Indians, Western	UTES
Indian title	RANEE,SRI
Indian, to cowboy	ENEMY
Indian tourist mecca	AGRA
Indian tribal unit	NATION
Indian tribe	ERIE,SAC
Indian V.I.P.	RAJAH
Indian weight	TOLA
Indian weights	SERS
Indian, Western	TETON
India: Prefix	INDO
Indication	SIGN
Indigence	NEED
Indigent	NEEDY
Indignant	IRATE
Indigo	ANIL
Indigos	DYES
In disagreement	ANTI
In disarray	MESSY
Indisposed	ILL
In the distance	AFAR
Indistinct	DIM

Indistinguishable SAME
Indites INKS
Individual SELF
Individually APART
Individual, Unique ONER
Indolent INERT
Indonesian island BALI
Indonesian ox ANOA
Induced LED
Inducing sleep OPIATE
Indulge SPOIL
Industrial area of Europe RUHR
Industrious one ANT
Inebriate SOT
In ecstasy RAPT
Ineffectual LAME,VAIN,WEAK
Inexorable STERN
Inexperienced GREEN
Infamous fiddler NERO
Infatuated GAGA
Infection, Eyelid STY
Inferior LESS
"Inferno" man DANTE
Infinite ENDLESS
Infinitive, Latin ESSE
Inflexible STERN
Info DOPE
Informally, Coffee JAVA
Informal taboos NONOS
Information DATA,NEWS
Informed AWARE
In a frenzied way AMOK
Infrequent RARE
In front AHEAD
Infuriates IRES
Ingenue, for one ROLE
Ingenuous NAIVE
Ingot BAR
Ingratiating OILY
Ingredient, Gumbo OKRA
Ingredient of beer MALT
Ingredient of ciders APPLE
Ingredient of girls SUGAR
Ingredients, Soap LYES
Ingredient, Varnish ELEMI,LAC
Ingress ENTRY
Inhabitant: Suffix ESE,ITE,OTE
In harmony ATONE
In Hawaii it's called aa LAVA
Initiate OPEN
Initiative DRIVE
Injurious EVIL
Ink kind INDIA
Inkling IDEA
In the know UPON,WISE
Ink producer SQUID
Inky EBON
In the least ATALL
Inlet ARM,COVE,RIA
In a line AROW
Inner: Prefix ENDO,ENTO
Innocent one BABE
In Oahu, Greeting ALOHA
In old days, Formerly ERST
In the past AGO
In pieces APART
In the pink HALE
In a predicament STUCK
In preference to OVER
Input, Computer DATA
Inquires ASKS
Inquiries ASKS
Inquisitive NOSY
In the red, Be OWE
In reserve ASIDE,ONICE
In the sandman's arms ASLEEP
Inscribed PENNED
In the secretary's drawer ONFILE
Insect FLEA,WASP
Insect abode HIVE
Insect eaters TOADS
Insect egg NIT
Insecticide DDT
Insects ANTS,BEES,GNATS
Insect stage IMAGO,LARVA
Insert mark CARET
Inside info TIP
Insincere talk CANT
Insipid TAME
Insist AVER
Insistent, Be URGE
Inspiration IDEA
Inspire ELATE
Inspired AWED
Inspiring fear EERIE,EERY
Instances TIMES
Instant TRICE
Instanter ATONCE
Instead of FOR
Instigate INCITE,URGE
Instruct TRAIN
Instruction, Steak RARE
Instructor TUTOR
Instrument REED
Instrument, Brass TUBA
Instrument, Measuring METER
Instrument, Musical OBOE
Instruments AGENTS,MEDIA
In style CHIC
In the style of: Fr. ALA
Insubstantial INANE
Insult SLAP
Insulting expression SNEER
Insurance man AGENT
Insurgent REBEL
Intelligent APT
Intended AIMED
Intense desires YENS
Intense zeal FLAME
Intention IDEA
Interdict BAN
Interdiction TABU
Interior artistry DECOR
Interjection in Bonn ACH
Internal: Prefix ENTO
Interpret READ
Interrupt STOP
Intersperse LARD
Interval SPACE
Intimate NEAR
Intimation HINT
Intimidate DAUNT,SCARE
Intimidates AWES
In a tizzy ATSEA
Into pieces APART
In turmoil AROAR
Intractable horse ROGUE
Intrepid BRAVE
Intrepidity NERVE
Intrigue PLOT
Intuitive ones SEERS
Inveigles (with "in") ROPES
Invent CREATE
Invented MADE
Invention IDEA
Inventor of diving bell EADS
Inventor, U.S. HOWE,OTIS
Inventory LIST
Invents COINS
Invest (with) ENDUE
In the vicinity NEAR
Invigorating VITAL
Invitation BID
Invited ASKED,BADE
Invites ASKS
In want NEEDY

In a way, Act EMOTE
In a way, Climb SHIN
In a way, Eye OGLE
In a way, Fish TROLL
In a way, Overcame AWED
In a way, Packaged BALED
In a way, Propelled OARED
In a way, Shelve TABLE
In a while ANON,LATER,SOON
In words ORAL
Ionian Sea gulf ARTA
I.O.U. NOTE
Iowa college COE
Iowa Indians SACS
Iowa religious sect AMANA
Iowa town AMES
Iranian export OIL
Irani bigwig SHAH
Iraq's neighbor IRAN
Ireland, Islands off ARAN
Iridescent substance NACRE
Iris part UVEA
Irish ERSE
Irish dramatist SHAW
Irish fuel PEAT
Irish hill TARA
Irish islands ARAN
Irish luck CESS
Irish poet MOORE,YEATS
Irish port SLIGO
Irish river ERNE
Iron PRESS
Iron and carbon STEEL
Iron and others AGES
Iron molds PIGS
Iron or teen AGE
Iroquoians ERIES
Irregular EROSE
Irresolute WEAK
Irritable EDGY
Irritate RILE
Irritates IRES,IRKS
Irritation, Sound of PSHAW
I.R.S. concern TAX
Irving's sleeper RIP
Irvin S. or Ty COBB
Irwin or Artie SHAW
Isaac's mother SARAH
Isaac's son and others ESAUS
Is beholden to OWES
Is done ENDS
Isfahan's country IRAN
Ishmael's skipper AHAB
Is in cahoots with ABETS
Isinglass MICA
Islamic priest IMAM
Island ATOLL
Island east of Java BALI
Island in Formosa Strait AMOY
Island in the Hebrides IONA
Island in N.Y. Bay ELLIS
Island, in Spain ISLA
Island land ERIN
Island nation JAPAN
Island near Corsica ELBA
Island off Alaska ADAK
Island off Donegal ARAN
Island of the kona OAHU
Island, Pacific YAP
Island republic EIRE,ICELAND
Island, River AIT
Islands, in France ILES
Islands in North Atlantic FAROE
Islands, South Pacific SAMOA
Isle, Greek SAMOS
Isle off England MAN
Islet CAY,KEY
Isolated APART,LONE
Isolated hill KNOB
Isolated rock SCAR
Is out of sorts AILS
Israel, Eban of ABBA
Israeli harbor ACRE
Israeli statesman EBAN
Is situated LIES
Issues EMITS
I stand: Lat. STO
Is wanting NEEDS
Italian black NERO
Italian bones OSSA
Italian cheese city PARMA
Italian city ASTI,PADUA,PISA
Italian coin LIRA
Italian composer TOSTI
Italian family ESTE
Italian finger game MORA
Italian island ELBA
Italian lake LAGO
Italian love AMORE
Italian map, City on ROMA
Italian poet TASSO
Italian port GENOA
Italian port on Adriatic BARI
Italian river ADDA,ARNO
Italian saint NERI
Italian star LOREN
Italian's who CHE
Italian three TRE
Italian today OGGI
Italian town ATRI
Italy, Six, in SEI
Itches YENS
Item UNIT
Item, Aloha LEI
Item at a luau POI
Item, Borsch BEET
Item, Breakfast CEREAL
Item, Camper's COT
Item for a vault POLE
Item, Fountain SODA
Item from Flint AUTO
Item, Golfbag IRON
Item in a cafe window MENU
Item in a librairie LIVRE
Item in a Paris bakery TARTE
Itemize LIST
Item, Kitchen OVEN,POT
Item, Ledger ASSET
Item, News OBIT
Item, Office DESK
Item often blown FUSE
Item on a Mexican menu TACO
Item on a repair bill LABOR
Item, Playground SEESAW
Item, Pub ALE
Item, Red ink IOU
Items, Book ENDS
Items, Collection of ANA
Items, Lab ETNAS
Items, Library TOMES
Items, Links TEES
Items measured in Calaveras County LEAPS
Items picked up by hosts TABS
Items, Smorgasbord EELS
Item, Table OLEO
Item that is slippery when wet SOAP
Item to talk through HAT
It has sweet in between HOME
It, in Italy ESSA
It's above the tibia KNEE
It's often burned at the beach SKIN
It's often golden RULE
"It tolls for thee" poet DONNE
It went a long way for George DOLLAR
Ivan TSAR

"Ivanhoe" girl ROWENA
Ivy Leaguers ELIS
"I warned you!" THERE
"I wasn't there," e.g. ALIBI

J

Jabber CHIN,YAP
"J'Accuse" author ZOLA
"J'Accuse" author Zola EMILE
Jack SPRAT
Jack and Jill's load PAIL
Jacket BOLERO
Jacket kind PEA
Jacket or collar ETON
Jackets ETONS
Jackie's former mate ARI
Jackknife DIVE
Jack of clubs PAM
Jack of TV PAAR
Jack's need PLAY
Jack Sprat or Peter EATER
Jacob's brother and others ESAUS
Jade TIRE
James Truslow or John Couch ADAMS
James Watt's medium STEAM
Jane PLAIN
Jane of fiction EYRE
Japanese case INRO
Japanese clogs GETA
Japanese coin SEN
Japanese fair city OSAKA
Japanese family badge MON
Japanese herb UDO
Japanese medicine case INRO
Japanese port OTARU
Japanese portal TORII
Japanese race AINU
Japanese statesman ITO
Japanese woman diver AMA
Jar, Earthen OLLA
Jargon CANT,LINGO
Jar parts LIDS
Jarring HARSH
Jason's ship ARGO
Jaunty PERT
Jaunty cap BERET
Java, Island off BALI
Javanese tree UPAS
Javelin SPEAR
Jaws away YAKS
Jazzman Hines EARL
Jeanne d'Arc, for one STE
Jeanne's summer ETE
Jefferson's V.P. BURR
Jejune ARID
Jelly flavor GRAPE
Jelly garnish ASPIC
Jelly, Grape SAPA
Jeopardy PERIL
Jester MIME
Jet ENGINE
Jeweler's weight CARAT
Jewelry item ONYX
Jewelry paint ENAMEL
Jewish festival SEDER
Jewish law TORAH
Jewish month ADAR,ELUL
Jewish months ABS
Jewish title ABBA
Jibs and lateens SAILS
Jig or buzz SAW
Job, Garden WEED
Job of sorts SNOW
Joey, for one PAL
Jog TROT
John in Cork SEAN
John, in Scotland IAN
Johnny CASH
Johnnycake PONE
John's relative IVAN
Joie de vivre ELAN
Join ABUT, ATTACH,ENTER,MEET,RELATE,SEAM
Join a card game SITIN
Join the choir SING
Joined forces with SIDED
Joining piece YOKE
Join the poker game ANTE
Joins UNITES,WEDS
Joint ANKLE,KNEE
Joint of a stem NODE
Joint, Pipe TEE
Josh RIB
Josip Broz TITO
Joss IDOL
Jostle ELBOW
Jot ATOM,MITE
Jot down NOTE
Jots IOTAS
Jotted up ADDED
Jotting MEMO
Journey TREK
Joyce JAMES
Jubilant ELATED
Jubilate CROW
Judge, Moslem CADI
Judge's call ORDER
Judge's seat BANC
Judgment TASTE
Judicial circuit EYRE
Judicial wear ROBES
Jug TOBY
Jug handles EARS
Juice SAP
Juicy fruit ORANGE
Juin, juillet et aout ETE
Julie Andrews movie STAR
July 4 event PARADE
July 4 sight FLAG
Jumble HASH,MESS
Jumbled, as type PIED
Jumbled mass HEAP
Jumna city AGRA
Jumps LEAPS
June bug DOR
June V.I.P. BRIDE
Jungfrau, for one ALP
Jungle dweller BEAST
Jungle neckpiece MANE
Jungle sound ROAR
Junior city TOWN
Junk TRASH
Junket TRIP
Juno, Greek HERA
Jury PANEL
Jutland people DANES
Jut out HANG
Jutting rock CRAG,TOR
Juvenile author ALGER

K

Kansas city IOLA
Karate's cousin JUDO
Karenina ANNA
Kashmir sight VALE
Kayak CANOE
Kazan ELIA

Keats et al. POETS
Keats specialty ODE
Keep SAVE
Keep company WOO
Keep informed POST
"Keep Off," for one SIGN
Keep out BAR
Keepsake RELIC
Kefauver ESTES
Keg wood OAK
Kelp ALGA
Kennedy TED
Kennel sound YAP,YELP
Kentucky bluegrass POA
Kept for reference ONFILE
Kerry's land EIRE
Kettles POTS
Key ISLAND,ISLE
Key Biscayne, for one ISLET
Keystone-cop event CHASE
Khan AGA
Khartoum's river NILE
Khayyam OMAR
Kick BOOT
Kicker TOE
Kicker's objective GOAL
Kiddie TOT
Kids RIBS
Kill SLAY
Killer whale ORCA
Kiln OAST
Kilns OSTS,OVENS
Kimono accessories OBIS
Kind GENRE,ILK,SORT
Kindled LIT
Kind of acid AMINO
Kind of anesthetic LOCAL
Kind of antenna RADAR
Kind of arch OGEE
Kind of arm or kick SIDE
Kind of assets REAL
Kind of bag KIT,TOTE
Kind of battle SHAM
Kind of bear POLAR,TEDDY
Kind of beer NEAR,ROOT
Kind of bell BAR
Kind of belt SEAT
Kind of bird EARLY,JAIL
Kind of blanket WET
Kind of blonde ASH
Kind of blue TRUE
Kind of bone WISH
Kind of bread RYE
Kind of brush SCRUB
Kind of burglar CAT
Kind of butter or brandy APPLE
Kind of button PANIC
Kind of cake YEAST
Kind of call ROLL
Kind of car USED
Kind of case SUIT
Kind of caterpillar TENT
Kind of chamber ECHO
Kind of change LOOSE
Kind of cheap DIRT
Kind of cheese EDAM
Kind of china BONE
Kind of closet CEDAR
Kind of cloth DISH
Kind of club GLEE
Kind of common denominator LEAST
Kind of corner AMEN
Kind of corporal LANCE
Kind of cotton PIMA
Kind of cross TAU
Kind of crow SCARE
Kind of cube ICE
Kind of cure REST
Kind of cut CREW
Kind of dance RAIN,TAP
Kind of dancer TAXI,TOE
Kind of dash or happy SLAP
Kind of demonstration SITIN
Kind of dive NOSE
Kind of dog CHOW
Kind of door TRAP
Kind of drab OLIVE
Kind of dream PIPE
Kind of drink FLIP
Kind of drop DEW,TEAR
Kind of drum BONGO,SNARE
Kind of egg NEST
Kind of eye EVIL
Kind of face FALSE
Kind of flight SOLO
Kind of floating ice PACK
Kind of flu ASIAN
Kind of football pass SPIRAL
Kind of fountain SODA
Kind of fund SLUSH
Kind of garden ROOF
Kind of generation BEAT
Kind of ground or blow LOW
Kind of guard REAR
Kind of gun STEN
Kind of head EGG
Kind of head or boat TOW
Kind of heat SOLAR
Kind of house PENT
Kind of iron SAD
Kind of jacket ETON
Kind of lamp OIL
Kind of land or world DREAM
Kind of leaf FIG
Kind of light NEON
Kind of look LEER
Kind of lot ODD
Kind of man YES
Kind of mark EASY
Kind of meal OAT
Kind of metabolism BASAL
Kind of mobile SNOW
Kind of nail HANG
Kind of numeral ARABIC
Kind of nut COLA
Kind of oak or poplar WHITE
Kind of offering PEACE
Kind of opera SOAP
Kind of orange OSAGE
Kind of orbit LUNAR
Kind of order LARGE
Kind of out, in football TIME
Kind of paper or ink INDIA
Kind of party HEN,STAG
Kind of pickle DILL
Kind of plate HOME
Kind of point or sister WEAK
Kind of poke SLOW
Kind of preservation SELF
Kind of pronoun PERSONAL
Kind of pupil or gazer STAR
Kind of quartz SARD
Kind of race RELAY,TROT
Kind of reckoning DEAD
Kind of renewal URBAN
Kind of review RAVE
Kind of road TOLL
Kind of roe SHAD
Kind of rubber FOAM
Kind of rug SHAG
Kind of sanctum INNER
Kind of saw RIP
Kind of sax ALTO
Kind of school PREP
Kind of score TIE
Kind of seal EARED

Kind of seamen ABLE
Kind of securities sale WASH
Kind of shooter PEA
Kind of show PEEP
Kind of skirt MINI
Kind of slipper CLOG
Kind of smasher ATOM
Kind of soup ONION
Kind of space OUTER
Kind of squash ACORN
Kind of stance AKIMBO
Kind of star NOVA
Kind of steamer TRAMP
Kind of stew or coffee IRISH
Kind of store COOP,MENS
Kind of story MYTH
Kind of straits DIRE
Kind of street or ticket ONEWAY
Kind of string GUT
Kind of strip DRAG
Kind of sugar CANE
Kind of suggestion AUTO
Kind of surgeon ORAL
Kind of talk IDLE,SHOP
Kind of tea ICED
Kind of telecast LIVE
Kind of theater ARENA
Kind of thief SNEAK
Kind of thing SURE
Kind of tide EBB
Kind of tiger PAPER
Kind of tire RECAP
Kind of tool RASP
Kind of transit RAPID
Kind of triangle ETERNAL
Kind of tribe NOMADIC
Kind of turkey ROAST
Kind of vote STRAW
Kind of waist WASP
Kind of waste DROSS
Kind of watch STOP
Kind of weed LOCO
Kind of wind TRADE
Kind of wing LEFT
Kind of wit DIM
Kind of worm INCH
Kind of writing IRONY
Kind of year LEAP
Kind of yell REBEL
King Cole NAT
King David opus PSALM
Kingfisher's home NEST
King: Fr. ROI
King, in drama LEAR
King, Iranian SHAH
King Mongkut's teacher ANNA
King of the Huns ATLI
King of Israel AHAB
King of Judah ASA
King of Norway OLAF,OLAV
King of Tyre HIRAM
King or Arkin ALAN
King's predecessor ALA
King's superior ACE
Kiosk STAND
Kipling words ARAG
Kirghiz range ALAI
Kitchen implement POT
Kitchen unit OVEN
Kitts and Louis STS
Kitty, Feed the ANTE
Kitty or Fido PET
Klemperer OTTO
Knack ART
Kneecap PATELLA
Knee: Lat. GENU
Kneel before ADORE
Knicks' Willis REED
Knife, Malayan KRIS
Knight's companion ROOK
Knights' wives DAMES
Knock down FELL
Knot NODE
Knot in fiber NEP
Knot in wood KNAR
Knot lace TAT
Knowing AWARE,WISE
Knowledge KEN,LORE
Knox or Wayne FORT
Knuckle sandwich FIST
Kodiak, for one BEAR
Kokomo product STEEL
Ko-Ko's weapon SNEE
K.O. number TEN
Korean metropolis SEOUL
Korean of note RHEE
Kudos, in Corrida OLE
Kuklapolitan hostess FRAN
Kwajalein ATOLL
Kyle ROTE

L

Labels TAGS
Lab equipment ETNA
Lab jobs TESTS
Lab medium AGAR
Laboratory fluid SERUM
Laborer PEON
Laborer, Anglo Saxon ESNE
Labor group ILO
Laboriously proceed WADE
Lab picture XRAY
Labyrinth MAZE
Lace VAL
Lace, Make TAT
Lacerated TORN
Laces TIES
Lack-a-day! ALAS
Lackawanna's old partner ERIE
Lacking harmony AJAR
Lacking interest ARID
Lacking motion INERT
Lack of vigor ANEMIA
Lacks NEEDS
Laconian capital SPARTA
Lacquered metalware TOLE
Lacrosse team TEN
Ladder feature RUNG
Ladd or King ALAN
Ladies in Lyons MMES
Ladies of Madrid SRAS
La Douce IRMA
Lady, Ivanhoe ROWENA
Lady of sonnets LAURA
Lady's hair accouterment RAT
Lady, Tennyson ENID
Lady Windermere's prop FAN
L.A. footballers RAMS
Lager BEER
Lager or Bock BEER
Lahr BERT
Lake ERIE
Lake for oread TARN
Lake in Africa CHAD
Lake in Andes INCA
Lake in Finland ENARE
Lake in Ireland ERNE
Lake: It. LAGO
Lake Tahoe city RENO
Lamb ELIA
Lambaste FLAIL
Lambkin's cry BAA

Lambs EWES
Lamech's wife ADAH
Lament MOAN
Lamentation sound ALAS
Lamps, Heating ETNAS
Lancelot or Galahad SIR
Lanchester ELSA
Land, African MALI
Land, Ancient ELAM
Land, Arab ADEN
Land area ISLE
Land area: Fr. ILE
Land, Biblical ARAM
Landed ALIT
Land, in France TERRE
Land known for cats SIAM
Land: Lat. AGER
Landlord's concern RENTAL
Land map PLAT
Landmark in Asia Minor TROY
Landmark, New Mexican TAOS
Landmark of China WALL
Landmark, Sicilian ETNA
Land mass, Large ASIA
Land measures ARES
Land of Baile Atha Cliath EIRE
Land of the Apennines ITALY
Land of the would-be free RENO
Landon ALF
Land on Caspian city IRAN
Land, Oslo's NORGE
Landowner, Scot LAIRD
Lands ACRES
Landscape SCENE
Land tax in Britain CESS
Lane ABBE
Language of Pakistan URDU
Language, South African TAAL
Language used in Jordan ARABIC
Languish PINE
Lansbury role MAME
Lapse ERROR,SLIP
Larch or carob TREE
Large amount TON
Large antelope ELAND
Large bird EMU,ERNE
Large deer ELK
Large dish TUREEN
Large hall SALA
Large jars OLLAS
Large number, informally SLEW
Large pill BOLUS
Large quantity MASS
Large red hog DUROC
Large-scale EPIC
Largest of seven ASIA
Large waves SEAS
Lariat LASSO,REATA,RIATA
La Scala highlights ARIAS
La Scala unit SCENA
Laser BEAM
Lass GIRL
Lasso REATA,RIATA,ROPE
Last OMEGA
Last, at, in Paris ENFIN
Lasted WORE
Last items OMEGAS
Last-minute study CRAM
Last stop on a diamond PLATE
Last straw LIMIT
Last traces ASHES
Last word AMEN
Latch device HASP
Late TARDY
Late cartoonist ARNO
Late Chinese leader MAO
Late comedian LAHR
Later ANON
Latest thing RAGE
Latest: Prefix NEO
Late writer and critic AGEE
Lather SOAP,SUDS
Latin American country PERU
Latin behold ECCE
Latin conjugation word AMAT,AMO
Latin field AGER
Latin god DEUS
Latin goddess DEA
Latin grammar word AMAS
Latin journey ITER
Latin love AMOR
Latin man VIR
Latin others ALII
Latin pronoun ILLE
Latin rhythm BOLERO
Latin roll-call reply ADSUM
Latin 6 SEX
Latin student's aid TROT
Latin thus SIC
Latin "to be" ESSE
Latin unless NISI
Latin verb ERAT
Latin wings ALAE
Latin years ANNI
Latvian gulf RIGA
Lauder, for one SCOT
Laughing RIANT
Laugh, in Lyons RIRE
Laughter HAHA
Launching pad for an acrobat MAT
Launching pad on the links TEE
Laurel STAN
Lava SLAG
Lava source ETNA
Laver opponent ASHE
Laver or McKuen ROD
Lavish fondness on DOTE
Lawful LICIT
Lawgiver SOLON
Lawman of West EARP
Lawn gear HOSE
Lawn nuisance WEED
Lawn wrecker MOLE
Lawyers' concerns CASES
Lay at anchor RODE
Layer COAT,HEN,PLY
Layer of the iris UVEA
Layer or sponge CAKE
Layer, Tissue TELA
Lazarus EMMA
Laze LOLL
Lead STAR
Lead and tin alloy TERNE
Leader, Chinese MAO
Leader, European TITO
Leader, Fishing SNELL
Leader, Hounds' HARE
Leader, Indian RAJAH
Leader, Israeli EBAN
Leader of Green Mountain Boys ALLEN
Leader, Steelworkers' ABEL
Leader, Stoics' ZENO
Leader, Turkish INONU
Leading AHEAD,ONTOP
Leading man HERO
Leading members of a group ELITE
Lead-off, for one BATTER
Leaf SEPAL
Leaf angle, in botany AXIL
Leaf-cutters ANTS
Leafless stalk SCAPE
Leaf nuisance APHID
League, Mideast ARAB
Leaguer, Ivy ELI
Leak OOZE
Leaks SEEPS

Leaky noise SSS
Lean CANT
Lean and leap YEARS
Leander's love HERO
Leap, for one YEAR
Learn HEAR
Learned HEARD
Learning LORE
Lear or Kong KING
Lease HIRE,RENT
Leases LETS
Lease-signer TENANT
Least particles IOTAS
Least skilled WORST
Leather CALF,ELK,KID,SUEDE
Leather thong STROP
Leaves out OMITS
Leavings ORTS
Ledger entry ASSET
Leeds's river AIRE
Lee J. or Ty COBB
Leer OGLE
Leeway ROOM
Left WENT
Left or U TURN
Leftward, at sea APORT
Legacy, Revoke a ADEEM
Legal action PLEA
Legal claim LIEN
Legal degree LLD
Legal document LEASE
Legal excuse ALIBI
Legal group BAR
Legal job CASE
Le Gallienne EVA
Legally prevent ESTOP
Legally revoke ADEEM
Legal papers DEEDS
Legal term INRE
Legal thing RES
Legal wrong TORT
Legatee HEIR
Legend MYTH
Legendary British princess URSULA
Legendary friend DAMON
Legendary Scandinavian ATLI
Legendary ship ARGO
Leghorn HEN
Leghorn city PISA
Leghorn, for one LAYER
Legislative body DIET
Legislative group BLOC
Leg joint ANKLE
Leg part KNEE,SHIN
Leg up HELP
Le Havre's river SEINE
Leisure EASE
Leks, leva and bahts COINS
Le Moko PEPE
Lemon part RIND
Lend a hand HELP
Length measure ELL
Length, Skirt MIDI,MINI
Lenient EASY
Lent a hand AIDED
Leporid HARE
Leprechaun land ERIN
Les femmes ELLES
Less challenging TAMER
Lessen ABATE,BATE
Lesser: Prefix DEMI
Let RENT
Lethargy SOPOR
Lets up EASES
Letter CEE,ELL
Letter, Greek BETA,ETA,PSI
Letters EES,EMS,ENS,ESSES,EXES,TEES
Letter-shaped beam IBAR
Levantine ketch SAIC
Level EVEN,RAZE
Level land PLAIN
Lever PEDAL
Leyden, for one JAR
Lhasa monk LAMA
Li'l Abner's boy ABE
Liberal FREE
Liberty LEAVE
Library contents TOMES
License-plate attachment TAB
License plates TAGS
Lichen MOSS
L.I. commuter word DASH
Lido money LIRE
Lie at anchor RIDE
Liebfraumilch WINE
Lie close NESTLE
Lieu STEAD
Life in Paris VIE
Life of the party CARD
Life substance DNA
Lifetimes AGES
Lifework CAREER
Lift RAISE
Lift, Ski TBAR
Light FAIR
Light as a feather GOSSAMER
Light brown BRAN
Light-bulb word WATT
Light cigar CLARO
Light color ECRU
Light-colored BLOND
Light colors TANS
Light craft CANOE
Lighten EASE
Lighter of a sort MATCH
Light-Horse Harry LEE
Lightly cooked RARE
Light or leap YEAR
Light precipitation TRACE
Light purple LILAC
Lights for stars ARCS
Light snack TEA
Light-switch positions ONS
Light upon HIT
Light wood BALSA
Like a babe in the woods NAIVE
Like a certain animal OVINE
Like certain tribes NOMADIC
Like fine lace DELICATE
Like George Apley LATE
Like good bourbon AGED
Like green apples TART
Like highly ADORE
Like Humpty Dumpty OVATE
Like a June day RARE
Like King Cole OLD
Likely APT
Like a million COOL
Likeminded ONE
Like the Mojave ARID
Like Munchausen titles UNTRUE
Like an old crone ANILE
Like old lettuce LIMP
Like a pro cager TALL
Like Richard of the almanac POOR
Like the Sahara SERE
Like some coffee TEPID
Like some college halls IVIED
Like some doors AJAR
Like some gasses INERT
Like some seals EARED
Like some shores these days OILY
Like some steaks RARE
Like some stories TALL
Like some tea ICED
Like some TV LIVE

Clue	Answer
Like: Suffix	INE
Like the twist or hula hoop	PASSE
Like unsafe ice	THIN
Like unto	AKIN
Like a wing	ALAR
Likewise	ALSO
Lillie	BEA
Lilliputian	WEE
Lily	SEGO
Lily Maid	ELAINE
Lily of opera	PONS
Lily of West	SEGO
Lily part	PAD
Lily plant	ALOE
Lima location	OHIO
Lima money	SOL
Limber	AGILE
Limerick land	ERIN
Limit	END
Limit, at times	SKY
Limited	NARROW
Limits	PALE
Limousine	AUTO
Limply hang	LOP
Lincoln Center unit	OPERA
Lindbergh's flight	SOLO
Linden	TEIL
Linden of TV	HAL
Line	QUEUE,ROPE
Line, Certain	DATE
Line, Diagonal	BIAS
Lined up	AROW
Line-marking material	LIME
Linemen	ENDS
Linen	TOILE
Line of movement	PATH
Line of soldiers	FILE
Lines made by compasses	ARCS
Linkletter and Carney	ARTS
Links	UNITES
Links locale	TEE
Linseed product	OIL
Lion	IDOL
Lioness	ELSA
Lion's pride	MANE
Lip	SASS
Lip-curling	SNEER
Lippo Lippi, for one	FRA
Liquefy	MELT
Liquefy by heat	FUSE
Liqueur flavor	ANISE,SLOE
Liquid container	CASK
Liquid fat	OLEIN
Liquor gulp	SWIG
Lisa	MONA
List	ROSTER,ROTA
Listen	HEED
Listing	ATILT
Listing in a playbill	CAST
List unit	ITEM
Literary conflict	AGON
Literary first name	EDGAR
Literary first name with "Edgar"	ALLAN
Literary name	TWAIN
Literary pseudonym	SAKI
Literary scraps	ANA
Literary signature	ELIA
Literary work	OPUS
Literary works	ODES
Litigant	SUER
Little	DAB,WEE
Little bear	URSA
Little bit	DAB
Little Eleanor	NELL
Little, in Scotland	SMA
Little one	TOT
Little terrors	IMPS
Little thing	MITE
Littoral	COAST
Liturgy	RITE
Live	ARE
Live coal	EMBER
Lived	WAS
Lively	PERT
Lively dance	CLOG,REEL
Lively wit	ESPRIT
Living-room piece	SOFA
Livorno love	AMORE
Lizard	GILA
Lizzie material	TIN
Llamas' home	ANDES
Llanos lasso	REATA
Load cargo	STEEVE
Loaf	IDLE
Loafer	DRONE,SHOE
Loath	AVERSE
Loathe	ABHOR,HATE
Lobster corals	ROES
Lobster roe	CORAL
Lobster source	MAINE
Locale	AREA,SCENE,SITE
Locale of Cork	EIRE
Locale of the Himalayas	ASIA
Localities	AREAS,TOWNS
Locality	SCENE
Locality: Suffix	ESE
Location	AREA,SCENE,SITE
Lock of hair	TRESS
Loch of note	NESS
Lock-up	JAIL
Lode yield	ORE
Lodge doorkeeper	TILER
Lodging of a kind	PAD
Lodging place	INN
Lofty	TALL
Lofty nest	AERIE
Lofty prefix	AERO
Logan	ELLA
"Lohengrin" heroine	ELSA
Loire summer	ETE
Lomond or Katrine	LOCH
London gallery	TATE
London park	HYDE
London quarter	SOHO
London street sight	TRAM
London spare	TYRE
Long	SENATOR
Long and short	TONS
Long aperture	RIMA
Long-billed bird	IBIS
Longfellow's contemporary	POE
Long for	ACHE
Longing	ITCH,YEN
Long-legged bird	CRANE
Long-napped cloth	SHAG
Long-necked birds	SWANS
Long-necked guitar	SITAR
Long-nosed animal	TAPIR
Long period	AEON
Long rod	CUE
Long-run shows	HITS
Longs	PINES
Long tale	ILIAD
Long time	AGE,YEARS
Long times	EONS
Look	SEEM
Look after	SEETO,TEND
Look ahead	PLAN
Look daggers at	GLARE
Looked at	EYED
Looked the place over	CASED
Look in a way	PEER
Look, in a way	OGLE
Look of sorts	LEER
Look over	SCAN

Clue	Answer
Looks up to	ADORES
Look up to	ESTEEM
Loom part	REED
Loops	TABS
Loop travelers	ELS
Loos	ANITA
Loose dress	TENT
Loose garment	SARI
Loose garments	ROBES
Loosely woven silk	TRAM
Loosely hangs	LOPS
Loosen	UNDO,UNTIE
Loosened	EASED
Loose robe	TOGA
Loot	SWAG
Loot, Hide the	STASH
Loot on the Spanish Main	ORO
Lopez number	NOLA
Lord Avon and others	EDENS
Lorna	DOONE
Los Angeles specialty	SMOG
Lose force	WANE
Lose interest	NOD
Lose no time	HIE
Lose power	WANE
Loses color	FADES
Lost	ASEA
Lost in delight	RAPT
Lot	FATE
Loud, in music	FORTE
Loud report	BANG
Loud sound	WHAM
Louis's weapon	FIST
Louis XIV, e.g.	ROI
Lounging spot	SOFA
Lout	OAF
Louvre name	LISA
Love	ADORE
Loved one	DEAR
Love, French	AMOUR
Love god	AMOR,EROS
Love, in Italy	AMORE
Lover	ROMEO
Love, Radames's	AIDA
Lover of Narcissus	ECHO
Love, Rose's	ABIE
Loves fatuously	DOTES
Low	BASE
Low-class Anglo-Saxons	ESNES
Low, hard-hit ball	LINER
Low-key lie	FIB
Low-lying land	VALE
Low or ebb	TIDE
Low or high	GEAR
Low-pitched	DEEP
Low pitch, for one	BALL
Low rating	POOR
Low: Sp.	BAJA
Low, Vulgar, or Late	LATIN
Loyal	FAST,TRUE
LSD user's experience	TRIP
Luau course	POI
Luau decor	LEIS
Luck: Irish	CESS
Ludwig	EMIL
Luge	SLED
Lugs	TOTES
Luise Rainer role	OLAN
Lukewarm	TEPID
Lumberjack gear	AXES
Luminary	STAR
Lummox	LOUT
Lump	MASS,NODULE
Luna, for one	MOTH
Lunar and leap	YEARS
Luncheon dish	OMELET
Luncheonette utensil	URN
Lupino	IDA
Lustrous cloth	PINA
Lutetia, today	PARIS
Luxor's river	NILE
Luxuriant	RICH
Luxuriant in growth	RANK
Luxury	EASE
Luzon town	IBA
Lycee's relative	ECOLE
Lynne's direction	EAST
Lyons' river	RHONE
Lyre, Hebrew	ASOR
Lyric drama	OPERA
Lyric form	EPODE
Lyrics to be sung	LAYS

M

Clue	Answer
Macadamia	NUT
Macaw	ARARA
Macaw, Brazilian	ARA
"Macbeth," for one	DRAMA
MacGraw	ALI
Machine cylinder	CAM
Machine of a sort	SLOT
Machine part	GEAR
Machine tool	LATHE
Mackerel's relative	CERO
Madagascar mammal	LEMUR
Madame Bovary	EMMA
Made the first play	LED
Made of a grain	OATEN
Made of a wood	ASHEN
Made a selection	CHOSE
Made sure of: Colloq.	ICED
Madison Ave. output	ADS
Madison Ave. suffix	WISE
Madrid bravo	OLE
Madrid love	AMOR
Madrid movie	CINE
Madrid this	ESTE
Madrigal	SONG
Mae West role	LIL
Magazine feature	SERIAL
Magazine: Fr.	REVUE
Maggiore	LAGO
Magic ritual	OBEAH
Maharishi	GURU
Maid, Cleopatra's	IRAS
Maid, Eastern	AMAH
Maiden	LASS
Maiden-name word	NEE
Maid of Astolat	ELAINE
Maid or butler part, usually	BIT
Mail	ARMOR,POST
Mail-chute areas	SLOTS
Mailed	SENT
Mailing address	APO
Mailman's hazard	BITE
Main	SEA
Main and Mott	STREETS
Maine symbol	PINE
Mainstay	ATLAS
Maintain	ASSERT,KEEP
Majolica item	VASE
Major Hoople's word	EGAD
Major name in the Prado	GOYA
Major or Minor	URSA
Make	CREATE
Make amends	ATONE
Make concise	PRUNE
Make a deal	SWAP
Make disappear	ERASE
Make edging	TAT
Make effervescent	AERATE
Make exultant	ELATE

Make fast	SECURE
Make feisty	RILE
Make fit	ADAPT,ALTER
Make fun of	KID
Make the grade	RATE
Make a lap	SIT
Make like a ghost	HAUNT
Make a living	EARN
Make merry	REVEL
Make money	MINT
Make one	WED
Make oneself scarce	FLEE
Make out	READ
Make over	REDO
Make right	MEND
Make rotten	ADDLE
Makers, Coffee	URNS
Maker, Silk	ERI
Makes accessible	OPENS
Makes an appearance	ENTERS
Make a scene	RANT
Makes do	EKES
Makes docile	TAMES
Make a second plan	REMAP
Makes a move at poker	SEES
Makes an out in baseball	TAGS
Make a speech	ORATE
Make a stab at	TRY
Make tracks	HIE
Make turbid	ROIL
Makeup: Colloq.	PAINT
Make up for	ATONE
Make use of	AVAIL
Make weary	PALL
Making all stops	LOCAL
Malayan dagger	KRIS
Malayan sir	TUAN
Malay gibbon	LAR
Malaysian vessel	PROA
"Male and Female" author	MEAD
Male gypsy	ROM
Male swan	COB
Malediction	CURSE
Maleficence	EVIL
Malt liquors	ALES
Mammal with webbed feet	OTTER
Manana	LATER
Man and horse contest	RODEO
Man at the plate	BATTER
Maneuver	PLOY
Maneuverable, as a ship	YARE
Man, for one	ISLE
Man from Korsor	DANE
Man from Lodz	POLE
Mangle	IRON
Mango or colima	TREE
Man, Gypsy	ROM
Manicure the lawn	MOW
Manicuring board	EMERY
Manifest	EVIDENT,OVERT
Man in a cast	ACTOR
Man in Entertainment	EMCEE
Man in Genesis	SETH
Man in the ring	REF
Manipulate	RIG,USE
Manitoba Indian	CREE
Manner	AIR,MIEN,MODE
Manner, In a frenzied	AMOK
Manner of expression	STYLE
Manner of, In the	ALA
Manners	SORTS
Man of action	DOER
Man of Avon	BARD
Man of Berlin	HERR
Man of the categorical imperative	KANT
Man of the church	ELDER
Man of the Civil War	REB

Man of easy life	RILEY
Man of the hour	HERO
Man of old Rome	VIR
Man of Spain	SENOR
Man of Tabriz	IRANI
Man on the beat	COP
Manor	ESTATE
Man or bird	BIPED
Man or boy	MALE
Mansard	ROOF
Man's name	ABEL, ADAM,ALAN,EMIL,ENOS,EVAN,IRA,OREN
Man's nickname	ABE,ALEX,ART, ARTIE,BERT,ERN,ERNIE,GUS,LEN,MOE, NAT,NED,PETE,STU,TED,TEDDY,TIM
Mantel decor	VASE
Mantle, Spanish	CAPA
Manufactured	MADE
Manuscript leaf	FOLIO
Man who comforted Job	ELIHU
Man, Wise	SAGE
Man with a load	ATLAS
Man without a country	NOLAN
Many	ALOT
Many times	OFTEN
Mao or Gandhi	ASIAN
Map	PLAT
Map addition	INSET
Map area	ASIA
Map explanation	KEY
Maple genus	ACER
Map line	ROAD
Map listings	RTES
Marathon	RACE
Marble	TAW
Marbles	AGATES
March and Holbrook	HALS
March animal	HARE
Marche or ton	BON
March girl	MEG
Marco	POLO
Margarine	OLEO
Margin	RIM
Margin of victory, sometimes	NOSE
Marianne or Grace	MOORE
Marienbad, e.g.	SPA
Marie or Therese	STE
Marine bird	ERNE
Marine hazards	REEFS
Marina sight	MAST
Marina visitor	YACHT
Mariner	GOB
Mariner's cry	AHOY
Mariner's guide, with "north"	STAR
Mariner's heading	SSE
Mariner's term	ALEE
Marionette man	SARG
Marital discards	EXES
Mark	SCAR
Market and Main	STREETS
Market declines	SAGS
Market, Flood the	GLUT
Market, Grain	PIT
Market purchase	OLEO
Market word	BEAR
Marketplace	AGORA
Mark in curling	TEE
Mark: Lat.	NOTA
Mark, Printing	CARET
Marks, Printing	STETS
Marks, reals, etc.	MONEY
Marmalade ingredient	RIND
Marner	SILAS
Marquette	PERE
Marriage prelims	BANNS
Marseilles relative	MERE

Marsh FEN
Marshall, for example PLAN
Marshal's badge STAR
Marsh birds SORAS
Marsh elder IVA
Marsh grass RUSH
Marsh growth REED
Mars: Prefix AREO
Martin DEAN
Martinique et al. ILES
Martinique volcano PELEE
Martyred saint URSULA
Marx KARL
Maryland campus USNA
Mary or Vincent ASTOR
Mary Todd's husband ABE
Mascaras DYES
Mascot, Fordham RAM
Mashie or wedge IRON
Masking and friction TAPES
Massage RUB
Massed group HORDE
Mast SPAR
Master of counterpoint BACH
Master, in Malaysia TUAN
Masts POLES
Mata HARI
Matador cheers OLES
Mata Hari, e.g. SPY
Match PAIR
Matched groups SETS
Matched pair MATES
Material, Blasting TNT
Material, Floor TILE
Material formed by fusion FRIT
Material for a punch card DATA
Material, Ribbed REP
Maternal relation ENATE
Mate, Rose's ABIE
Math branch TRIG
Mathematical association RATIO
Math ratio SINE
Matinee time TWO
Mat or mate word AUTO
Matriculate ENROL
Matterhorn, for one ALP
Matter, in law RES
Matty of baseball ALOU
Mature ADULT,RIPEN
Matured AGED
Mature, More OLDER
Matures AGES
Maugham story RAIN
Maui greeting ALOHA
Mauna Loa coating LAVA
Maurice of stage note EVANS
Mausoleum city AGRA
Mavourneen's place ERIN
Maxim GNOME
Maxwell ELSA
Maxwell or Reo CAR
Mayday SOS
May of the theater ELAINE
May or Ann CAPE
McCarthy, to friends GENE
McKuen and Serling RODS
McNamara's outfit BAND
Meadow creature HARE
Meadowlands LEAS
Meadow mouse VOLE
Meadow sounds BAAS
Meager POOR
Meaning SENSE
Meaning: Colloq. HANG
Mean ones OGRES
Measure LITRE,METER,OUNCE,PACE,PINT
Measure in Europe METRE
Measure, Metric ARE
Measure of capacity STERE
Measure of length ROD
Measure, Old ELL
Measure, Paper REAM
Measures of yarn LEAS
Measure with the hand SPAN
Meat cut LOIN
Meat jelly ASPIC
Meat order CHOP
Meat spread PATE
Mecca native ARAB
Mechanical device ENGINE
Mechanical method ROTE
Med DARN
Medal of Honor man HERO
Medals AWARDS
Meddle NOSE
Medicates DOSES
Medicinal plant ALOE,SENNA
Medicine or old HAT
Medieval poem ALBA
Medieval shield ECU
Medieval stone throwers ONAGERS
Mediocre SOSO
Meditates PORES
Mediterranean island ELBA
Mediterranean port ORAN
Mediterranean resort NICE
Mediterranean sailboat SAIC
Mediterranee, for one MER
Medit. port SAID,TUNIS
Medit. vessel XEBEC
Medium, Art OILS
Medium's medium SEANCE
Medium's messages RAPS
Medley OLIO
Meetings TRYSTS
Meets SITS
Me, in France MOI
Me, in Munich MIR
Mel HONEY
Melchior and companions MAGI
Mellow AGE
Melody ARIA,TUNE
Mel of baseball OTT
Melt THAW
Melville captain AHAB
Melville hero AHAB
Melville novel OMOO
Member, Eastern-church UNIAT
Member of the electorate VOTER
Member of the family MOM
Member of an Iroquois union NATION
Member, Orchestra OBOE
Member, Party DEMOCRAT
Members, Choir ALTOS
Members, Fraternal ELKS
Memberships SEATS
Members of a blind trio MICE
Members of a crew OARS
Member, Staff AIDE
Memento RELIC
Memento of a scrape SCAB
Memo NOTE
Memorable actor Paul MUNI
Memorable Cowardly Lion LAHR
Men CREW,HES,SEW
Menander's Muse ERATO
Mend SEW
Men, Fraternal ELKS
Men from Aarhus DANES
Men, Ivy League ELIS
Men's gathering STAG
Men, Staff AIDES
Menswear purchase SUIT
Mention, Fail to OMIT
Mentions CITES
Menu CARTE

Menu favorites STEWS
Menu item EGG, ENTREE, OMELETTE, ROAST, SALAD, VEAL
Menu offering HASH
Men, Wall St. TRADERS
Mercator product MAP
Merchandise WARE
Mere VERY
Mere indication WISP
Merganser SMEW
Merit EARN
Merkel UNA
Merriman and others NANS
Merriment GLEE
Merriment sounds HAHA
Merry RIANT
Merry sounds HAHAS
Merry, in Marseilles GAI
Meshed fabrics NETS
Meshed's country IRAN
Mesozoic et al. ERAS
Mess fare CHOW
Met SAT
Metal bolt RIVET
Metal clasping piece TNUT
Metal, Decorated NIELLO
Metal disk part PATEN
Metal dross SLAG
Metal loop DEE
Metal piece TBAR
Metal ring EYELET
Metals ORES
Metal tag AGLET
Metalware TOLE
Meted out DOLED
Meter and printer prefix TELE
Meter prefix ALTI
Met head on DARED
Method WAY
Methods SYSTEMS
Me-tooer APER
Met rendition ARIA
Metrical stress ARSIS
Metric measure STERE
Metric unit GRAM, LITRE
Metric volume STERE
Metroliner TRAIN
Mets' arena SHEA
Mets' league NAT
Mets or Braves NINE
Mexican aunts TIAS
Mexican gentleman SENOR
Mexican home ADOBE
Mexican nothing NADA
Mexican stew OLLA
Mexican tidbit TACO
Michelangelo work DAVID
Michigan locks, for short SOO
Michigan town IONIA
Middies USNA
Middle-ear bone ANVIL
Middle East seaport GAZA
Middle or Far EAST
Mideast capital ANKARA, SANA
Mideasterner IRANI, IRAQI
Mideasterners ARABS
Mideast land IRAN
Mideast motel SERAI
Mideast port ACRE, ADEN, BASRA
Midges GNATS
Midi summers ETES
Midnight, to some LATE
Midwest college COE
Midwestern city OMAHA
Midwest Indian HURON
Midwest state IOWA
Miff RILE
Mighty mite ATOM
Migrant worker OKIE
Migrate MOVE
Migration TREK
Migratory birds GEESE
Milady's concern MODE
Milan money LIRE
Mild cheese EDAM
Mild expletive EGAD, PSHAW
Mild oath DARN, EGAD
Milieu, Bowler's LANES
Milieu, Pickles' BRINE
Milieu, Scarlett's TARA
Milieu, Technician's LAB
Military address APO
Military attack man RAIDER
Military body UNIT
Military halting place ETAPE
Military installation FORT
Military man AIDE
Military post FORT
Military truant AWOL
Milk: Fr. LAIT
Milking, for one CHORE
Millay EDNA
Millinery HATS
Mill materials ORES
Milton and Keats POETS
Mime APER
Mimics APERS
Mince or humble PIE
Mind HEED, OBEY, TEND
Mindanao native ATA
Mine approach ADIT
Mine gas DAMP
Mine guardian of fable GNOME
Mine, in France AMOI
Mineo SAL
Mine output ORE
Mineral SPAR, TALC
Mineral deposits LODES
Minerals ORES
Mineral, Soft TALC
Miner's nail SPAD
Miner's prize LODE
Minestrone ingredient PEAS
Mine vehicle TRAM
Mine yields ORES
Minimal BARE
Minimum LEAST
Mining city in Kansas ARMA
Mining nail SPAD
Mini or maxi STYLE
Mini or midi DRESS
Miniscule WEE
Miniskirt, of a sort TUTU
Mink piece STOLE
Minnesota product IRON
Minnow's role LURE
Minor or Major URSA
Minor taboo NONO
Minted money SPECIE
Mints COINS
Minus LESS
Minus-yardage in football LOSS
Minute amount TINGE
Minutia MOTE
Miquelon et St. Pierre ILES
Mirrored APED
Mirth GLEE
Misbehave ACTUP
Miscalculate ERR
Miscellanies ANAS
Miscellany OLIO
Mischief makers IMPS
Misdemeanor, Military AWOL
Misdo ERR
Misdoubt FEAR

Miser's forte GREED
Misfortunes ILLS
Mishmash OLIO
Mislay LOSE
Misplaces LOSES
Misrepresent BELIE
Misrepresenter LIAR
Miss GIRL,LASS
Miss Adams EDIE
Miss Arden EVE
Miss Baxter ANNE
Miss the blue ribbon LOSE
Miss Cinders ELLA
Miss Claire and others INAS
Miss Dunne IRENE
Misses a fly ball ERRS
Misses out on LOSES
Miss Foch NINA
Miss Hagen UTA
Missile ATLAS,NIKE
Missile for Washington DOLLAR
Missile housing SILO
Missile part NOSECONE
Missiles DARTS
Mission CRUSADE
Mississippi name TWAIN
Miss Kett of comics ETTA
Miss kind NEAR
Miss Lanchester ELSA
Miss Logan ELLA
Miss Murray of silents MAE
Miss O'Grady ROSIE
Miss Sommer ELKE
Miss Stevens INGER
Miss St. Johns ADELA
Misstepped ERRED
Miss Turner LANA
Miss Vaughan SARAH
Miss West MAE
Mistook ERRED
Mistress, "Contrary" MARY
Mitch Miller's instrument OBOE
Mitigate EASE
Mix, Drink SODA
Mixed up, as type PIED
Mix rapidly BEAT
Mixture OLIO
Mix-up MESS
Mock DERIDE
Model IDEAL,NORM
Mode of life STYLE
Moderate BATE
Modern author URIS
Modern Christiania OSLO
Modern hospice MOTEL
Modern Lutetia PARIS
Modern painter DALI
Modern: Prefix NEO
Modern serais MOTELS
Modified TONED
Modify ADAPT,AMEND
Mohammedan beauty HOURI
Mohammedan name ALI
Mohammedan priest IMAM
Moist DAMP
Moisten in a way BASTE
Moisture DEW
Moki Indian HOPI
Mold DIE
Molding OVOLO
Molding, Curved OGEE
Moldings, Column TORI
Mole gray TAUPE
"Moll Flanders" author DEFOE
Mollusk delicacy MUSSEL
Molt SHED
Moment TRICE
Momentous words IDO

Momentum SPEED
Monad ATOM,UNIT
Mona Lisa characteristic SMILE
Monarch PRINCE,TSAR
Monarch in Norse legend ATLI
Monastery man PRIOR
Monday mood BLAH
Money-changing fee AGIO
Money for Loren LIRA
Money, for one ASSET
Money handler TELLER
Money in coin SPECIE
Money in Iran RIAL
Money in Lille FRANC
Money, in Lima SOL
Money in Modena LIRE
Money in Monterrey PESO
Money, Thai BAHT
Mongkut's tutor ANNA
Mongol, for one ASIAN
Mongrel MUTT
Moniker NAME
Monk LAMA
Monkey TITI
Monk parrot LORO
Monkshood ATIS
Monk's title FRA
Monopolized, with "up" SEWED
Monotone DRONE
Monster GILA
Monsters OGRES
Monster's habitat LOCH
Monster's Loch NESS
Montague ROMEO
Montez LOLA
Montgomery's river ALABAMA
Month APRIL
Month in Biarritz MAI
Moo LOW
Mood TONE
Moolah SCRATCH
Moon, Of the LUNAR
Moon phenomena HALOS
Moon site RILL
Moonlight and others SONATAS
Moonlighting group NASA
Moonshot sponsor NASA
Moral value ETHIC
Morals man AESOP
More effective ABLER
More exceptional RARER
More experienced OLDER
More pay RAISE
More singular ODDER
More stable SANER
Morning-after eyes RED
Morning moisture DEW
Moroccan port RABAT
Morose GLUM,SAD
Morph or plasm prefix ECTO
Morsel ORT
Morsels BITES
Morse symbol DOT
Mortarboards CAPS
Mortar tray HOD
Mortgage LIEN
Mortise's companion TENON
Mosaic gold ORMOLU
Mosarrat's cruel domain SEA
Moses' spokesman AARON
Moslem leader IMAM,OMAR
Moslem magistrate CADI
Moslem nobleman AMEER
Moslem nymph HOURI
Moslem prince AMIR,EMEER
Moslem religion ISLAM
Moslem ruler EMIR
Moslem V.I.P. AGA

Mosque priest	IMAM	Mr. Burr	AARON
Mostel	ZERO	Mr. Eban	ABBA
Motel of yore	INN	Mrs. Copperfield	DORA
Mother Goose character	SPRAT	Mrs. Dick Tracy	TESS
Mother Hubbard's lack	BONE	Mrs. Helmer	NORA
Mother of Artemis	LETO	Mrs. Lindbergh	ANNE
Mother of Helen of Troy	LEDA	Mrs. Roosevelt	SARA
Mother of Isaac	SARAH	Mrs. Sprat's choice	FAT
Mother of Julie	PAT	Mrs. Truman	BESS
Mother of Learchus	INO	Mr. Wolfe	NERO
Mother of mankind	EVE	Mt. Telpos-iz and others	URALS
Mother-of-pearl	NACRE	Much: Prefix	ERI
Mother-of-pearl mollusk	ABALONE	Mucilages	GELS
Mother of Peer Gynt	ASE	Mud	MIRE
Mother of the Titans	GAEA	Muddy	ROIL
Mother of Zeus	RHEA	Muddy deposit	SILT
Mother or Good	EARTH	Muffin	GEM
Mother's command	EAT	Muhammed	ALI
Mother's common word	DONT	Mulberry bark	TAPA
Motion, Be in	STIR	Mule parts	SOLES
Motion picture	CINE	Mulligans	STEWS
Motivate strongly	URGE	Multiplication word	TIMES
Motive	CAUSE	Multitude	ARMY,HORDE
Motor	DRIVE	Munich's river	ISAR
Motorized caddie	CART	Municipality	TOWN
Motto	SAW	Munificent	OPENHANDED
Mound	HEAP	Munitions	AMMO
Mount	STEED	Munro	SAKI
Mountain	ALP	Muralist	SERT
Mountain, Buddhist	OMEI	Murky	DIM
Mountain climber's reward	VIEW	Murmur	COO
Mountain crest	ARETE	Muscle twitches	TICS
Mountain goat	IBEX	Muse	CLIO,ERATO
Mountain of Crete	IDA	Muses, e.g.	NINE
Mountain of Nepal	API	Museum offering	ART
Mountain of Thessaly	OSSA	Musial	STAN
Mountain pass	GHAT	Musical and bank	NOTES
Mountain pool	TARN	Musical end	FINE
Mountain: Prefix	OREO,ORO	Musical exercise	ETUDE
Mountain ramble	HIKE	Musical family	BACH
Mountain range	ANDES	Musical finale	CODA
Mountains, Soviet	URALS	Musical group	CHOIR,NONET,OCTET
Mountain stronghold	AERIE	Musical instruction	LENTO
Mountbatten or Avon	EARL	Musical instrument	ORGAN,REED,SAX
Mournful piece	DIRGE	Musical instruments	LUTES,OBOES
Mournful sound	MOAN	Musical mark	SLUR
Mouselike rodent	VOLE	Musical note	SOL
Mouthful, as of rum	SWIG	Musical notes	FAS,TIS
Mouth, in Madrid	BOCA	Musical piece	DUET,MOTET,SOLO
Mouth: Prefix	ORI	Musical refrain	LALA
Mouths	ORA	Musical show	REVUE
Movable barrier	GATE	Musical sign	REST
Movable property	GEAR	Musical sound	TING
Move aimlessly	COAST	Musical sounds	TONES
Move, as a camera	PAN	Musical syllable	TRA
Move heavily	DRAG	Musical symbol	CLEF,DOT
Move, Poker	BET,RAISE	Musical tempo direction	ASSAI
Move quietly	STEAL	Musical term	TONAL
Moves	STIRS	Musical work	OPERA,OPUS,TRIO
Moves cautiously	EDGES	Musical works	SONATAS
Move slowly	INCH	Music group	OCTET,TRIO
Move strongly, with "through"	PLOW	Music halls	ODEA
Move suddenly	DART,START	Music, High in	ALT
Move unsteadily	TEETER	Music, Pauses in	RESTS
Move with care	EASE	Music-room item	ALBUM
Movie accolade	OSCAR	Music, Slow in	LENTO
Movie-ad word	EPIC	Music style	JAZZ
Movie canine	ASTA	Music, Upbeat in	ARSIS
Movie classification	ADULT	Muskie's state	MAINE
Movie local	SET	Muslim beauty	HOURI
Movie marquee word	TODAY	Muslim ruler	AMIR
Movie name	LADD	Muslim title	IMAM
Movie-palace feature	ORGAN	Mussorgsky's mountain	BALD
Movie, Paul Newman	HUD	Mutineer	REBEL
Movies, in Roma	CINE	My gal	SAL
Moving	ASTIR	Myrna	LOY
Moving line	TRAIN	Mysteries, First name in	ERLE
M.P.H.	SPEED	Mysterious	WEIRD

Mystery pioneer POE

Mythomaniac LIAR

N

Nabokov heroine ADA
Nader subject AUTO
Nag CARP
Nagger SHREW
Nail SPAD
Nail or secret FILE
Naldi of old films NITA
Name, Arabic ABOU
Name, Argentine PERON
Name, Automotive OLDS
Name, Baseball ALOU
Name, Biblical ABEL,ELI
Name, Chinese MAO
Name, Cremona AMATI
Name, Fashion DIOR
Name for Alcatraz ROCK
Name for a dog SPOT
Name for an English queen BESS
Name for Henry V HAL
Name for an island ERIN
Name for a pooch ROVER
Name for a Western horse PAINT
Name, French RENE
Name, Genesis ENOS,ESAU
Name, Girl's ETTA,MELANIE,TESS,TONI
Name, Golfing SNEAD
Name in baseball, First TRIS
Name in boxing ALI
Name in detective fiction ERLE
Name in fashion FATH
Name in French history MARAT
Name in journalism OCHS
Name in long-run show ABIE
Name in map-making RAND
Name in tennis ASHE
Name in U.N. lore LIE
Name in U.S. poetry BENET
Name, Israeli EBAN
Name, Korean RHEE
Name, Literary ELIA
Name, London art TATE
Name meaning grace ANN
Name of Ancient Syria ARAM
Name, Opera TOSCA
Name, Persian OMAR
Name, Presidential ABE
Name, Russian IVAN
Name, Russian girl's OLGA
Namesakes of Isaac's son ESAUS
Name, Scottish RAE
Names formally CITES
Names, Girls' NANS
Name, "Zhivago" LARA
Nanny's offspring KID
Napery LINEN
Naples evening SERA
Naples port AMALFI
Naples she ESSA
Napoleon's sentence EXILE
Narcotic OPIATE
Narcotics-squad man at times RAIDER
Narrative SAGA,YARN
Narrative, Long ILIAD
Narrow boat CANOE
Narrow crest ARETE
Narrow groove STRIA
Narrow inlet RIA
Narrowly look PEER
Narrow passage STRAIT
Narrow peninsula NECK
Narrow shoal SPIT
Narrow valley GLEN
Mystic cards TAROT
Myth, Nymph of ECHO

Nash and Dickinson POETS
Nasty SNIDE
Nasty look LEER
Natch SURE
Nathan HALE
Nation, Asian IRAK,LAOS
Native, Australian ABO
Native, Caucasian OSSET
Native craft PROA
Native, Nigerian ARO
Native of Bangkok THAI
Native of Mosul IRAQI
Native of: Suffix ITE,OTE
Native of Tabriz IRANI
Native of Yemen ARAB
Natives of Cracow POLES
Natives: Suffix ITES
Native: Suffix ITE
Nativity figures MAGI
NATO and SEATO PACTS
NATO member ITALY
Natterjack TOAD
Natty SMART
Naturally spoken ALOUD
Naturalness EASE
Nature SORT
Nature's replay ECHO
Naught NIL
Naughty word OATH
Nautical direction ALEE
Nautical man SALT
Nautical position ABEAM
Nautical reading ENE,ESE
Nautical ropes SHEETS
Nautical speed unit KNOT
Nautical term ALEE
Nautical word LEE
Nautics prefix AERO
Naval apparatus SONAR
Naval base, Algerian ORAN
Naval direction APORT
Naval historian MAHAN
Naval term AFT
Navigational aid LORAN
Navy boats LSTS
Nazimova ALLA
N.C. college ELON
Neap or rip TIDE
Near ABOUT
Nearby ABOUT,AROUND
Near the end LATTER
Near-flunking mark POOR
Nearly ABOUT
Near or Far EAST
Near or Ole MISS
Near to: Prefix EPI
Neat PRIM
Nebraska Indian OTOE
Nebraskan Indian OTO
Neckline VEE
Neckpiece of sorts ADAMSAPPLE
Neckpieces BOAS,NAPES
Neck, Stretch one's CRANE
Neckwear ASCOT
Need, Baker's OVEN
Need, Computer DATA
Need, Diplomat's TACT
Need for Jack, A PLAY
Needle case ETUI
Needlefish GAR
Needlework, Do SEW
Need, Printer's INK
Need, Rower's OAR
Need, Weaver's SLEY

Clue	Answer
Negation, Emphatic	NEVER
Negative, Certain	XRAY
Negative contraction of sorts	AINT
Negative prefix	NON
Negative, Scottish	NAE
Negative, Slangy	NOPE
Neglect	OMIT
Negligent	LAX
Negotiate	TREAT
Negri of the silents	POLA
Neighbor of Caledonia	EIRE
Neighbor of Des Moines	AMES
Neighbor of Ida	ORE
Neighbor of Pakistan	IRAN
Neighbor of Sverige	NORGE
Neighbor of Virginia City	RENO
Neighborhoods	AREAS
Neighbor's child	BRAT
Neither's companion	NOR
Nemo, translated	NOONE
Neon, for one	SIGN
Neon, Like	INERT
Nepal peak	API
Nerve	GRIT
Nerve networks	RETIA
Nervous	EDGY,TENSE
Nervous movements	TICS
Ness	LOCH
Nessen	RON
Nest	AERIE,AERY
Nested boxes	INRO
Nester on crags	EAGLE
Nestling	EYAS
Nest of sorts	MARES
Net	GAIN,SEINE
Netherlands commune	EDE
Netherlands town	EDAM
Netherworld	HADES
Netman Lacoste	RENE
Net's partner	GROSS
Nettle	PIQUE
Network	RETE,SYSTEM,WEB
Networks	RETIA
Nevada city	RENO
Never, in Bonn	NIE
Newcastle's river	TYNE
New charts, Make	REMAP
New England city	BARRE
New England, etc.	EAST
New England sights	ELMS
Newest news	LATEST
New frontier	SPACE
New Guinea port	LAE
New Havenite	ELI
Newlywed	BRIDE
New-math units	SETS
New Mexico resort	TAOS
New Rochelle college	IONA
News brief	ITEM
News hot off the press	LATEST
News story of a kind	SOB
Newspaper item	OBIT
Newspaper items	ADS
Newspaper, familiarly	SHEET
Newspapers	PRESS
Newsroom man	EDITOR
Newsworthy jet	SST
Newts	EFTS
New World capital	LIMA
New York city	OLEAN
New York county	TIOGA
New York time	EST
New Zealand parrot	KEA
Next in order	THEN
Next to, Be	ABUT
N.F.L. team	RAMS
Nice school	ECOLE
Nice summers	ETES

Clue	Answer
Niche	SLOT
Nicholas or Peter	TSAR
Nichols' hero	ABIE
Nick	DENT
Nick Charles's wife	NORA
Nickname for a Greek	ARI
Nicotines' partners	TARS
Nigerian town	EDE
Nigerian tribe	IBO
Nigerian tribesman	ARO
Night fliers	BATS
Nightingale symbol	LAMP
Nights before	EVES
Night spot	CAFE
Nile bird	IBIS
Nimble	AGILE,SPRY
Nimbus	AURA,HALO
Nincompoop	ASS
Nincompoops	SAPS
Nine: Prefix	ENNE
1945 conference site	YALTA
1947 Nobel writer	GIDE
1943 Bogart movie	SAHARA
Nineteenth hole	BAR
1930 Nobelist in literature	LEWIS
1912 Peace Nobelist	ROOT
Ninny	SAP
Nixon V.P.	AGNEW
N.L. player	ASTRO
N.L. team	METS,REDS
N.M. art colony	TAOS
Noah's landfall	ARARAT
Noah's son	SHEM
Nobel author, 1930	LEWIS
Nobelist writer, 1947	GIDE
Nobel physicist	RABI
Nobleman	EARL,LORD
Nobleman in France	DUC
Noblemen	PEERS
Noble, Moslem	AMEER,AMIR
Nocturnal mammal	LEMUR
Noel	CAROL
No gentleman	CAD
Nog ingredient	EGG
No, in Glasgow	NAE
No, in Munich	NEIN
Noise	BLARE
Noise of a kind	SNORE
Noise of a sort	STATIC
Noise, Sudden	CLAP
Noisy	AROAR
Noncocktail party	TEA
Noncoms	PFCS,SGTS
Nonflying bird	EMU
Nonplused	STUCK
Nonprofessional	LAIC
Nonsense	TRASH
Nonsense!	RATS,ROT
Nonthoroughbred	MUTT
Non-waiter	TIDE,TIME
Nonworking	IDLE
No other than	ONLY
No place for apple eating	EDEN
No point, in tennis	LET
Nordhoff co-author	HALL
"No-returns" warning	ASIS
Normal	PAR
Normally five to the foot	TOES
Normandy beach	UTAH
Normandy town	STLO
Normandy river	ORNE
Norse god	LOKI,ODIN
Norse goddess	RAN
Norse goddess of fate	NORN
Norse gods, Race of	AESIR
Norse king	OLAF
Norse name	OLE
Norse navigator	ERIC

Norse poem RUNE
North Africa, Gully, in WADI
North African MOOR
North African port ORAN,SFAX,TUNIS
North Atlantic fish COD
North Atlantic island group FAROE
North Carolina college ELON
Northern capital OSLO
Northern shrub ALDER
North or Ross SEA
North or South POLE
North Sea river YSER,ELBE,MEUSE
North Sea tributary WESER
Norwegian coin ORE
Norwegian dramatist IBSEN
Norwegian saint OLAV
Nose PRY
Nosegay POSY
Nostradamus et al. SEERS
Not alert ASLEEP
Notation on an envelope PERSONAL
Not brand-new USED
Notch DENT
Notched EROSE
Not citified RURAL
Not competent UNFIT
Not dissonant TONAL
Not down ARISEN
Noted SEEN
Noted British family EDENS
Noted cartoonist NAST
Noted Italian DANTE
Noted marsupial POGO
Noted Ohio family TAFT
Noted publisher OCHS
Noted Russian LENIN
Noted sculptor RODIN
Noted traveler POLO
Note, Office MEMO
Note of Guido ELA
Notes of the scale FAS
Noteworthy EMINENT
Not flabby TAUT
"Not guilty," for one PLEA
Nothing NIL
Nothing, in Spain NADA
Nothing for Pierre RIEN
Nothing to marry in HASTE
Notice ESPY,HEED,SIGN
Noticed SEEN
Notices, Certain ADS
Not in use IDLE
Not in vogue OUT
Notion IDEA
Notion, in Nines IDEE
Not the king's English SLANG
Not mad SANE
Not more than MERE
Not much DROPINTHEBUCKET
Not new USED
Notorious marquis SADE
Not a one NARY
Not partial ENTIRE
Not recorded LIVE
Not ruddy PALE
Not settled MOOT
Not shut OPEN
Not so hot TEPID
Not sweet SEC
Not talking MUM
Not taped LIVE
Not this OTHER
Not a tyro PRO
Not up ABED
Not well ILL
Not written ORAL
Noun ending ATOR,EER,ENCE,ERY,ION,NESS,URE
Noun endings ERS
Noun suffix INE,ING,ITE,SIS
Noun suffixes ATES
Nourished FED
Novarro RAMON
Novel heroine EMMA
Novelist Glasgow ELLEN
Novel, Nabokov ADA
Novel of 1880 NANA
Novel, Scott IVANHOE
Novel title SHE
Novice TIRO
No-voter ANTI
Now ATONCE,TODAY
Now, For PROTEM
Now's companion HERE
Noxious weed LOCO
Nuance SHADE,TRACE
Nuisance PEST
Nuisance, Urban SMOG
Nullify UNDO,VOID
Number THREE
Number ending TEEN
Number, Italian TRE
Number, Large SLEW
Numbers FOURS,ONES,TENS
Numbers man CPA
Numbskull DOLT,IDIOT
Numerals, Certain ARABIC
Numeral, Spanish SEIS
Numerical prefix DECA,OCTA,OCTO,TER,TRI
Nureyev specialties LEAPS
Nurse TEND
Nursemaid, Oriental AMAH
Nursery item CRIB
Nursery-rhyme burden PAIL
Nursery-rhyme porridge PEASE
Nurture REAR
Nut COLA,KOLA
N.Y.C. college PACE
N.Y.C. events of 1863 RIOTS
N.Y. county TIOGA
N.Y. five NETS
Nymph ECHO,OREAD
Nymph loved by Apollo ARIA
N.Y. nine METS
N.Y.S.E. trader BEAR
N.Y. sports place SHEA
N.Y. team METS
N.Y.-Wash. liner METRO
N.Z. parrot KEA

O

Oaf IDIOT,LOUT
Oahu dance HULA
Oahu fare POI
Oahu greeting ALOHA
Oakley ANNIE
Oak or elm TREE
Oar part LOOM
Oast OVEN
Oath, Old EGAD
Oath-taker's words IDO
Obdurate STONY
Obi SASH
Obi accessory INRO
Objective END
Objective, for one CASE
Objective, Scout's good DEED
Object of devotion IDOL
Object of exorcism DEMON
Object pettily CAVIL
Obligated, Is NEEDS,OWES

Clue	Answer
Obligation	ONUS
Obligations	NEEDS
Obliquely drive a nail	TOE
Obliteration	ERASURE
Oblivion	LETHE
Oboe	REED
Obscenity	SMUT
Obscure	DEEP,VEIL
Obsequies	RITES
Observances	RITES
Observe	SEE
Observed	EYED,NOTED,SEEN
Obsess	HAUNT
Obsolescent wedding word	OBEY
Obsolete	DATED,DEAD
Obstacle	RUB
Obstacles	SNAGS
Obstreperous one	BRAT
Obstruct	BAR,CLOG
Obtains	GETS
Obvious	EVIDENT
O'Casey	SEAN
O'Casey, for one	IRISH
O'Casey milieu	EIRE
Occasion	TIME
Occasional bonnet occupant	BEE
Occasional sky sighting	UFO
Occasion, Social	TEA
Occupant	TENANT
Occupation	LINE
Occupied	INUSE
Occur	RISE
Occurred	WAS
Ocean area	BED
Ocean-bottom covering	OOZE
Ocean food fish	OPAH
Ocean route	LANE
Ocean swell	SEA
Ocean vessel	LINER
October event	SERIES
October stone	OPAL
Odd, in Scotland	ORRA
Odds and ends	ANA
Odds and ends case	ETUI
Ode subject	URN
Odin and followers	AESIR
Odists' instruments	LYRES
"Odyssey," for one	EPIC
Of an Asian nation	SINO
Of birds	AVIAN
Of a certain grain	OATEN
Of the ear	OTIC
Off, Cut	LOP
Offense	PIQUE,SIN
Offensive	EVIL
Offer	BID
Offering, Ad	SALE
Offering, Stage	OPERA
Off, Give	EMIT
Offhand	GLIB
Office communication	MEMO
Officeholders	INS
Office need	DESK
Official, City	MAYOR
Official, Mosque	IMAM
Official notice	EDICT
Official, Roman	EDILE
Officials, Moslem	AGAS
Official stamp	SEAL
Off key	FLAT
Of flying	AERO
Off the mark	AMISS
Off on the Elizabeth 2	ASEA
Off a ship's middle	ABEAM
Off-target	STRAY
Of a geological epoch	ERIAN
Of the glacial side	STOSS
Of grandparents	AVAL

Clue	Answer
O'Flaherty	LIAM
Of Mars: Prefix	AREO
Of the mouth	ORAL
Of musical keys	TONAL
Of old, Market place	AGORA
Of a poetic form	ODIC
Of secondary importance	SIDE
Of Selene's realm	LUNAR
Of the shoulder	ALAR
Of a sort, Bookmark	DOGEAR
Of a sort, Industrialists	ANTS
Of a sort, Suit	ARMOR
Of a space	AREAL
Often-drawn object	STRAW
Often-lent thing	EAR
Of a time interval	HORAL
Of a time period	ERAL
Oft-quoted Persian	OMAR
Of yore	OLDEN
Of yore, of yore	ERST
Ogden's state	UTAH
Ogles	EYES
O'Grady	ROSIE
O'Hara's Joey	PAL
"Oh, my!"	ALAS
Ohio city	LIMA
Ohio name	TAFT
Ohio river	MIAMI
Ohio team	REDS
Oil city of Oklahoma	ADA
Oil country	IRAN
Oil receptacle	TANK
Oil source	OLIVE,SHALE
Oil-well equipment	RIG
Ointment	BALM,NARD
Oka city	OREL
O.K. by radio	ROGER
Okinawan city	NAHA
Oklahoma fort	SILL
Oklahoman city	ENID
Olaf's capital	OSLO
Old ale jug	TOBY
Old auto	NASH,REO
Old card	TAROT
Old card game	LOO
Old Chinese bowl	TING
Old Chinese money	TAEL
Old Chinese treaty port	AMOY
Old cloth measures	ELLS
Old coin of India	ANNA
Old coin of Spain	REAL
Old corset support	STAY
Old dagger	SNEE
Old draft agency	SSS
Olden days	YORE
Old English coin	ORA
Old English court	LEET
Old enough	ENOW
Old expletive	EGAD
Old fogy	DODO
Old French ballad	LAI
Old French coin	ECU
Old gray one	MARE
Old Greek coin	OBOL
Old Greek contest	AGON
Old Greek district	IONIA
Old Greek platform	BEMA
Old hat	TRITE
Old-hat	PASSE,STALE
Old humor magazine	LIFE
Old instrument	LUTE
Old man, in Berlin	ALTE
Old man, Wise	NESTOR
Old market place	AGORA
Old music hall	ODEUM
Old name for one of Irani	MEDE
Old name for Tokyo	EDO
Old nautical term	YARE

Old port of Rome OSTIA
Old road ITER
Old saw, with "Fool me once, shame on" and "fool me twice, shame on me", An THEE
Old saw, with "Fool me once, shame on thee" and "me twice, shame on me", An FOOL
Old saw, with "Fool me once, shame on thee, fool me twice" and "on me", An SHAME
Old saw, with "Fool me once, shame on thee, fool me twice, shame", An ONME
Old school necessity SLATE
Old Siamese coin ATT
Old style anoint ANELE
Old style awry AGEE
Old style former ERST
Old style reveal OPE
Old style reward MEED
Old style temple FANE
Old swimming hole POND
Old Syria ARAM
Old $10 coin EAGLE
Old term of address SIRE
Old Testament book EZRA
Old-time slave ESNE
Old-time sorceror MAGE
Old Times Sq. hotel ASTOR
Old Turkish coin ASPER
Old Turkish title BEY
Old verb ending ETH
Old Versailles resident ROI
Old weapon LANCE
Old-womanish ANILE
Old World blackbird OUSEL
Old-World capital PARIS
Old-World duck SMEW
Old wound SCAR
Old writing SAGA
Olga's boyfriend IVAN
Olio STEW
Olive or pea GREEN
Olive shrub OLEA
Olympian ARES,ATHENA,EROS,HEBE
Olympian goddess HERA
Olympians GODS
Omani ARAB
Omar's rhyme for "thou" ENOW
Omit ELIDE
Onagers ASSES
Onassis ARI
On the briny ASEA
Once-around LAP
Once more ANEW
Once more, Western style AGIN
Once named NEE
Once: Scot ANES
Once-snazzy footwear SPATS
One ANY,UNIT
One and only LONE
One-armed bandits SLOTS
One-armed bandits city RENO
One at the polls VOTER
One, Be as UNITE
One beyond belief LIAR
One bite ended it EDEN
One bringing a case SUER
One club, for example BID
One, Holes in ACES
100 centavos PESO
100 centesimi LIRA
100-yard item DASH
O'Neill OONA
O'Neill heroine ANNA
O'Neill subject APE
O'Neill work PLAY
O'Neill's field DRAMA
One, in Paris UNE
One kind of book SCRAP
One kind of comic SERIO
One kind of keeper BEE
One kind of mill TREAD
One kind of order LARGE
One kind of seat AISLE
One man, many women HAREM
One, Mean OGRE
One, Nagging SHREW
One, Not NARY
One of the Bears PAPA
One of the Carsons KIT
One of Churchill's four offerings TOIL
One of an eager trio ABLE
One of five SENSE
One of five little pigs TOE
One of the five W's WHERE
One of the Gardners ERLE
One of Ghent's rivers LYS
One of the Hagens UTA
One of the Hebrides SKYE
One of "H.O.M.E.S." ERIE
One of the Horae IRENE
One of the Keys LARGO
One of a Kipling trio ARAG
One of a Latin trio AMO
One of the Little Women MEG
One of the media PRESS,RADIO
One of the Muses ERATO
One of Omar's wishes WINE
One of a pair DIE,EAR,MATE
One of the Plinys ELDER
One of a radio pair AMOS
One of the senses SMELL
One of the sins PRIDE
One of the Sporades SAMOS
One of the Three Stooges MOE
One of a Tolstoi pair PEACE
One of a world seven ASIA,SEA
One opposed ANTI
One or two word STEP
One past recovery GONER
Ones, Cherished DEARS
One's companion ALL
One: Scot. AIN
One, Scottish ANE
One-sided wins ROUTS
One's share QUOTA
Ones, Slippery EELS
Ones, Young LADS
One-time actor Milton SILLS
Onetime, old style ERST
One-time vamp BARA
One to a shay HOSS
One-two subject SHOE
Oneupmanship word PLOY
One was Attila HUN
One way to marry ELOPE
One way to walk ALONE
One who does: Suffix ATOR
One who stares GAPER
On the glacial side STOSS
On a grand scale EPIC
On hand ALONG
Onion's cousin LEEK
On the level EVEN
Only SOLE
On the move, Fish TROLL
On one's side FOR
On the qui vive ALERT
On reserve ASIDE
On the rocks ICED
On the short end, Be LOSE
On top AHEAD
On vacation AWAY

On view	OPEN
Onward	AHEAD
Oodles	SCADS
Oolong and Bohea	TEAS
Oozes	SEEPS
Open	AJAR,OVERT
Open a barrel	TAP
Open footwear	SANDAL
Opening	GAP,SLIT
Opening words for Caesar	ICAME
Openings	GATES,PORES
Openings, Small	EYELETS
Open-mouthed one	GAPER
Open space	AREA
Open spaces	LEAS
Open-weave fabric	LENO
Opera-box headgear	TIARAS
Opera by Verdi	AIDA
Opera cycle	RING
Opera role	IGOR,MIMI,TOSCA
Opera segment	SCENA
Opera star, Former	ALDA
Operate	ACT
Operated	RAN
Operatic segment	SCENA
Operatic solo	ARIA
Operation, Coin	TOSS
Operation, Police	RAID
Opinions	TENETS
Oporto export	WINE
Opportunity	DOOR
Opposed	ANTI,AVERSE
Opposed, cowpoke style	AGIN
Opposite of aweather	ALEE
Opposite of "Here, kitty"	SCAT
Opposite of nadir	NOON
Opposite of post	ANTE
Opposite of vive	ABAS
Opposite the wind	ALEE
Oppress	LOAD
Ops's daughter	CERES
Opt	ELECT
Opted	CHOSE
Optical device	LASER
Optimism, in Soho	OPE
Optimistic	ROSY
Option	CHOICE
Oral, e.g.	EXAM
Orally	ALOUD
Orbed	LUNAR
Orchestra members	OBOES
Orchestra sections	PITS
Orchestrate	ARRANGE
Orchid tubers	SALEP
Ordain	ENACT
Order, Fountain	MALT
Order, Pub	ALE
Order, Secret	KLAN
Orders, Fountain	SODAS
Order to a broker	SELL
Order to a dog	SIT,SPEAK
Ordinal ending	ETH
Ordinary	SOSO
Ordnance: Slang.	AMMO
Organ part	STOP
Organic compound	ENOL
Organic compounds	ESTERS
Organist	BACH
Organized group	PACK
Organized patterns	SYSTEMS
Organs often lent	EARS
Orgy	REVEL
Oriental	ASIAN
Oriental case	INRO
Oriental coins	YENS
Oriental gateway	TORII
Oriental heroine	OLAN
Oriental holiday	TET

Oriental name	ABOU,ALI,MAO
Oriental notable	AGA
Oriental nurses	AMAHS
Oriental V.I.P.	RAJAH
Orifice	PORE
Origami need	PAPER
Origin	SEED
Originate, with "from"	STEM
Oriole's home	NEST
Ornamental alloy	NIELLO
Ornamental piece	CAMEO
Ornamentation	DECOR
Ornament, Roof	EPI
Orphan	ANNIE
Orphant Annie's creator	RILEY
Or's relative	AND
Ort	BIT
Orthodontist's concerns	BITES
Oscar's cousin	TONY
Oscars, e.g.	AWARDS
Oscar-winning film	OLIVER
Oslo's land, to natives	NORGE
Ostrichlike bird	RHEA
O.T. book	PSALMS
Othello	MOOR
"Othello" role	IAGO
Other shoe	MATE
Others, in Rome	ALII
Otherwise	ALIAS,ELSE
Otiose	IDLE
Otis of baseball	AMOS
Otologist's concern	EAR
Ott	MEL
O.T. teacher	ELI
Our: Fr.	NOS
Oust	EVICT,EXPEL
Out	AWAY,NOTIN
Outbreak	RASH,RIOT
Outburst	FLARE,GALE
Outcome	EVENT
Outcries	HUES
Outcry	NOISE
Out, Deal	METE
Outdistance	LOSE
Outdo	BEST
Outdoor game	POLO
Outer: Pref.	ECTO
Outfield chance	FLY
Outfielder Felipe	ALOU
Outfit	RIG
Outgrowth of hair	MANE
Outing	RIDE
Outing spoiler	RAIN
Outlanders	ALIENS
Out, Leak	OOZE
Out, Leave	OMIT
Outlet	STORE
Outline	LIMN
Outlook	VIEW
Out, Make	EKE
Out, Mete	DOLE
Out of date	PASSE
Out of harmony	AJAR
Out of, in Munich	AUS
Out-of-luck person	GONER
Out of the ordinary	NOVEL
Out of play, as a ball	DEAD
Out of range	AFAR
Out of sorts	ILL,IRED
Out of the way	ASIDE
Output, Mauna Loa	LAVA
Output, Poetic	ODE
Outrigger	PROA
Outside: Prefix	ECTO
Outsiders	ALIENS
Outstanding	EMINENT
Outstanding one	STAR
Outstanding person	ONER

Clue	Answer
Outstanding thing: Slang	LULU
Outstanding, Was	SHONE
Outward bound	ASEA
Out West, Friend	PARD
Out West, Opposed	AGIN
Out, Wipe	ERASE
Oval cake	PONE
Oven	OAST
Over	ANEW,ATOP,DONE,ENDED,PAST
Overabundance	GLUT
Overact	EMOTE
Overboard for, Goes	DOTES
Overcome a fly	SWAT
Overdo the steaks	CHAR
Overdrinks	TOPES
Overdue	LATE
Overfills	SATES
Over, Fix	REDO,RESET
Overgrown, in a way	IVIED
Overhang	EAVE
Overhead	ATOP
Overhead item	ROOF
Overindulge	TOPE
Overlook	OMIT
Overly	TOO
Overplay	EMOTE
Overthrow	RUIN
Over, to Germans	UBER
Overused	TRITE
Overweight	OBESE
Overwhelm, informally	SLAY
Overwhelms	AWES
Owing	DUE
Own	HAVE
Owned	HAD
Owns	HAS
Own: Scot.	AIN
Oxford	SHOE
Oxford fellow	DON
Oxidizes	RUSTS
Oyster product	NACRE
"Oz" dog	TOTO

P

Clue	Answer
Pace	GAIT,RATE
Paced	LED
Pacific bark cloth	TAPA
Pacific fish	UNIE
Pacific, for one	OCEAN
Pacific herb	REA
Pacific island	BALI,OAHU
Pacific island group	SAMOA
Pacific islet	YAP
Pacific neckpiece	LEI
Pacific outrigger	PROA
Pacific porgy	TAI
Pacific sea	JAVA,SULU
Pacific sight	ATOLL
Pack	STOW
Packaged	BALED
Pack tightly	TAMP
Paddleboat, in a way	CANOE
Paddles	OARS
Paderewski	IGNACE
Pad, Hair	RAT
Paducah river	OHIO
Paganini's birthplace	GENOA
Page	LEAF
Page number	FOLIO
Pagoda ornament	TEE
Paid attendance	GATE
Paid notices	ADS
Pain	AGONY
Pain-in-the-neck	PEST
Pains	AILS
Pain sharply	STING
Pains' partners	ACHES
Painter famed for pastels	DEGAS
Painter, French	MATISSE,MONET
Painter's need	EASEL
Painter, Spanish	DALI,GOYA
Painter, Swiss	KLEE
Painter, U.S.	PEALE
Painting	NUDE
Painting effects	TONES
Painting or sculpture	ART
Paintings	OILS
Pair	BRACE,DUET,SPAN
Pakistani coin	ANNA
Pakistani tongue	URDU
Pakistan's neighbor	IRAN
Pal	PARD
Pale	ASHEN,ASHY
Pale color	AQUA
Palestine port	ACRE
Pale tan	ECRU
Palindrome word	ERE
Pallas	ATHENA
Pallid	ASHY,WAN
Palm	ARECA
Palm cockatoo	ARARA
Palmer, Golfer	ARNIE
Palmer's need	TEE
Palm fiber	TAL
Palm leaf	OLA
Palm of Brazil	ASSAI
Palm product	DATE
Palms	NIPAS
Palm, Starch	SAGO
Pal, Paris	AMI
Pals, in Paree	AMIS
Pamaps weapon	BOLA
Panay natives	ATIS
Pandowdy	PIE
Pant	GASP
Pantheon	GODS
Panther, for one	FELINE
Papal name	URBAN
Papal veil	ORALE
Paper quantity	REAM
Paper, Legal	DEED,LEASE
Papers, Work on	EDIT
Papyrus, for one	REED
Parade unit	BAND
Paradise	BLISS
Paradises	EDENS
Paragon	IDEAL
Paragraph	ITEM
Parcae	TRIO
Parcel out	DOLE,METE
Parched	ARID
Pardon	REMIT
"Pardon me!"	AHEM
Pare	PEEL
Parenthetical comment	ASIDE
Parents' word	DONT
Pari-mutuel item	BET
Paris area	PARC
Paris bank	LEFT
Paris cup	TASSE
Paris designer	FATH
Paris' field	ORLY
Paris here	ICI
Parisian assent	OUI
Parisian friend	AMIE
Parisian friends	AMIS
Parisian husband	MARI
Parisian night	NUIT
Parisian notion	IDEE
Parisian pate	TETE
Parisian's dream	REVE
Parisian seasons	ETES

Parisian's one	UNE
Parisian's stocking	BAS
Parisian sweetmeat	TARTE
Parisian water	EAU
Paris laugh	RIRE
Paris mine	AMOI
Paris nothing	RIEN
Paris, Plaster of	GESSO
Paris river near	MARNE
Paris school	ECOLE
Paris state	ETAT
Paris time	SOIR
Paris transport	METRO
Paris with	AVEC
Parker House, for one	ROLL
Park features	TREES
Parking problem	AUTO
Park in West	ESTES
Parlor piece	SOFA
Parochial	LOCAL
Parrot	KEA,MACAW
Parrot fish	LORO
Parseghian	ARA
Part	SEPARATE
Part, Battery	ANODE
Part, Bristlelike	SETA
Part, Chair	SPLAT
Part, Choice	ELITE
Part, Chorus	ALTO
Part, Church	AISLE,ALTAR,APSE
Part, Coat	LAPEL
Part, Corolla	PETAL
Parted	RENT
Part, Face	BROW
Part, Forelimb	ULNA
Part for Theda Bara	SIREN
Part, House	DEN,ELL
Participate	SITIN
Participating	INON
Particle, Charged	ION
Particles	ATOMS,IOTAS
Particles, Tiny	ATOMS
Particular	POINT
Particulars	ITEMS
Parties	BEES,GALAS,TEAS
Parting word	ADIEU
Parting words	TATA
Partisan: Suffix	CRAT
Partition	WALL
Partitioned-off area	LOGE
Part, Kimono	OBI
Part, Knee	PATELLA
Partly open	AJAR
Partly: Prefix	SEMI
Partly round	OVATE
Part, Machine	CAM
Part, Mailbox	SLOT
Part, Neck	NAPE
Partner, Andy's	AMOS
Partner, Bill's	COO
Partner, Now's	HERE
Partner of cut	DRIED
Partner of dash	DOT
Partner of 'earty	ALE
Partner of feather	TAR
Partner of flow	EBB
Partner of here	NOW
Partner of Larry and Curly	MOE
Partner of neither	NOR
Partner of nice	EASY
Partner of Ollie	FRAN
Partner of quo	QUID
Partner of ram	EWE
Partner of Scotch	SODA
Partner of snick	SNEE
Partner of tattered	TORN
Partner of to	FRO
Partner of yep	NOPE
Partners	MATES
Part of	SOME
Part of A.D.	ANNO
Part of A.M.	ANTE
Part of an auto	AXLE
Part of a basket	SLEW
Part of a building	STAIR
Part of a coop	ROOST
Part of the court scene	NET
Part of a decade	YEAR
Part of a Dickens title	ATALE
Part of a dog's foot	PAD
Part of dovetail joint	TENON
Part of D.V.	DEO
Part of a D.W. Griffith title	NATION
Part of an Eastern church	BEMA
Part of an ephah	OMER
Part of et al.	ALII
Part of etc.	AND
Part of the eye	UVEA
Part of a fairy tale beginning	UPON
Part of the fauna	AVES
Part of a fence	RAIL
Part of a fishline	SNELL
Part of a football team	LINE
Part of a fork	TINE
Part of a gem	FACET
Part of a golf club	TOE
Part of a Greek clan	OBE
Part of a Grieg title	ASES
Part of the hand	PALM
Part of handwriting on the wall	MENE
Part of a harness	HAME
Part of the head	SCALP
Part of a hearth	HOB
Part of H.M.S.	HER
Part of a horseman's gear	REIN
Part of a horseshoe	CALK
Part of H.S.H.	SERENE
Part of I.O.U.	OWE
Part of K.K.K.	KLAN
Part of Las Vegas	STRIP
Part of Latin "to be"	ERAT
Part of a Latin trio	AMAT
Part of l.c.m.	LEAST
Part of the leg	ANKLE,SHIN
Part of a Louvre name	LISA,MONA
Part of Mao's name	TSE
Part of a map	INSET
Part of the media	PRESS
Part of a molecule	ATOM
Part of a movie dog's name	TIN
Part of NASA	SPACE
Part of O.D.	OLIVE
Part of an old alphabet	RUNE
Part of an opener	SESAME
Part of an opera	SCENA
Part of a parrot's bill	CERE
Part of a poem	CANTO,STAVE
Part of a poetic trio	ARAG
Part of the psyche	EGO
Part of a race	LAP
Part of R and R	REST
Part of R.F.D.	RURAL
Part of R.S.V.P.	SIL
Part of S.A.R.	SONS
Part of Saturn's rings	ANSA
Part of SEATO	ASIA
Part of a ship	PROW
Part of ship or nut	HULL
Part of a space vehicle	NOSECONE
Part of the street scene	BUSES,TAXI
Part of a toast	SANTE
Part of a trunk	LID
Part of U.S.S.R.	UNION
Part of a Venetian blind	SLAT
Part of "veni, vidi, vici"	ICAME
Part of a wedding gown	TRAIN

Part of W.W.	WAR
Partook of	ATE
Part, Play	ACT
Part, Refrain	TRA
Part, Roof	EAVE
Parts	ROLES
Parts, Church	NAVES
Parts, Curve	ARCS
Part, Seed	ARIL
Part, Shoe	LACE,LAST
Part, Shoelace	AGLET
Parts, Jug	EARS
Parts of dancing shoes	TAPS
Parts of horses	MANES
Parts of an inning	OUTS
Parts of a match, in a game	SETS
Parts of a pad	SHEETS
Parts of the psyche	IDS
Parts of speech	NOUNS
Part song	GLEE
Parts, Skirt	GORES
Parts, Truck	CABS
Part suddenly	SNAP
Parts, Window	SILLS
Parts, Winglike	ALAE
Part, Telephone	DIAL
Part, Tire	TREAD
Party, Certain	STAG
Partygoers	GUESTS
Party man	DEMOCRAT
Pasha and Baba	ALIS
Pass	ELAPSE
Passable	SOSO
Passage	AISLE,ALLEY,GAP,LANE
Passage, French	ALLEE
Passage in anatomy	ITER
Passage, Mine	ADIT
Passage, Musical	CODA
Passage on a farm	STILE
Passe	DATED,OUT,STALE
Passe dance	SHAG
Passengers	FARES
Passion	ANGER,ARDOR,ZEAL
Pass lightly	FLIT
Pass over	ELIDE
Passover rite	SEDER
Pass the peak	FADE
Pass a rope through	REEVE
Past	AGO,OVER
Pasteboard	CARD
Pasternak character	LARA
Pastiche	OLIO
Pastoral poem	IDYL
Past or present	TENSE
Pastry	FLAN
Pastry chef's concern	ICING
Pastry item	TART
Pasture animal	EWE
Pastured	FED
Pastures	LEAS
Pasture sound	MOO
Pasture sounds	BAAS
Patella	KNEE
Path	LANE
Patisserie item	FLAN,TORTE
Patron saint of sailors	ELMO
Pattern, Confusing	MAZE
Patterns, Star-shaped	ETOILES
Pauline's problem	PERIL
Paul Newman film	HUD
Pause	REST
Paved the way for	EASED
Payable	DUE
Pay attention to	HEAR
Payment, Certain	ANTE,RENT
Payments, Certain	DUES
Payne subject	HOME
Pay phone feature	SLOT

Pay up	ANTE,REMIT
Peaceful	CALM,SERENE
Peaceful places	EDENS
Peace goddess	IRENE
Peak	ACME,TOR
Peaked	PALE
Peak in Thessaly	OSSA
Peaks	ALPS
Peak, Sicilian	ETNA
Peaks, Russian	URALS
Pealed	RANG
Pea or egg	COAL
Pea or hazel	NUT
Pea pod	HULL
Pear	BOSC
Pearl Buck heroine	OLAN
Pearl of the perils	WHITE
Pearl or Bermuda	ONION
Pearl-shell substance	NACRE
Peary's conquest	POLE
Pebble, in England	SCREE
Pecan-shaped	OVAL
Peculiar: Prefix	IDIO
Peddler, Street	ARAB
Pedestal part	DADO
Peel	RIND
Peel in a way	FLAKE
Peer	EARL
Peer Gynt's creator	IBSEN
Peer Gynt's mother and others	ASES
Peeve	RILE
Peeved: Colloq.	SORE
Peewee or Della	REESE
Pegasus	STEED
Pegs	TEES
Pekoe	TEA
Pelee overflow	LAVA
Pelion's companion	OSSA
Pelt	HIDE
Pelt of sorts	SCALP
Pelvic bones	ILIA
Pen	STY
Pencil part	ERASER
Pen name	ELIA
Penna. port	ERIE
Pen pal	INK
Penpoints	NIBS
Pens	STIES
Pentateuch	TORAH
Penthouse	AERY
Penthouse for birds	AERIE
Penurious	NEEDY
People	MEN,ONES
People, African	BANTU
People, Baltic	LETTS
People born in July and August	LEOS
People, Cardiff	WELSH
People, Certain	MALES
People, Middle East	IRANI
People, Nigerian	ARO,IBO
People of Sonora	SERI
People of Tierra del Fuego	ONA
People, Staff	AIDES
People who take advantage	USERS
People, Young	LADS
Pepper, in Rome	PEPE
Pepper-pot ingredient	TRIPE
Peppery	HOT
Perceive	ESPY
Perceived	SEEN
Perceives	NOTES
Perched	SAT
Perches	ROOSTS,SITS
Percolate	SEEP
Perennial TV show	TODAY
Perfect	IDEAL
Perform	ACT,ENACT,PLAY
Performed	DID

Performing group TRIO
Performs DOES
Perfume ATTAR,ODOR,SCENT
Perfume ingredient ASPIC
Perfumes ESSENCES
Pericarp ARIL
"Perils of Pauline," for instance SERIAL
Period STOP
Period, Duty TOUR
Period of human culture IRONAGE
Period, Roman IDES
Periods AGES,EONS,ERAS
Periods, Time YEARS
Perk up ANIMATE
Permeate SEEP
Permissive LAX
Permits LETS
Permitted LICIT
Pernicious EVIL
Perpetual ENDLESS,ETERNAL
Perplexed ATSEA
Perry, e.g. CIDER
Perry Mason's detective DRAKE
Persian ally MEDE
Persian elf PERI
Persian gazelle CORA
Persian Gulf port BASRA
Persian Gulf sight OILER
Persian poet OMAR
Persian tiger SHER
Persia, today IRAN
Person BEING
Personalities EGOS
Personal: Prefix IDIO
Person, Enigmatic SPHINX
Personification of man ADAM
Persons MEN,ONES
Person: Slang, Disagreeable PILL
Person, Unique ONER
Pertaining to an epoch ERAL
Pertaining to pitch TONAL
Pertinent: Lat. ADREM
Peru Indian INCA
Perused READ
Peruvian INCA
Peruvian coin SOL
Peruvian river ICA
Pesky insects GNATS
Pester NAG,TEASE
Pet IRE
Peter ARNO
Peter and others NEROS
Peter I, for example TSAR
Peter of nursery rhyme, for one EATER
"Peter Pan" pirate SMEE
Petition PRAY
Petitioned SUED
Petitions ASKS
Pet name SUGAR
Pet peeves HATES
Pews SEATS
Pewter, for one ALLOY
P.G.A. player PRO
Pharaoh, for one ANT
Pharmacy honey MEL
Phase STEP
Phidias statue ATHENA
Philatelist's need ALBUM
Philippine cloth PINA
Philippine dye tree IPIL
Philippine island LEYTE
Philippine money PESO
Philippine tree DAO,IBA
Philippine volcano TAAL
Philosopher KANT
Philosopher of Elea ZENO
Philosophy existence ESSE
Phoenicia's capital TYRE
Phone CALL,DIAL
Phoned RANG
Phone greeting, in Paris ALLO
Phone or photo prefix TELE
Phonetically smooth LENE
Phonograph record DISC
Phony FAKE
Phosgene GAS
Photo SNAP
Photo, Certain XRAY
Photography plate NEGATIVE
Physicist Edward TELLER
Physics prefix META
Pianist Peter NERO
Piano part PEDAL
Piano player's standby NOLA
Piano's opposite FORTE
Pickable RIPE
Picked CHOSE
Pickling solution BRINE
"Picnic" author INGE
Picnic pest GNAT
Picnic spoiler RAIN
Picnic spoilers ANTS
Picture border MAT
Pictured SEEN
Piece BIT
Piece, Armor TASSE
Piece, Chair-back SPLAT
Piece for nine NONET
Piece in a game TILE
Piece, Musical OPUS
Piece, News ITEM
Piece of gossip TALE
Piece of hardware TNUT
Piece of jewelry PIN
Piece of music ETUDE,LARGO
Piece of statuary TORSO
Piece of sugar LUMP
Piece out EKE
Piece, Piano NOLA
Piece, Small SNIP
Piece, Thick SLAB
Piedmont city ASTI
Pie flavor LEMON
Pier MOLE
Pierce ENTER,STAB
Pier, in architecture ANTA
P.I. fruit tree IBA
Pig and fountain PENS
Pigeon breeds NUNS
Pigment, Brown SEPIA
Pigmented liquid INK
Pilaf ingredient RICE
Pilaster ANTA
Pile HEAP,NAP
Pile: Fr. AMAS
Pile up AMASS
Pilfers STEALS
Pillar's counterpart POST
Pillbox HAT
Pill for animals BOLUS
Pilot CONN
Pilotless ship DRONE
Pilots STEERS
Pilot, Top ACE
Pinafore TIER
Pinball expression TILT
Pinch NIP
Pindaric ODE
Pinnacle ACME,SPIRE,TOR
Pinochle maneuver MELD
Pintails SMEES
Pinza EZIO
Pioneer, Auto OLDS
Pioneer, Norse ERIC
Pipe joints TEES

Pipe smoker's device	REAMER	Plain	EVIDENT
Pipesmoker's tool	TAMP	Plain of S.A.	LLANO
Pipes up	SAYS	Plain or deckle	EDGE
Pips on cards	SPOTS	Plains Indian	OTOE
Piquancy	ZEST	Plan	IDEA,MAP
Pique	IRE,PET	Plane-boarding staircase	RAMP
Piqued: Colloq.	SORE	Plane, Certain	SST
Pirate's gold	ORO	Planes, Russian	MIGS
Pistachio	NUT	Planet	EARTH,MARS
Pit	MINE,STONE	Plankton	ALGA
Pitch	HURL,TAR	Plant	HERB,SEED,SOW
Pitcher	EWER	Plant, Aromatic	NARD
Pitcher feature	LIP	Plant beards	AWNS
Pitchers and walls have them	EARS	Plant, Cereal	OAT
Pitches	TONES	Plant, Climbing	LIANA
Pitches in	AIDS	Plant disease	SMUT
Pitch, High in	ALT	Plant fluids	SAPS
Pitching rubber	SLAB	Plant, Forage	RAPE
Pitching statistics	ERAS	Plant, Indigo	ANIL
Pitch's tag-along	TOSS	Plant louse	APHID
Pitfall	TRAP	Plant, Marsh	RUSH
Pithy saying	ADAGE	Plant of lily family	ALOE
Pitiful	SAD,SORRY	Plant part	STEM
P.I. tree	DAO,IPIL	Plant pore	STOMA
P.I. tribesman	MORO	Plant, Sea	ALGA
Pity word	ALAS	Plant shoot	BINE
Pivotal	POLAR	Plant stalk	STIPE
Pivots	SLUES	Plants, Western	SEGOS
Pixie	ELF	Plasm prefix	ECTO
Pizza	PIE	Plaster of Paris	GESSO
Place	LIEU,SITE	Plateau	MESA
Place again	RESET	Plate, Certain	HOME
Place, Confusing	MAZE	Plate, Pitcher's	SLAB
Placed	LAID	Platform for Demosthenes	BEMA
Place, Drinking	BAR	Play direction	ENTER
Place for certain combs	HIVE	Player, A.L.	ORIOLE
Place for a chapeau	TETE	Player, L.A.	RAM
Place for coal	BIN	Player on dealer's right	PONE
Place for a coin	SLOT	Players	CAST
Place for darjeeling	TEAPOT	Player, Tennis	ASHE
Place for a flash	PAN	Playful animal	OTTER
Place for French teacher	ECOLE	Playground device	SEESAW
Place for high notes	ARIA	Playing card	TEN
Place for a marina	COVE	Playing marble	AGATE
Place for medals	CHEST	Play the lead	STAR
Place for missiles	SILO	Play, Name in long-run	ABIE
Place for a nest	LIMB	Play or band prefix	DIS
Place for an oda	HAREM	Play part	SCENE
Place for Peggy Fleming	RINK	Play the part of	ACT
Place for photos	ALBUM	Play parts	ROLES
Place for research	LAB	Play, Pinochle	MELD
Place for a ring	EAR	Play role	HERO
Place for a rose	VASE	Plaything	DOLL
Place for woof	LOOM	Play to the gallery	EMOTE
Place, Hiding	LAIR	Playwright	SHAW
Place, Hot	OVEN	Playwright, Norwegian	IBSEN
Place, Market	AGORA	Playwright, U.S.	INGE,ODETS
Place of action	SCENE	Plead	URGE
Place of interest	BANK	Pleasant	ROSY
Places, as a cue ball	SPOTS	Pleasant emotion	LOVE
Places, Bowling	LANES	Pleasant place	EDEN
Places, Cozy	NESTS	Pleased	ELATED,GLAD
Place, Secret	CACHE	Pleased look	GRIN
Places for antes	POTS	Pleasing, to a Parisian	JOLIE
Places, Grassy	LEAS	Pleasure craft	YACHT
Place, Shopping	MART	Plectrum	PICK
Places in competition	PITS	Plenty, to Omar	ENOW
Places, in law	LOCI	Plexus	RETE
Places of refuge	ARKS	Plinth	ORLO
Place, Sports	ARENA	Pliny, One	ELDER
Place, Suffix of	ERY	Plod heavily	SLOG
Place, Teller's	CAGE	Plucky	GAME
Place to get out from	UNDER	Plume	EGRET
Place to watch a game	SHEA	Plump	OBESE
Place, Vacation	CAMP	Plum varieties	GAGES
Placid	SERENE	Plunder	LOOT,RIFLE,ROB,SPOIL
Plagiarize	LIFT	Plural ending	IES
Plagiarize: Colloq.	CRIB	Plural suffix	ATA

Plus AND
Plus values ASSETS
Pluto HADES
Pocket nuisance LINT
Podium DAIS
Poe family name ALLAN
Poem by Keats LAMIA
Poem division CANTO
Poem, Pindaric ODE
Poems, Formerly, in ERST
Poe's pendulum choice PIT
Poet ODIST
Poet, Famous OMAR
Poetically, Close to ANEAR
Poetically, Sufficient ENOW
Poetic form EPODE
Poetic times of day EVES
Poetic word NEER
Poet Lowell AMY
Poet Marianne MOORE
Poet Millay EDNA
Poet, Norwegian IBSEN
Poetry, Analyze SCAN
Poetry, Certain EPOS
Poetry, Lined up, in AROW
Poetry, Muse of ERATO
Poet's adverb EEN
Poet's command HEST
Poet's concern METER
Poet's ended OER
Poets' land ERIN
Poet Stephen or William BENET
Poet's valley VALE
Poet's word ERE
Poets' word EER,TIS
Poet Teasdale SARA
Point, Compass ESE,NNE,SSE
Point, Culminating ACME
Pointed AIMED
Pointed arch OGEE,OGIVE
Pointed instruments PRODS
Pointed tool PICK
Point in one's favor ASSET
Pointless INANE
Point of land SPIT
Points TIPS
Points won by a single stroke ACES
Point, Tennis ACE
Poise COOL,TACT
Poison ivy aftermath ITCH
Poisonous snake KRAIT
Poker STUD
Poker holding PAIR
Poker money ANTE
Poker moves BETS,RAISES
Poker round POT
Poker term CALL,OPEN,SEE
Pokes JABS
Polaris, for one STAR
Pole or Czech SLAV
Police blotter entry ALIAS
Policeman, at times RAIDER
Police problem RIOT
Police rounds BEAT
Polish SAND
Polite word for a falsehood STORY
Political cartoonist NAST
Political group BLOC
Poll man ROPER
Pollux STAR
Pollux's mother LEDA
Polly, to Tom Sawyer AUNT
Polytheist PAGAN
Pomade OIL
Pompeii heroine IONE
Pompey supporter CATO
Pompous one PRIG
Ponder PORE
Ponies up ANTES
Ponselle ROSA
Pony PINTO,TROT
Pooh's cousins BEARS
Pool MERE,POND
Pool-table shot MASSE
Poop deck STERN
Poor, as an excuse LAME
Pop SODA
Poplar ABELE,ALAMO
Poppy product OPIATE
Popular article THE
Popular color AQUA
Popular garnish MINT,OLIVE
Popular hairdo AFRO
Popular instrument SITAR
Popular kind of fur FAKE
Popular material ORLON
Popular pets CATS
Popular scent LILAC
Popular signature ANON
Popular transformation WIG
Popular tune HIT
Porch STOA,STOOP
Porch of Oahu LANAI
Pornography SMUT
Porous rock SHALE
Porridge SAMP
Porsena LARS
Port HAVEN
Port, Alaskan NOME
Port, Algerian ORAN
Port and vermilion REDS
Port Authority income source TOLL
Portend BODE
Portent OMEN
Portico STOA
Port in Hanover EMDEN
Port in Norway OSLO
Port in Tunisia SFAX
Port in Yemen ADEN
Portion, Tiny ATOM
Portions DOSES
Port, Israeli ACRE
Portland, City south of SALEM
Port, Latvian RIGA
Portly OBESE
Portman ERIC
Port of ancient Rome OSTIA
Port of Brazil NATAL
Port of Guam APRA
Port of Iraq BASRA
Port of Italy BARI
Port of Samoa APIA
Port, Okinawan NAHA
Port on Gulf of Salerno AMALFI
Port or hock WINE
Port or lance, Word with FREE
Portray ENACT,LIMN
Portuguese navigator GAMA
Posed SAT
Position LIE,SEAT,SITE,STAND
Position, Bridge EAST
Position, Debater's NEGATIVE
Position, Difficult STRAIT
Position, Football END
Positive SURE
Positively QUITE
Positively state AVER
Positive negatives NONOS
Posse BAND
Possess OWN
Possesses HAS
Possess, in Scotland AIN
Possessive HER,OURS
Poss. pronoun ONES
Post ENTER,MAIL
Post-Bronze period IRONAGE

Post-impressionist	MATISSE	Prefix, Movie	CINE
Post office wall word	ALIAS	Prefix, Of an Asian race	SINO
Postpone	REMIT,TABLE	Prefix, Thrice	TER
Posts	MAILS	Prefix, Through	PER
Postulate	ASSERT	Prefix with circle or colon	SEMI
Potato	SPUD	Prefix with classic or mycin	NEO
Potato bud	EYE	Prefix with date or cede	ANTE
Potatoes, Certain	IRISH	Prefix with freeze or body	ANTI
Potentate	RAJAH	Prefix with meter or tude	ALTI
Potent, Prefix for	OMNI	Prefix with meter or vise	TELE
Pother	STIR	Prefix with morph or plasm	ECTO
Pothers	ADOS	Prefix with phile or stat	HEMO
Pot, Mexican	OLLA	Prefix with skirt	MINI
Pot part	LID	Prefix with space or naut	AERO
Potpourri	OLIO	Prehistoric ax	CELT
Po tributary	ADDA	Prejudice	BIAS
Pottage buyer	ESAU	Pre-marital title	MISS
Pouch	SAC	Pre-med subject	ANAT
Poultry	HENS	Preminger	OTTO
Pound	EZRA	Premium, Exchange	AGIO
Pounds and marks	MONEY	Prepare, as fruit	CORE
Pour	RAIN	Prepare, as potatoes	PEEL
Pourboires	TIPS	Prepare butter for lobster	MELT
Pours	TEEMS	Prepare copy	EDIT
Powder	TALC	Prepared to drive	TEED
Powder for a dog	FLEA	Prepared, as potatoes	RICED
Power agency	TVA	Prepare fish	SCALE
Powerless	INERT	Prepare for action	ARM
Power source	ATOM,STEAM	Prepare for finals	CRAM
Powers, W.W.II	AXIS	Prepare for takeoff	TAXI
Power unit	WATT	Prepare for a test, with "up"	BONE
Practice	USAGE	Prepare fruit	PIT
Practices	USES	Prepare ice in a way	SHAVE
Praise	LAUD	Prepares apples	CORES
Praise: Fr.	ELOGE	Preposition	INTO,ONTO,UNTO
Prank	CAPER	Presage	BODE
Prankish spirit	ARIEL	Present	HERE,TODAY
Prayer	PLEA	Present an idea	OPINE
Prayer word	AMEN	Present at, Be	ATTEND
Preamble, for short	INTRO	Present-day netman	ASHE
Precarious spot	PERCH	Present, in Soho	ERE
Precedent, Refer to	CITE	Present or past	TENSE
Precept	RULE	Preservative	SALT
Precious ones	DEARS	Preserve	CURE,JAM
Precious stone	GEM	Preserve container	JAR
Precipice, in Hawaii	PALI	Preserves	CANS
Precipitateness	HASTE	Presidential nickname	
Precipitation	HAIL		ABE,CAL,IKE,TEDDY
Precipitous	STEEP	President's prerogative	VETO
Precise	EXACT,NICE,PRIM,TRUE	Presides	SITS
Predatory fishes	GARS	Press	IRON,URGE
Predecessors of Virgos	LEOS	Press agency	TASS
Predicament	HOLE,MESS	Press agent's concern	IMAGE
Pre-diesel power	STEAM	Press close	NESTLE
Prefix, Eight	OCTO	Presses	URGES
Prefix for angle	TRI	Press, radio, etc.	MEDIA
Prefix for bar or tope	ISO	Presume	DARE
Prefix for crine or carp	ENDO	Pretend	FAKE,LETON
Prefix for derm or gram	EPI	Pretense	SHAM
Prefix for gate or dome	ASTRO	Pretext	PLEA
Prefix for god or monde	DEMI	Pretty	CUTE
Prefix for graduate or handed	UNDER	Pretty: Fr.	JOLIE
Prefix for gram	ANA	Prevalent	RIFE
Prefix for gram or meter	KILO	Prevent	AVERT,ESTOP
Prefix for gram or naut	AERO	Preview, Kind of	SNEAK
Prefix for hap or deed	MIS	Previous	OLD,PRIOR
Prefix for logue	DECA	Price	RATE
Prefix for mate or graph	AUTO	Price declines	SAGS
Prefix for matic	IDIO	Pride member	LION
Prefix for med or meditate	PRE	Priest, Hebrew	ELI
Prefix for motive	LOCO	Priestly garment	ALB
Prefix for parage or jointed	DIS	Priestly vestment	ORALE
Prefix for physics or phor	META	Priest of Mideast	IMAM
Prefix for potent or present	OMNI	Priest, Tibetan	LAMA
Prefix for pret or cession	INTER	Prima principia	ABCS
Prefix for a subcontinent	INDO	Primal chaos	ABYSS
Prefix for thermy and lect	DIA	Primate	APE
Prefix meaning height	ACRO	Primate genus	HOMO

Prime AONE
Primers ABCS
Primitive chisel CELT
Primitive home TEPEE
Primitive Japanese AINU
Prince RAJA
Prince, Arab EMIR
Princely REGAL
Princely family ESTE
Prince, Oriental AGA
Princess ANNE
Princess Anne to Margaret NIECE
Princess in myth IOLE
Princess of Brabant ELSA
Princess of India RANI
Princeton player TIGER
Principles TENETS
Printemps month MAI
Printer's direction STET
Printer's mark CARET
Printer's measure NUT
Printers' measures ENS
Printer's needs INKS
Printing direction DELE
Prison JAIL,STIR
Prison, British GAOL
Prisoner's concern TERM
Prison sentence LIFE
Prissy PRIM
"Private Lives" woman AMANDA
Privation NEED
Prize ESTEEM
Prize, Coveted OSCAR
Prized zoo exhibit PANDA
Prizefight program CARD
Prize for a brave SCALP
Prize, Trapper's PELT
Pro FOR
Proa or kayak CANOE
Probabilities ODDS
Problem in the city SMOG
Problem of Lady Macbeth SPOT
Procedure STEP
Proceed PASS
Proceeding EVENT
Proceedings ACTA
Proceed with difficulty WADE
Processes in a way TANS
Procession PARADE,TRAIN
Proclaim loudly BLARE
Procure GET
Prod SPUR
Produced, Biblically BEGAT
Produce (with "up") SCARE
Producing: Suffix OTIC
Productively, Thinks IDEATES
Product of Alencon LACE
Product of Newark, N.Y. ROSE
Product, Pelee LAVA
Product, Seaweed AGAR
Profane, in Hawaii NOA
Profession BAR
Profits NETS
Pro football team RAMS
Progenitor SIRE
Progeny SEED
Prognostic OMEN
Prognosticators SEERS
Program AGENDA
Progression STEP
Prohibit BAN
Prohibition DONT,TABU
Prohibition opponent WET
Projecting window ORIEL
Projections EARS
Prolific writer ANON
Promenade PARADE
Promenades MALLS
Prominent clergyman PEALE
Promontory NESS
Promptly SOON
Prong TINE
Pronoun HER, HIM,ITS,ONE,ONES,OURS,SHE,THEM
Pronouncements DICTA
Pronoun, French ELLE,UNE
Pronoun, Spanish ESTA,LAS,LOS
Proofreaders' words STETS
Proofreading mark CARET
Prop SHORE
Propeller OAR
Propel a punt POLE
Property ASSET
Property right LIEN
Prop for Aladdin LAMP
Prophets SEERS
Proportional changes RATES
Proprietor, Scottish LAIRD
Prop up SHORE
Pros ACES
Proscribe BAN
Pro's opposite ANTI
Prospector's quest LODE
Prosperous FAT
Protagonist HERO
Protagonist, Corrida TORO
Protagonist, Uris ARI
Protected ALEE
Protection CARE
Protective cover, for short TARP
Protective covering ARMOR
Protracts SPINS
Protruding window ORIEL
Protuberance NODE
Proud, Make ELATE
Prove false BELIE
Proverb ADAGE
Proverbially, a trifle GNAT
Proverbial waste-maker HASTE
Provided LENT
Province in Tuscany PISA
Provoke ANGER
Provoked IRATE,IRED
Pro vote YES
Prow STEM
Prowler, Sea UBOAT
Proxy suitor ALDEN
Prudent SAFE
Prussian town EMS
Pry NOSE,SNOOP
Pseudonym ALIAS
Psyche's lover EROS
Psychiatric concern EGO
Psychoanalyst's concerns IDS
Pub drinks ALES
Public OVERT
Public carriers BUSES
Public disorder RIOT
Public houses INNS
Publicizes AIRS
Public official MAYOR
Public square of old AGORA
Pub serving PINT
Pub weapon DART
Pudding starch SAGO
Puddle, Mud MIRE
Puerto Rican drink RON
Puffed BLEW
Puff up ELATE
Pulitzer historian (1934) AGAR
Pulitzer winner, 1958 AGEE
Pull a boner GOOF
Pulled DREW
Pullets HENS
Pulsate PANT

Pump SHOE
Pumpkin or squash PEPO
Punch, Fruit ADE
Pung SLED
Pungent bulb ONION
Pungent flavor TANG
Punkie MIDGE
Punky or midge GNAT
Pupil's need ERASER
Puppet DOLL
Puppeteer SARG
Pure NEAT
Purify CLEAN
Purloined STOLE
Purplish red LAKE
Purport TENOR
Purpose END
Purposes USES
Pursue CHASE
Push aside ELBOW
Put aside SAVE
Put away STORE,STOW
Put down LAID
Put forth EXERT
Put in hock PAWN
Put in a new place RESET
Put in order ARRANGE
Put in a row ALINE
Put into circulation EMIT
Put on DON,STAGE
Put-on SHAM
Put on cargo LADE
Puts down QUASHES
Puts in appearance ENTERS
Puts out a base runner TAGS
Put to trial ASSAY
Put 2 and 2 together ADD
Put up ANTE
Put up with, if you don't like it LUMP
PX STORE
Pyle ERNIE
Pyramid name TUT

Q

Q.E.D. word ERAT
QE2, for one LINER
Quadruped BEAST
Quaff DRINK
Quagmire MORASS
Quahogs CLAMS
Quaker pronoun THEE
Quaker William PENN
Qualified ABLE
Quality AURA,ODOR,TRAIT
Quality, Normal PAR
Quality, Taste SAPOR
Quantity, Determinate UNIT
Quarrel ROW,SPAT
Quarry, Certain HARE
Quarterback play SNEAK
Quarterback's specialty PASS
Quartet member TENOR
Quasi ASIF
Quaver TRILL
Quebec's neighbor MAINE
Quechua INCA
Queen, Egyptian SATI
Queens landmark SHEA
Queries ASKS
Question, Reporter's WHERE
Quest, Squirrel's ACORN
Queued up AROW
Quick RAPID
Quick blows RAPS
Quick-lunch stop DINER
Quickly SOON
Quickly break SNAP
Quickly pass FLIT
Quickly read SCAN
Quidnuncs HENS
Quiet EASE
Quiet spell LULL
Quill PEN
Quip MOT
Quixote's foes EVILS
Quoits peg HOB
Quote CITE
Quotes, Collection of ANA

R

Rabbit, Female DOE
Rabbit's cousin HARE
Rabbit's title BRER
Raccoon's relative COATI
Race RELAY
Raced TORE
Race kind DRAG
Race led by Odin AESIR
Race of a sort ARMS
Racetrack item TIP
Racetrack pest TOUT
Racetrack position RAIL
Racetrack staple OATS
Racetracks OVALS
Race-track term ODDS
Racing term LAPS
Racing-shell needs OARS
Racket BAT,NOISE
Rack's partner RUIN
Radames's beloved AIDA
Radiate BEAM
Radio buffs HAMS
Radio nuisance STATIC
Radio term OVER,ROGER
Radius's neighbor ULNA
Rafter BEAM
Rage ANGER
Ragtime JAZZ
Ragweed genus IVA
Rails SORAS
Rail support TIE
Railway place DEPOT
Raiment TOGS
Rainbow IRIS
Rainbows ARCS
Rain cover, for short TARP
Rainy-day cry TAXI
Rainy spells WETS
Raise ELEVATE,ERECT
Raise the spirits ELATE
Raises the pot UPS
Rajah's spouse RANI
Rajah's wife RANEE
Rake ROUE
Ram ARIES
Ramble ROVE
Ramlike OVINE
Rampart area REDAN
Ram's mate EWE
Ranch rope RIATA
Ranee's attire SARI
Range ANDES,ROAM,ROVE
Range animal STEER
Range of sight KEN
Range parts OVENS
Ranger or wolf LONE

Clue	Answer
Rangers' milieu	RINK
Range, Russian	URAL
Rank, as contestants	SEED
Rank high	RATE
Ran madly	TORE
Ransack	RIFLE
Rapid	FAST
Rapid rodent	HARE
Rapidly	APACE
Rapiers	EPEES
Rapunzel's pride	HAIR
Rarebit ingredient	BEER
Rare golf-hole score	ONE
Rare person	ONER
Rascals	IMPS
Rate, Exchange	AGIO
Rates	FARES
Rational, More	SANER
Rattan	CANE
Rattle on	PRATE
Ravelings	LINT
Rave's pal	RANT
Raw	CRUDE
Raw-boned	LEAN
Raw materials	ORES
Rayburn or Spade	SAM
Ray, Certain	BETA
Razor, Sharpen the	STROP
Reach	GETAT,SPAN
Reach a conclusion	ENDUP
React suddenly	START
React to a dull speech	NOD
Readily	SOON
Reading, Compass	NNE
Reading, for one	GAOL
Read meter	SCAN
Reads closely	PORES
Ready	RIPE
Ready, as a golf ball	TEED
Ready for mildew	DAMP
Ready money	CASH
Ready to act	ALERT
Real bargain	STEAL
Real estate sign	SOLD,TOLET
Real gone birds	DODOS
Realized	SEEN
Realm	EMPIRE
Realtor's unit	ACRE
Realty matter	LEASE
Realty sign	TOLET
Realty unit	LOT
Reaper's wake	SWATH
Rear	RISE
Rearward	AFT
Reasoned, More	SANER
Rebecca or Mae	WEST
Rebel	RISE
Rebelled	AROSE
Rebound	ECHO
Rebuff	SLAP
Rebuke	RAP
Rebuke word	TUT
Recaps	TIRES
Receded	EBBED
Receive	GREET
Receiver	DONEE
Receives	GETS
Receiving set	RADIO
Recent	LATE,LATTER
Recent: Prefix	NEO
Receptacle: Fr.	URNE
Receptacles	CANS
Recess	APSE,NICHE
Recess activity	PLAY
Recesses	RESTS
"Recessional" word	LEST
Recipe direction	STIR
Recipient	DONEE
Recital piece	SOLO
Reckon	ESTIMATE
Recline	REST
Recognition	HONOR
Recoil	SHY,WINCE
Recollections	MEMORIES
Recompense, old style	MEED
Reconcile	HEAL
Record	DISC,ENROL,ENTER,LOG,TAPE
Recorded proceedings	ACTA
Recording system	STEREO
Record, old style	ANNAL
Record player	STEREO
Records	TAPES
Records of debt	IOUS
Recover	MEND
Rectifier	DIODE
Rectify	AMEND
Red, The	ERIC
Red, among others	RIVER
Red and Coral	SEAS
Red Baron, for one	ACE
Red-coated cheese	EDAM
Reddish shade	RUST
Red dye	EOSIN
Red hog	DUROC
Red-ink symbols	IOUS
Red item	CENT
Red-letter word	EXIT
Redolence	AROMA,ODOR
Red or black insect	ANT
Red or green	COLOR
Red or roe	DEER
Red or White	SEA
Redoubtable person	ONER
Red planet	MARS
Red quartz	SARD
Reds or Mets	NINE
Red Square name	LENIN
Reduce	ABATE,PARE,SHAVE
Reedlike grass	GAMA
Reeds	OBOES
Reel	DANCE
Reels' companions	RODS
Reference book	ATLAS
Refers to	CITES
Refined	PURE
Refined jujitsu	JUDO
Reflection	IMAGE
Reflect on	PORE
Reflux	EBB
Refrain syllable	TRA
Refrain words	LALA
Refuge	HAVEN
Refuge, Place of	ARK
Refusals	NOES
Refuse	DENY,DROSS,TRASH
Regale	DINE
Regal name	CLEO
Regan's father	LEAR
Regard	SEE
Regarding	ANENT,ASTO,INRE
Regards	EYES
Regards, As	ANENT
Regime	SYSTEM
Regimen	DIET
Region, Of	AREAL
Region of Africa	SUDAN
Region of Arabia	ADEN
Region of Asia Minor	IONIA
Region of India	GOA
Region, Old Greek	IONIA
Regions	AREAS
Register	ENTER,READ
Regret	RUE
Regulus or Polaris	STAR
Rehan	ADA
Reichenbach's electrical force	ELOD

Reign of Claudius I year	LIII	Remnant	TAGEND
Reign, in India	RAJ	Remnant of a sort	EMBER
Reine's counterpart	ROI	Remnants	ASHES,ENDS
Related	AKIN	Remotely	AFAR
Related items	SERIES	Removes	ERASES
Related through one's mother	ENATE	Renaissance instruments	LUTES
Relative	MAMA,NIECE,UNCLE	Rend	TEAR
Relative, Alpaca's	LLAMA	Render a decision	RULE
Relative, Cod's	HAKE	Rendered	MADE
Relative, familiarly	GRAMP	Rendezvous	TRYSTS
Relative, for short	SIS	Rendezvous rocket	AGENA
Relative, Giraffe's	OKAPI	Rene of France	COTY
Relative, Gnat's	MIDGE	Reno departers	EXES
Relative of adieu	ALOHA	Renounce	DENY
Relative of applejack	CIDER	Renovate	REDO
Relative of "are"	WAS	Renown	KUDOS
Relative of the cassowary	EMU	Renowned	NOTED
Relative of Cheddar	EDAM	Renowned novel	NANA
Relative of a circle	OVAL	Renowned Roman	CATO
Relative of corn	CAMP	Rent	LEASE,TORE
Relative of cortisone	ACTH	Renter	TENANT
Relative of deary	HON	Rents	LETS
Relative of drat	DARN	Reo or Hudson	CAR
Relative of eterne	EER	Repaired	SEWN
Relative of exempli gratita	IDEST	Repast	MEAL,TEA
Relative of fable	MYTH	Repeat	ITERATE
Relative of groovy	NEAT	Repeated passages	QUOTES
Relative of honey	DEAR	Repeatedly	OFTEN
Relative of a hornpipe	REEL	Repeat a printing job	RESET
Relative of the ibis	STORK	Repent	RUE
Relative of itty-bitty	TEENY	Repetition	ECHO,ROTE
Relative of karate	JUDO	Replace	RESET
Relative of largo	LENTO	Replay medium	TAPE
Relative of Mayday	SOS	Reply	YES
Relative of roger	OKAY	Reply, Understanding	ISEE
Relative of "Say cheese"	SMILE	Reporter's query	WHERE
Relative of scads	SLEW	Reporter's question	WHAT
Relative of soir	NUIT	Repose	REST
Relative of telepathy	ESP	Representative	AGENT
Relative of via	ITER	Reptiles	ASPS
Relative of warbler	ROBIN	Republic, African	CHAD
Relative of wheaten	OATEN	Republic, Arab	YEMEN
Relative, Onion's	LEEK	Repulsive	UGLY
Relatives	AUNTS,KIN	Reputation	NAME,ODOR
Relatives, Grackles'	DAWS	Request	ASK
Relatives, Scottish	EMES	Requested	BADE
Relatives, Spanish	TIAS	Requiem	DIRGE
Relative, Stout's	ALE	Requirement	NEED
Relaxation	EASE,REST	Requires	ASKS
Relay-race sections	LEGS	Requisites	NEEDS
Release	UNDO,UNTIE	Rescue	SAVE
Release, News	ITEM	Research rooms	LABS
Relent	MELT	Resembling: Suffix	OID,ULAR
Relief, Sound of	SIGH	Resentment	PIQUE
Relief, in Britain	DOLE	Residence	ABODE
Relieve	SPELL	Residence, First	EDEN
Religion, Eastern	ISLAM	Residence, in Soho	OME
Religious cape	ORALE	Resident of: Suffix	ESE
Religious feast	SEDER	Resident: Suffix	ITE
Religious object	ICON	Residue	ASH,ASHES
Religious order	SECT	Resign	QUIT
Religious plate	PATEN	Resiliency	TONE
Religious superior	PRIOR	Resinous substance	LAC
Religious title	FRA	Resins, Varnish	ELEMIS
Relinquish	CEDE	Resister	REBEL
Relish	ZEST	Resort	MIAMI
Relish-tray standby	OLIVE	Resorts	SPAS
Relocate	MOVE	Resound	ECHO
Reluctant	AVERSE	Resounded	RANG
Rely, with "on"	BANK	Resource	ASSET
Remainder	REST	Resources, Certain	ORES
Remained resolute	STOOD	Resources, Draw on, as	TAP
Remaining	OVER	Respect	ESTEEM
Remains	ASHES	Respecting	ANENT
Remains inactive	SITS	Respect, Word of	MAAM
Remark	NOTE	Respite	LETUP
Remick	LEE	Responds	REACTS
Remiss	LAX	Response to an explanation	ISEE

Responsible citizen	VOTER
Rest	SLEEP
Restaurant bill	TAB
Resting	ABED
Resting places	BEDS
Restless desire	ITCH
Restrain	BATE,STAY,STEM
Restrained eating	DIET
Restraint	LEASH,REIN
Restrict	LIMIT,TIE
Rests (on)	SITS
Result	ENSUE
Result of cerebral activity	IDEA
Result of a clench	FIST
Results	ENDS
Resume	RENEW
Retail	SELL
Retain	KEEP
Retained	HELD
Retardations	LAGS
Retiarius' milieu	ARENA
Reticule	ETUI
Retina features	RODS
Retired	ABED
Retired valley	DELL
Retreats	DENS,NESTS
Retribution goddess	ATE
Returns after expenses	NETS
Reveals	BARES,OPENS
Revelry	ORGY
Revelry cry	EVOE
Reverberation	ECHO
Revered object	RELIC
Revered one	IDOL
Revere took one	RIDE
Reverie	DREAM
Reversal: Prefix	ALLO
Reviewer of a sort	CENSOR
Revises	EDITS
Revived an old film	RERAN
Revived the fire	RELIT
Revoke	ADEEM
Revolt	ARISE
Revolutionary figure	OTIS
Revolutionary name	REVERE
Revolutionary patriot	OTIS
Revolutionary War general	GATES
Revolutionist, French	MARAT
Revue skit	TURN
Reward for a good horse	PAT
Reward, in old days	MEED
Rhino's relative	TAPIR
Rhone tributary	ISERE
Rhyme scheme	ABA,ABBA
Rhythm	LILT
Rhythm, British style	METRE
Rialto offering	PLAY
Rialto sign	SRO
Riatas	ROPES
Rib	COSTA
Ribbed fabric	REP
Rice or Davis	ELMER
Richard's need	AHORSE
Rich cake	TORTE
Riches' predecessor	RAGS
Rich in silica	ACID
Richmond's river	JAMES
Rich repast	FEAST
Rider, Rods	HOBO
Riders	FARES
Ridged plate	GRID
Ridge, Mountain	ARETE
Ridges on shells	LIRAS
Ridicule	DERIDE
Rifle range: Fr.	TIR
Right angles	ELLS
Rights and lefts	JABS
Riled	SORE

Rill	STREAM
Rim of a pitcher	LIP
Rind	SKIN
Ring	HALO
Ring enclosures	ROPES
Ring man	REF
Ring, Solar	ATEN
Rinse	LAVE
Riot weapon	MACE
Rip	REND
Ripens	AGES
Ripped	TORE,TORN
Rise	EMERGE
Riser	STAIR
Rises up	REARS
Rising agent	YEAST
Risk	PERIL
Rita or Bravo	RIO
Rite words	IDO
Ritual promise	OATH
Rival of Pisa and Venice	GENOA
River area, in France	ILE
River, Asian	AMUR
River, Austrian	ENNS
River basin, European	SAAR
River called Labe by Czechs	ELBE
River called Ohre by Czechs	EGER
River, Czech	ISER
River feature	DELTA
River fish	SHAD
River in Bavaria	ISAR
River in central Africa	UELE
River in England	AVON
River in France	LOIRE
River in Kenya	TANA
River in Scotland	AYR
River in Tell's land	AARE
River in upstate New York	TIOGA
River in Yorkshire	OUSE
River islands	AITS
River of Africa	NILE
River of Asia	ILI
River of Belgium	YSER
River of Berlin	SPREE
River of England	DEE
River of Florence	ARNO
River of France	ISERE
River of Germany	EDER
River of Italy	ADDA
River of the Left Bank	SEINE
River of myth	STYX
River of oblivion	LETHE
River of Venezuela	AROA
River of W.W.I	MARNE
River of W.W.I note	MEUSE
River: Sp.	RIO
River through Lake Geneva	RHONE
River to the Amazon	ICA
River to the Baltic	ODER
River to the Caspian	URAL
River to the Colorado	GILA
River to the Mediterranean	EBRO
River to the Missouri	OSAGE
River to the Moselle	ORNE
River to North Sea	TYNE
River to the Oise	AISNE
River to the Rhine	RUHR
River to the Rhone	AIN,SAONE
River to Rio Grande	PECOS
River to the Seine	EURE,OISE
Rivulet	STREAM
Road curves	ESSES
Road for Caesar	ITER
Roadside rest	DINER
Roadside sign	GAS
Road sign	SLO
Road surface	TAR
Roast: Fr.	ROTI

Clue	Answer
Roast slightly	PARCH
Robbers' persuaders	GATS
Robe, Priest's	ALB
Robert E. et al.	LEES
Robes, Arabs'	ABAS
Robust	HALE
Rochester's waterfront	ONTARIO
Rock	CRAG
Rock debris	SCREE
Rocket fuel	LOX
Rocket projection	VANE
Rocket stage	AGENA
Rockfish	RENA
Rockingham ratios	ODDS
Rockweed	ALGA
Rocky debris	SCREE
Rocky height	TOR
Rocky Mountains of Wyoming	TETON
Rocky ridge	ARETE
Rodent	HARE,RAT
Rodeo man	ROPER
Rod-rider	HOBO
Rods	POLES
Roentgen discovery	XRAY
Roe source	SHAD
Roger!	OKAY
Roger's companion	OVER
Roguish	ARCH,SLY
Roil	STIR
Roise-colored dye	EOSIN
Role	HERO,PART
Role, Ibsen	NORA
Role in "Othello"	IAGO
Role, Opera	AIDA
Role, Wagnerian	ERDA,SENTA
Roll	BUN,ROSTER
Roll-call answer	ADSUM
Roll-call reply in Soho	ERE
Roll-call response	HERE
Rollcall word	PRESENT
Rolled tea	CHA
Roll logs	BIRL
Roll of cloth	BOLT
Roll of stamps	COIL
Roman bronze	AES
Roman courtyards	ATRIA
Roman date	NONES
Roman dates	IDES
Roman 53	LIII
Roman 506	DVI
Roman god	LAR,SOL
Roman goddess	CERES
Roman gods	LARES
Roman halls	ATRIA
Roman magistrate	EDILE
Roman poet	OVID
Roman raiment	TOGA
Roman violinist	NERO
Roman way	ITER
Roma was one	URBS
Rome, Black, in	NERO
Rome's Censor	CATO
Roof edge	EAVE
Roofing	TILE
Roofing material	SLATE
Roof ornaments	EPIS
Room	DEN
Room in a casa	SALA
Room in a harem	ODA
Rooms, for Cicero	ATRIA
Roomy	LARGE
Roosevelt and Hoover	DAMS
Root	CAUSE,ELIHU,TARO
Rope	LASSO,REATA,RIATA
Rope fiber	SISAL
Ropes, Bind with	FRAP
Rorschach material	INK
Rose dye	EOSIN

Clue	Answer
Rose oil	ATTAR
Rose's beloved	ABIE
Rosinante, for one	NAG
Ross and Coral	SEAS
Roster	LIST
Rotate	SPIN
Rotate, as a TV camera	PAN
Rotating machine part	CAM
Rothschild's pride	SONS
Rotund	OBESE
Rouen, Very, in	TRES
Rouen, Weapon in	ARME
Rouge's sidekick	NOIR
Rough	COARSE,RUDE
Rough calculation	ESTIMATE
Rough cliff	CRAG
Rough it	CAMP
Roulade	RUN
Roulette bet	ODD,RED
Roulette color	NOIR
Rounded hill	KNOB
Round, in music	ROTA
Roundish	OVAL,OVATE
Rouses	STIRS
Rousseau's fictional pupil	EMILE
Routing word	VIA
Rover	NOMAD
Rover or Spot	PET
Row	OAR,TIER
Rowan tree	ASH
Roy	ROB
Royal headpiece	DIADEM
Royalist of '76	TORY
Royal kind of highness	SERENE
Rubber	PARA
Rubber trees	ULES
Rubbish	TRIPE
Rubies	STONES
Rub out	ERASE
Ruby	GEM
Ruby or Sandra	DEE
Rudely awaken	ROUST
Rude word of dismissal	SCRAM
Rudiments	ABCS
Ruffle	ROIL
Rugged	HAIRY
Rugged rocks	CRAGS
Rug surface	PILE
Rug type	SHAG
Ruhr city	ESSEN
Ruin	SPOIL,UNDO
Ruined: Colloq.	SHOT
Ruining agent	BANE
Rule out	BAN
Ruler, Iranian	SHAH
Ruler of the Aesir	ODIN
Rulers	REGENTS,TSARS
Rules	LAWS
Rumanian coin	BAN
Rumbullions	RIOTS
Rum cake	BABA
Ruminant	DEER
Rummage	ROUT
Rummage and fire	SALES
Rumor	TALE
Rumor about	NOISE
Run	FLEE
Run-down	SEEDY
Rung	STEP
Run off	ELOPE
Run out	LAPSE
Runner	SKI
Running game	TAG
Running knot	NOOSE
Runs, Trial	TESTS
Run swiftly	DART,HARE
Run, in England	STAND
Runyon	DAMON

Rupanco or Puyehue LAGO
Rural highway hazard DEER
Rural overpass STILE
Rushed SPED,TORE
Russian agency TASS
Russian assent DADA
Russian body RADA
Russian city OREL
Russian commune MIR
Russian czar IVAN
Russian fighters MIGS
Russian great divide URALS
Russian name IGOR
Russian peninsula KOLA
Russian press agency TASS
Russian queen OLGA
Russian reply NYET
Russian river LENA
Russian sea ARAL
Russian stockade ETAPE
Rustic RURAL
Rustler's wear NOOSE
Ruth BABE
Rx datum DOSE
Rye fungus ERGOT
Ryun or Liquori MILER

S

Saarinen EERO
Sabbath utterance AMEN
S.A. bird RHEA
S.A. copper center AROA
S.A. country PERU
Sacrament PENANCE
Sacred ICON
Sacred bird IBIS
Sacred Buddhist mountain OMEI
Sacred bull APIS
Sacred chests ARKS
Sad DREAR
Safe SECURE
S. African village DORP
Saga TALE
Sage WISE
Sailboat CAT,SLOOP
Sailing ASEA
Sailing ship BRIG
Sailing vessel SLOOP
Sailor TAR
Sailor's call ALEE
Sailors' saint ELMO
Sails SHEETS
Sails, Shortens REEFS
Saint, Sailor's ELMO
Saint-Tropez is one SPA
Salad SLAW
Salad fish TUNA
Salad gelatin ASPIC
Salad ingredient ONION
Salad plant KALE
Salad topping OIL
Salamanders EFTS
Salerno money LIRE
Salesman's samples LINE
Sale stipulation ASIS
Sal, for one GAL
Salk's place LAB
Sally Rand's prop FAN
Salt TAR
Saltate LEAP
Salt, Chemical ESTER
Salt in fatty substances OLEATE
Saltpeter NITER
Salt tree ATLE
Salty relish ROE
Salutations AVES
Salvador DALI
Salver TRAY
S.A. metropolis LIMA
Samoan port APIA
Samovar URN
Sample TASTE
Samuel's teacher ELI
San Antonio sight ALAMO
Sancta DENS
Sanctify BLESS
Sandarac ARAR
Sandburg POET
Sand hill, in Britain DENE
Sandra DEE
Sandusky's county ERIE
Sandwich HERO
Sandwich staple TUNA
Sandy ridge OSAR
Sandy's sound ARF
San Luis and Grand Coulee DAMS
Sap BOOB
S.A. plain LLANO
Sapling TREE
Saratoga SPA
Saratoga purchase FOAL
Sarazen GENE
Sarcasm IRONY
Sardine locale CAN
Sardines, Like OILY
Sardonic humor IRONY
S.A. rodent PACA
S.A. rubber PARA
S.A. ruminant LLAMA
Sashes OBIS
Sass LIP
Sassafras TREE
Sassafras tree AGUE
Sassy FLIP,PERT
Satan's specialties EVILS
Satellite MOON
Satellite, Planet with one EARTH
Satiate GLUT
Satisfaction, Exact AVENGE
Satisfy SATE
S.A. tree MORA
Sauce SOY
Sauce, Kind of APPLE
Saucy PERT,SASSY
Saul's grandfather NER
Savage FERAL
Save, with "away" SALT
Savoir faire TACT
Savor TASTE
Savory TASTY
Savvy remark ISEE
Saw ADAGE
Sawbuck TEN
Saw, old, with "me once, shame on thee, fool me twice, shame on me" FOOL
Sawtoothed EROSE
Saying ADAGE
Say yes, informally OKAY
Scale CLIMB
Scale degree STEP
Scaloppine ingredient VEAL
Scan READ
Scandinavian NORSE
Scandinavian money ORE
Scandinavian name OLAF
Scarce RARE
Scarlet RED
Scarlett OHARA
Scarlett's friend MELANIE
Scarlett's manse TARA
Scarves BOAS

Clue	Answer
Scary	EERY
Scary sound	BOO
Scatter	STREW
Scatters	TEDS
Scene, Exile	ELBA
Scene of action	SITE,THEATER
Scene of Perry victory	ERIE
Scenery	SETS
Scenery, Theater	DECOR
Scenic town near Naples	AMALFI
Scenic view	SCAPE
Scenite or Arab	NOMAD
Scent	AROMA,ODOR,SMELL
Scented	OLENT
Scents	ESSENCES
Schedule	SLATE
Scheme	PLAN,PLOT
Schism	RENT
Schlemiels	SAPS
Scholar's arrival time	TEN
School course	LATIN
School dance	PROM
School-day hurdles	TESTS
School, for short	PREP
School in England	ETON
School in France	ECOLE
School item	ERASER
School of thought	ISM
School subject	ART,MATH
Schoolwork, Does	ADDS
Schuss	SKI
Scientist-author	SNOW
Scientist's places	LABS
Scions	SONS
Scoff	SNEER
Scold	RATE
Scoop up	ROUT
Scope	AREA,ROOM
Scope and vise prefix	TELE
Scorch	CHAR,PARCH,SEAR
Score	GOAL,RATE
Scoreboard listing	OOO
Scoreboard statistics	RUNS
Scoreboard trio	III
Score, Bridge	SLAM
Scored a point	ACED
Score, Evens the	TIES
Score, Golf	EAGLE
Score, rare, on a golf hole	ONE
Scoria	LAVA
Scornful look	SNEER
Scotch's friend	SODA
Scotland, Uncles, in	EMES
Scotsman's since	SYNE
Scotsman's so	SAE
Scotsman's tiny	SMA
Scotsman's to	TAE
Scott	DRED
Scott creation	NOVEL
Scott hero	IVANHOE
Scottish	ERSE
Scottish answer	NAE
Scottish delicacy	SCONE
Scottish explorer	RAE
Scottish eyes	EES
Scottish hillside	BRAE
Scottish inventor	WATT
Scottish island	IONA
Scottish landowner	LAIRD
Scottish loch	NESS
Scottish name	IAN
Scottish noble	THANE
Scottish odd	ORRA
Scottish port	PERTH
Scottish river	DEE
Scottish shire	AYR
Scottish uncle	EME
Scottish units	ANES
Scoundrel	ROGUE
Scourge	LASH
Scout activity	HIKE
Scout's good thing	DEED
Scouts' founder	BEARD
Scout unit	DEN
Scows	ARKS
Scrammed	BLEW
Scrap	END,RAG
Scrap, Table	ORT
Scratch and tear	CLAW
Scratch out	EKE
Scream, in Nice	CRI
Screen	HIDE,SIFT
Screw pines of Pacific	IES
Scrimp	SAVE
Script direction	ENTER
Scrooge's word	BAH
Scruff	NAPE
Scrutinize	SCAN
Scuffle	MELEE
Scull	OAR
Sculling group	CREW
Sculptor	RODIN
Sculpture piece	TORSO
Scuttle	DART,HOD
Sea	CORAL,ROSS
Sea areas	ARMS
Sea bird	ERN
Sea call	AHOY,SOS
Sea cook's relative	SON
Sea cow	MANATEE
Sea creature, Inky	SQUID
Sea duck	EIDER
Sea eagle	ERNE
Sea east of Caspian	ARAL
Seafood	CLAMS,CRAB,TUNA
Seafood, Calif.	ABALONE
Seafood delicacy	EEL
Seafood item	MUSSEL
Sea: Fr.	MER
Sea god	LER
Sea goddess	RAN
Seagoing ears	RADIO
Seagoing jail	BRIG
Sea gull	TERN
Sea, Left, at	APORT
Seam	DART
Seaman	GOB,TAR
Seaman, Kind of	ABLE
Sea marauder	UBOAT
Seamstress work, Does	SEWS
Sea off Borneo	SULU
Seaport in Israel	ACRE
Seaport of Eire	SLIGO
Seaport of Scotland	AYR
Search	COMB
Sea, Sheltered, at	ALEE
Season	SALT,YULE
Seasonal period	LENT
Seasonal song	CAROL
Seasonal time	NOEL
Season, in Nice	ETE
Sea-story writer	DANA
Seat of Nobel Institute	OSLO
Seats of a sort	LAPS
Seaweed	AGAR
Seaweed plant	ALGA
Secluded valley	GLEN
Secondhand	USED
Second-hand	OLD
Second in evildoing	ABET
Second-rate stuff	TRIPE
Second-stringer	SCRUB
Secret	INNER
Secretary	DESK
Secret meetings	TRYSTS
Secret store	CACHE

Clue	Answer
Secret U.S. group	KLAN
Section	AREA,PANEL,UNIT
Sections, Flat	PANES
Section, Theater	LOGE
Secular	LAIC
Secure, as a line	LASH
Secures a ship	MOORS
Sedan	CAR
Sediment	LEES,SILT
See	ESPY
Seed coat	BRAN
Seed covering	ARIL
Seed for rolls	SESAME
Seed, Flavorful	ANISE
Seed, Grain	OAT
Seeger	ALAN
Seek office	RUN
Seek to find out	TEST
See-through item	LENS
See-through material	NET
Seine	NET
Seine features	ILES
Seine seasons	ETES
Seine tributary	EURE,OISE
Seize	NAB,NAIL
Seized	TOOK
S.E. Kansas, City in	IOLA
Select	CHOICE
Selected	CHOSE
Selection, Concert	ARIA
Self-appointed adviser	TOUT
Self-esteem	EGO,PRIDE
Self-flagellation	PENANCE
Semblance	IMAGE
Semester	TERM
Semicircular recess	APSE
Seminar product	IDEA
Semitic deity	BAAL
Senator from Indiana	BAYH
Send out	EMIT
Seneca's pupil	NERO
Senora's palce	CASA
Senor's coin	PESO
Senor's greeting	HOLA
Sense	SMELL
Sensible	SANE
Sensitive	SORE
Sentiment: Fr.	AME
Sent to another club	TRADED
Separate	REND
Separated	APART
Separate, with "out"	SPACE
Sepulchral sound	TOLL
Sequel to "Typee"	OMOO
Sequence	SERIES
Sequence, End of a	OMEGA
Seraglio	HAREM
Serais	INNS
Serb or Croat	SLAV
Sere	ARID,DRIED
Serf	ESNE
Serge's plague	LINT
Series of questions	TEST
Series of woes	ILIAD
Series, Wagner	RING
Serpents	ASPS
Servant, Indian	AMAH
Serve	AVAIL
Served well, at tennis	ACED
Server	TRAY
Serves, Certain	ACES
Service branch	WAC
Service club	LIONS
Service, Jewish	SEDER
Servicemen's mecca	USO
Service station giveaway	AIR
Servicewoman of Britain	WREN
Servicewomen	SPARS
Sesame	TIL
Sesame product	SEED
Set	PAIR
Set apart	SPACE
Set aside	STORE
Set down	LAND
Seth's father	ADAM
Seth's son	ENOS
Set in operation	START
Set on	ASSAIL
Sets	GELS
Sets of boxes	NESTS
Sets of three	TRINES
Set straight	ALINE
Set system	ROTE
Setter, Kind of	IRISH
Setting	DECOR,SCENE
Settle	LOCATE
Settled	ALIT
Settled habits	RUTS
Settled places	TOWNS
Settlement, Greenland	ETAH
Settles down	ROOSTS
Set up a golf ball	TEED
Seven of eleven on offense	LINE
17th, The	OHIO
Seventh sons	SEERS
Severe	HARSH,RIGID
Sew	BASTE
"Seward's Folly"	ALASKA
S.F. hill	NOB
Shade	HUE,RED,TINGE,TINT
Shade, Brownish	SEPIA
Shaded	TONED
Shaded area	ARBOR
Shaded walk	ALAMEDA
Shade of blue	NAVY,PARIS
Shade of gray	SLATE
Shade of green	NILE
Shade tree	ASH
Shade trees	ELMS
Shadow	TAIL
Shadowbox	SPAR
Shady middleman	FENCE
Shaft	AXLE
Shah's land	IRAN
Shake	JAR
Shakespeare	BARD
Shakespearean character	ARIEL,IAGO
Shakespearean forest	ARDEN
Shakespearean hero	ROMEO
Shakespearean role	LEAR
Shallow	INANE
Sham	LETON
Sham gem	PASTE
Shampoo cycle	RINSE
Shamrock land	ERIN,EIRE
"Shane", Alan of	LADD
Shannon flows, Where the	EIRE
Shaped a certain way	OVAL
Shaped beam	IBAR
Shaped, in a way	OVATE
Shaped like: Suffix	OID
Shaped molding	OGEE
Shapely miss	DISH
Shapes, Bow	ARCS
Shaping device	DIE
Shaping machine	LATHE
Share	QUOTA
Share for Mother Hubbard's dog	NONE
Share in	ENTER
Sharif	OMAR
Sharp	KEEN
Sharp cold	NIP
Sharp cry	YELP
Sharpen	HONE,WHET
Sharpener	STROP
Sharp feeling	PANG

Sharp flavor	TANG
Sharply watched	EYED
Sharpness	BITE,EDGE
Sharp pain	STAB
Sharp ridge	ARETE
Sharps and flats	KEYS
Sharp sound	HISS
Sharp turn	ZAG
Shave off	PARE
Shaw	ARTIE
Shawl	STOLE
Shawl or scarf	WRAP
Shay's motive power	HOSS
Shea players	METS
Shebat's follower	ADAR
Shed	MOLT
Sheen	PATINA
Sheep	EWE,EWES
Sheep-killing parrot	KEA
Sheeplike	OVINE
Sheep of Asia, Wild	SHA
Sheep sound	BAA
Sheer	PURE
Sheer cloth	PINA
Sheet of stamps	PANE
She: Ger.	SIE
Sheiks, e.g.	ARABS
She, in Calabria	ESSA
She, in Paris	ELLE
Shell occupants	CREW
She loved Narcissus	ECHO
Shelter	HAVEN,LEE
Sheltered	ALEE
Sheltered nook	COVE
Shelter, in Soho	OME
Shelters	LEES
Shelve	TABLE
Shepard of space fame	ALAN
Sheridan or Harding	ANN
Sheriff's men	POSSE
She was born free	ELSA
She was a lady	EDIE
Shield	EGIS
Shield border, Heraldic	ORLE
Shiftless one	TRAMP
Shillong's state	ASSAM
Shimmying sister	KATE
Shinto gateway	TORII
Ship	OILER,SEND
Shipbuilding wood	TEAK
Ship designation	SHE
Ship direction	APORT
Ship launcher of legend	HELEN
Ship, Medit.	XEBEC
Ship officer	MATE
Ship or plane	LINER
Ship part	HULL,KEEL,PROW
Shipped	SENT
Shipping-room item	TWINE
Ship pole	SPAR
Ship's officer	MATE
Ship stowaway, of sorts	RAT
Ship to remember	MAINE
Shiraz resident	IRANI
Shirk	EVADE
Shirt material	PIMA
Shish kebab ingredient	ONION
Shoal	REEF
Shoddy merchandise	BORAX
Shoe	SANDAL
Shoe-factory worker	LACER
Shoe form	LAST
Shoelace, for one	TIER
Shoelace tip	AGLET
Shoe material	SUEDE
Shoe or slipper	FLAT
Shoe part	TOE
Shoe parts	EYELETS,SOLES
Shoe preserver	TREE
Shoe sizes	TENS
Shoes or stockings	PAIR
"Shoo!"	SCAT
Shoot the dice	ROLL
Shooter	TAW
Shooter fodder	PEA
Shooting match: Fr.	TIR
Shoots of a woody plant	RODS
Shop	MART
Shoppe word	OLDE
Shopper's aid	CART
Shopper's guide	LIST
Shopper's word	SEND
Shopping centers	MALLS
Shopping-mall unit	STORE
Shore bird	RAIL
Shoreline feature	INLET
Short-billed rail	SORA
Short, Cut	CROP
Short distance	STEP
Short-eared dog, in heraldry	ALAN
Shorten, as a sail	REEF
Shortening	LARD,OLEO
Short featured role	CAMEO
Short jacket	ETON
Shortly	ANON
Short message	LINE
Short or long	TON
Short rail extension	SPUR
Short ride	SPIN
Short-story writer	POE
Shoshonean	UTE
Shostakovich's land	USSR
Shot	DRINK
Shot and shell	AMMO
Shot, Billiard	MASSE
Shote's area	STY
Shot, Golf	PUTT
Shot of redeye	SNORT
Shotput, for one	EVENT
Shoulders squared	ERECT
Shout	CRY
Shout: Fr.	CRI
Show	BARE,POMP
Show biz chap	ACTOR
Show-business name	COHAN
Showed an old movie	RERAN
Showed the way	LED
Shower	RAIN
Showery time	APRIL
Show fondness	DOTE
Showiness	GLARE
Showing no pain	STOIC
Showman Edwards	GUS
Show off	PARADE
Show of sorts	RODEO
Show place	SALON
Shows boredom	NODS
Shows durability	LASTS
Shows, Successful	HITS
Show surprise	START
Showy butterfly	URSULA
Showy display	ECLAT
Shred	RAG,TEAR
Shrewd	CUTE
Shrew of musical	KATE
Shrine	ALAMO
Shrink	WINCE
Shrub	ALDER
Shrub, Popular	LILAC
Shrub, Virginia	ITEA
Shrub yielding indigo	ANIL
Shun	ELUDE,FLEE
Shut in	PENT
Siamese	CAT,TAI
Siamese money	ATS
Siamese twin	ENG

Sib	CLAN
Siberian river	AMUR,LENA
Sicilian resort	ENNA
Sicilians' Mongibello	ETNA
Sideboard item	TUREEN
Side dish	SALAD,SLAW
Side, Flat	PANE
Sidekick	AIDE,PAL
Sidekick, Andy's	AMOS
Sidestep	AVOID,ELUDE,EVADE
Sidewalk fixture	METER
Sieved	RICED
Sight, City-sky	SMOG
Sight, Cleveland	ERIE
Sight, Congo	HIPPO
Sight from Finsteraarhorn	ALPS
Sight from Sugar Loaf	RIO
Sight, Opera-box	TIARA
Sight or touch	SENSE
Sight, Sicilian	ETNA
Sights in the Bronx	ELS
Sight, Thessaly	OSSA
Sigmoids	ESSES
Sign	INK,OMEN
Signal	CUE,FLARE
Signal flare of W.W.I	VERY
Signal in bridge	ECHO
Signals in a way	NODS
Signal, Warning	ALERT
Sign at a through street	STOP
Signature on some writings	ANON
Signboard symbol	ARROW
Sign, Diner	EATS
Sign, Kind of	NEON
Sign, Music	CLEF
Sign of a hit	SRO
Sign on	HIRE
Sign on a door	ENTER
Signore's money	LIRA
Sign, Road	GAS
Sign, Sale	ASIS
Sign up	ENROL
Sign, Zodiac	LEO
Silent	MUM,TACIT
Silent actor	MIME
Silent movie fare	SERIAL
Silent one	CLAM
Silent salute	WAVE
Silents' Negri	POLA
Silents' Naldi	NITA
Silents' vamp	BARA
Silk fabric	MOIRE
Silk thread	TRAM
Silkworm	ERI,ERIA
Silly	APISH,INANE
Silly creatures	GEESE
Silly: Slang	GAGA
Silly talk	SLUSH
Silvery fish	SMELT
Similar	AKIN
Simple	EASY,MERE,PLAIN
Simple Simon's quest	PIES
Simpleton	BOOB
Simplify	EASE
Simplon Pass locale	ALPS
Sin	ENVY
Since	AGO
Since, in Scotland	SYNE
Sincere	HONEST,REAL
Sinecure	SNAP
Sinew: Prefix	TENO
Singer	ALTO
Singer Eames	EMMA
Singer Horne	LENA
Singer Joan	BAEZ
Singer Stevens	RISE
Singer Torme	MEL
Singing brothers	AMES
Singing group	OCTET,TRIO
Singing voice	ALTO
Single	ONE,UNAL
Single or double	FILE
Single out	NAME
Singly	ALONE
Sinister	EVIL
Sinister glance	LEER
Sinkiang river	ILI
Sins	ERRS,EVILS
Siouan language	OSAGE
Sioux	OTO,OTOE
Sioux City gal	SUE
Sip	TASTE
Sired, Biblically	BEGAT
Siren	ALARM
Sir in Singapore	TUAN
Sir Thomas	MORE
Sir Walter was one	SCOT
Sister of Ares	ERIS
Sister of Calliope	ERATO
Sisters	NUNS
Site of Expo 70	OSAKA
Site of Napoleonic victory	LODI
Site of the Quirinal	ROME
Site of Sugar Loaf	RIO
Site of Taj Mahal	AGRA
Site of Tell fable	URI
Site of Tree of Life	EDEN
Site of W.W.II battle	STLO
Sitka vehicles	SLEDS
Situate	PUT
Situated, Be	LIE
Situation	CASE
Situation, Adjust to	ORIENT
Siva's wife	DEVI
Six cubits	REED
Six dits and three dahs	SOS
Six, in Napoli	SEI
Six or seven, in bridge	SLAM
Six: Span.	SEIS
Sixth century date	DVI
Sixth sense	ESP
Sixty grains	DRAM
Size AAAA	NARROW
Size of coal	PEA
Size of type	PICA,AGATE
Skelton	RED
Skewed	ALOP
Skid	SLUE
Skiers' aid	TOW
Skiers' lift	TBAR
Skier's quest	SNOW
Skill	ART
Skilled	ABLE
Skilled hand	ACE
Skilled one	ARTIST
Skilled worker	ARTISAN
Skill, in Italy	ARTE
Ski maneuver	STEM
Skinner	OTIS
Skip	OMIT
Skip out	DECAMP
Skirt	AVOID,MIDI
Skirt, Ballet	TUTU
Skirt panels	GORES
Skirt style	ALINE,MINI
Skits	ACTS
Skull and dunce	CAPS
Sky	ETHER
Sky bear	URSA
Sky god	ANU
Sky, in Naples	CIELO
Sky sight	MARS
Sky sight for some	UFO
Slabs of glass	PANES
Slack	LAX,LOOSE
Slacken	ABATE,EASE,RELAX

Slackening LETUP
Slalom SKI
Slander SMEAR
Slanders SLURS
Slangy diamonds ICE
Slangy hats LIDS
Slangy loot SWAG
Slangy negative AINT
Slangy reply NOPE
Slant BIAS,TILT
Slave SERF
Slave, Early ESNE
Slavishly, Copies APES
Sled's milieu SNOW
Sleeper RIP
Sleeps RESTS
Sleep uneasily TOSS
Sleepy-head's land NOD
Sleeveless garment VEST
Sleuth MOTO
Sleuth, Fictional MOTO
Sleuth Wolfe NERO
Slicer's cry FORE
Slick OILY
Slick chick DISH
Slide, Golden or RULE
Slight NEGLECT
Slighter LESS
Slightest LEAST
Slight hollow DENT
Slime OOZE
Slip ERR,LAPSE
Slip away ELOPE
Slip away from ELUDE
Slip by ELAPSE
Slippery one EEL
Slippery trees ELMS
Slips over SLURS
Slips up ERRS
Slip up GOOF
Slope BANK,CANT,GRADE,RISE
Slope, Scottish BRAE
Sloping way RAMP
Sloppy MESSY
Sloppy stuff SLUSH
Sloth UNAU
Slough BOG
Slow LATE
Slow, in music LARGO
Slowly, Moved EDGED
Slowly: Music LENTO
Slugger Hank AARON
Sluggish INERT
Slum problem RAT
Slur over ELIDE
Small TEENY
Small amount DAB,GRAM
Small animal HARE
Small ape LAR
Small aperture, in botany STOMA
Small bird TIT,WREN
Small bit SNIP
Small bits IOTAS
Small boat CAT
Small boy TAD
Small carrying case ETUI
Small cask KEG
Small change CENT
Small city TOWN
Small container VIAL
Small craft CANOE
Small dogs TOYS
Small draught DRAM
Small drink NIP
Small drum BONGO
Small fiddle KIT
Small fish IDE,SMELT
Small game for tabby MICE
Small handful WISP
Small harps LYRES
Small hole EYELET
Small inlet RIA
Small insect GNAT
Small island AIT,CAY
Small jug TOBY
Small land areas KEYS
Small lizards EFTS
Small lump NODULE
Small missile DART
Small monkey TITI
Small or grand SLAM
Small pocket FOB
Small porch STOOP
Small portion TOT
Small shark TOPE
Small shield ECU
Small spring SEEP
Small stream RILL
Small: Suffix ETTE,ULE
Small sums MITES
Small thrush CHAT
Small type AGATE
Small valley GLEN
Small whales SEIS
Smart CHIC,STING
Smart one ALEC
Smart remark MOT
Smash signs SROS
Smears SOILS,TARS
Smetana character BRIDE
Smidgen DAB,IOTA
Smith KATE
Smitten: Colloq. GAGA
Smoke byproduct SOOT
Smoker's item PIPE
Smokers' product ASHES
Smooth SATIN
Smooth consonants LENES
Smorgasbord item EEL
Smudge SMEAR
Smutch STAIN
Smuts was one BOER
Smyrna product FIG
Snack BITE
Snack, Mexican TACO
Snacked ATE
Snake ADDER,ASP,URAEUS
Snake's home EDEN
Snake's warning HISS
Snare ENTRAP,NET,TRAP
Sneaky name PETE
Snick's partner SNEE
Sniff NOSE
Snoop PRY
Snoopy NOSY
Snoopy's Baron RED
Snooze NAP
Snow field NEVE
Snow leopard OUNCE
Snow vehicles SLEDS
Snowy or lulu OWL
Snug harbor HAVEN
Snuggle up to NESTLE
Soak STEEP
Soaked WET
Soak flax RET
Soak up ABSORB
Soap ingredient LYE
Soap opera, e.g. DRAMA
Sobeit AMEN
Social asset TACT
Social climber SNOB
Social division CASTE
Social event BALL
Social group CLAN,SEPT
Social insect WASP

Clue	Answer
Socials	TEAS
Social stratum	CLASS
Social V.I.P.	LION
Society event	DEBUT
Society page word	NEE
Society, Secret	KLAN
Socratic approach	IRONY
Sod	TURF
Soda adjunct	STRAW
Soda flavor	COLA
Sodium hydroxide	LYE
Soft cheese	BRIE
Soft down	EIDER
Soft drink	COLA
Soft drinks	ADES
Soften	THAW
Softened	EASED
Soft food	PAP
Soft-grain sheepskin	ROAN
Soft mass	BOLUS
Soft or no	SOAP
Soft speech sounds	LENES
Soft stone	TALC
Soho residence	OME
Soil	DIRT,LOAM
Soil for fuel	PEAT
Soiled	MESSY
Sojourn	STAY
Solar disc	ATEN
Solar disk	ATON
Soldiers	GIS
Soldiers, Certain	PFCS
Soldier's equipment	KIT
Solemn assent	AMEN
Solemn declaration	OATH
Solemnity	RITE
Solemn: Prefix	SERIO
Solicitous	CARING
Solicits	ASKS
Solid	CONE
Solidifies	GELS,SETS
"So-long!"	TATA
Solo, Opera	ARIA
Solution	BRINE
Solutions, Strong	LYES
Somber: Prefix	SERIO
Some	ANY
Some are blue	LAWS
Some are split	PEAS
Some bills	ONES,TENS
Some cards	TWOS
Some Coloradans	UTES
Some dives	SWANS
Some fliers	ACES
Some funds	SLUSH
Some iron	SCRAP
Some is soft	SOAP
Some jewelry	PASTE
Some paintings	OILS
Some people	MALES
Some people's headgear	TAMS
Some playing fields	OVALS
Some railroads	ELS
Some streets	ONEWAY
Something destructive	BANE
Something easy	PIE
Something extra	PLUS
Something of value	ASSET
Something pleasant	TREAT
Something to bolster	EGO
Something to clean up	MESS
Something to follow	NOSE
Something to grind	ANAX
Something to study for	TEST
Sometimes dry item	ROT
Sometimes it's dim	PAST
Some users' aim	TRIP
Some votes	AYES,MAYS,NOES,NOS
Sommer	ELKE
Son	HEIR
Song	ARIA,GLEE
Song and movie title	LAURA
Song, Cheery	LILT
Song, Lopez	NOLA
Song of joy	CAROL
Song of praise	PAEAN
Song of sorrow	DIRGE
Song syllable	TRA
Songs	LAYS
Songstress Adams	EDIE
Sonnet source	POET
Son of Adam	CAIN,SETH
Son of Aphrodite	EROS
Son of Gad	ERI
Son of Hera	ARES
Son of Isaac	ESAU
Son of Jacob	LEVI
Son of Noah	SHEM
Son of Priam	PARIS
Son of Seth	ENOS
Sonoran people	SERI
So, old style	SAE
Soon	ANON
Soon after	THEN
Sooner	OKIE
Sooner than	ERE
Soot	SMUT
Soothe	LULL
Soothsayer's need	OMEN
Sophia	LOREN
Sophisticated	BLASE
Sora	RAIL
Sorcerer	MAGE
Sorcery, West Indian	OBEAH
Sorensen and Kennedy	TEDS
Sorrow sound	SIGH
Sorry, Word with	OOPS
Sort	ILK,KIND
So-so	TEPID
So-so grade	CEE
Sotto or viva	VOCE
Sotto voce	ASIDE
Souchong	TEA
Soul buyer	SATAN
Soul, in France	AME
Sound	HALE,SANE
Sound, Barn	MOO
Sound, Bullfight	OLE
Sounded	RANG
Sound, Farm	BAA
Sound, Horsy	SNORT
Sound, Loud	BANG
Sound loudly	BLARE
Sound, Of	TONAL
Sound of disbelief	PSHAW
Sound of disgust	UGH
Sound off	ORATE
Sound of impact	WHAM
Sound of longing	SIGH
Sound of relief	PHEW
Sound of sorrow	MOAN,SOB
Sound of surprise	GASP
Sound of thunder	CLAP
Sound of traffic	DIN
Sound phenomenon	ECHO
Sounds	TONES
Sounds, Attention-getting	PSTS
Sounds, Hesitating	ERS
Sounds of amusement	HAHA
Sounds of discovery	AHAS
Sound, Sudden	SNAP
Sound, Surf	ROTE
Sound to gain attention	AHEM
Soup	PUREE
Soup ingredient	OKRA
Soup spoon	LADLE

Soupy of TV SALES
Sour TART
Source ROOT
Source, Fuel PEAT
Source of formic acid ANT
Source of harm BANE
Source of heat STEAM
Source of indigo ANIL
Source of power ATOM
Source of the Blue Nile TANA
Source, Plume EGRET
Sources, Ego IDS
Source, Tallow SUET
Sour fruit SLOE
South African BOER
South African Dutch TAAL
South African iris IXIA
South African province NATAL
South African village DORP,STAD
South American beverage MATE
South American, Early INCA
South American range ANDES
South and North POLES
Southern cape FEAR,HORN
Southern college ELON
Southern constellation ARGO
Southern favorite PONE
Southern sea ROSS,SULU
Southern tree TITI
South European currency LIRA
South of France MIDI
South Pacific island TAHITI
South Pacific isle SAMOA
"South Pacific" or "Wayside Inn" TALES
"South Pacific" role EMILE
South Sea export COPRA
South Sea staple TARO
Souvenir RELIC
Soviet chain URALS
Soviet chessmaster TAL
Soviet city OREL
Soviet lake ARAL
Soviet press agency TASS
Soviet range ALAI
Spa EVIAN
Space AREA,GAP,ROOM
Space agency NASA
Space-age platforms PADS
Spacecraft booster AGENA
Space fuel LOX
Space hero GLENN
Spaceship, Part of a NOSECONE
Spade SAM
Spad or brad NAIL
Spanish article LAS,LOS,UNA
Spanish artist GOYA
Spanish bit of land ISLA
Spanish cat GATO
Spanish city AVILA
Spanish cloak CAPA
Spanish coin, Old REAL
Spanish dance BOLERO
Spanish direction ESTE
Spanish dukedom ALBA
Spanish exclamation OLE
Spanish greeting HOLA
Spanish half dozen SEIS
Spanish hall SALA
Spanish healthy SANO
Spanish hero CID
Spanish home CASA
Spanish jar OLLA
Spanish lake LAGO
Spanish liquid AGUA
Spanish month ENERO
Spanish mouth BOCA
Spanish name RAMON
Spanish nickname PEPE
Spanish nothing NADA
Spanish numeral DOS
Spanish painter MIRO,SERT
Spanish preposition POR
Spanish queen ENA
Spanish relative TIA,TIO
Spanish river EBRO,RIO
Spanish surrealist DALI
Spanish title SENOR
Spanish treasure ORO
Spanish verb ESTA
Spanish weight ONZA
Spar MAST,POLE
Spare, in Soho TYRE
Spares TIRES
Sparkle GLEAM
Sparks of films NED
Spark stream ARC
Sparse THIN
"Spartacus" author FAST
Sparta, Portico, in STOA
Spasm PANG
Spatiate ROAM
Speaker of baseball TRIS
Speak falteringly LISP
Speak: Fr. PARLE
Speak pompously ORATE
Spear LANCE
Special-interest group BLOC
Specialized strip of wood SKI
Special quality TRAIT
Special treat FEAST
Specialty, Met ARIA
Specialty, Southern PONE
Specific quantity UNIT
Specify CITE
Speck IOTA,MOTE
Sped TORE
Speech fault LISP
Speechify ORATE
Speech, Part of NOUN
Speech sounds ERS
Speed horse ARAB
Speed unit KNOT
Speedy, Be RUN
Speedy one HARE
Spenserian lady UNA
Spent TIRED,USED
Sphere ORB
Sphere of activity ARENA
Spica or Rigel STAR
Spice MACE
Spicy stew OLIO
Spied SEEN
Spigot TAP
Spike EAR
Spiked staff MACE
Spikes, as a drink LACES
Spill SLOP
Spill the beans SING
Spin a floating log BIRL
Spinner TOP
Spinning air EDDY
Spirit ELAN,GENIE
Spirit lamps ETNAS
Spirit, Roman LAR
Spirits ESSENCES
Spiritual nourishment MANNA
Spiro AGNEW
Spiteful woman CAT
Splashes against LAPS
Spleen IRE
Splendid REGAL
Splendor POMP
Split RIP,RIVE
Spoil MAR,ROT
Spoiler BANE

Spoils LOOT
Spoken ORAL
Sponsorship EGIS
Spooky EERY
Spool REEL
Spoon LADLE
Spoon or spinner LURE
Sported WORE
Sport, Horsy POLO
Sports area OVAL
Sportscaster Kyle ROTE
Sports enclosure ARENA
Sports equipment SKIS
Sports event MEET
Sports meet EVENT
Sports name BABE
Sports place RINK
Sports trophy CUP
Sportswear TOGS
Spot ESPY
Spot, Roadside DINER
Spots SEES
Spotted cavy PACA
Spotted and snowy OWLS
Spouse, Chaplin OONA
Spouse, Reine's ROI
Spouse, Rose's ABIE
Spouses, Certain EXES
Spray, Insect DDT
Spread JAM
Spread, Appetizer PATE
Spread outward FLARE
Spread, Table OLEO
Spread to dry TED
Spree TOOT
Sprightliness ESPRIT
Sprightly CRISP,PERT
Spring ARISE,LEAP
Springe TRAP
Spring flower IRIS,LILAC
Spring from EMANATE
Spring month APRIL
Spring period LENT
Spring riser SAP
Spring time EASTER
Spring up and down DANCE
Sprinkled, in heraldry SEME
Sprinter's pathway LANE
Sprite ELF
Sprite, Persian PERI
Sprout, as a tree LEAVE
Spruce's cousin FIR
Spry AGILE
Spume FOAM
Spunky GAME
Spurious FALSE,SHAM
Spur on a peak ARETE
Spy AGENT,HARI
Squabble ROW,SPAT
Squander LOSE,SPEND
Square footage AREA
Square, Granny or KNOT
Squash or melon PEPO
Squeaky door, Fixed a OILED
Squeeze PRESS
Squeeze out EKE
Squelch SITON
Squelched SATON
Squid's fluid INK
Squirrels tidbit ACORN
S-shaped molding OGEE
Stadium ARENA,OVAL,SHEA
Stadium feature TIER
Stadium receipts GATE
Stadium shout BOO
Stadium sounds RAHS
Staff magazine ORGAN
Staffmen AIDES
Staff on a green PIN
Stage PHASE
Stage and screen name MUNI
Stage award TONY
Stage designs SETS
Stage direction ENTER,EXIT,SOLA
Stage fare DRAMAS,OPERA,REVUE
Stage group ANTA
Stage husband ABIE
Stage of life ESTATE
Stage remark ASIDE
Stage signal CUE
Stage, Skinner of OTIS
Stage turn ACT
Stage villain IAGO
Stain DYE
Stains SOILS
Stair STEP
Staircase, Plane RAMP
Stake ANTE,BET
Stakes PALES
Stakes, Put up ANTE
Stale TRITE
Stalemate DRAW
Stalk STEM,STIPE
Stall LOGE
Stamp DIE,TENOR
Stand TENET
Standard NORM,PAR
Standard of perfection IDEAL
Standing ERECT
Standing, Has a good RATES
Standish stand-in ALDEN
Standoff TIE
Standout ONER
St. Andrews sport GOLF
Stanley, for one CAR
Stanza STAVE,VERSE
Staple RICE
Star NOVA
Starch SAGO
Starchy PRIM
Starchy plant TARO
Star, Corrida TORO
Stare in a way LEER
Star: Fr. ETOILE
Star, Golf ARNIE
Star in Cetus MIRA
Star in Cygnus DENEB
Star of India, e.g. GEM
Star or cat POLE
Starr RINGO
Starr of football BART
Star's light NEON
Star-spangled, in heraldry SEME
Start ONSET
Start a card game DEAL
Start the day ARISE
Started the fire LIT
Started a hole TEED
Started up a dead fire RELIT
Startle SCARE
Start of the Grande RIO
Starts, Companion of FITS
State AVER,IOWA,UTAH
State admitted in 1803 OHIO
State, Inactive SLEEP
State in Brazil ACRE
State, in Saint-Etienne ETAT
Stately REGAL
Stately music LARGO
State of being: Suffix NESS
State of India ASSAM
State of irritation SNIT
State of snafu MESS
States, as prices QUOTES
Statesman, British EDEN
Statesman, Roman CATO

State Street's city, for short	CHI	Stood for election	RAN
Stationery item	PEN	Stop	CEASE,QUIT,STAY
Stationery items	INKS	Stop: Fr.	ARRET
Statistical gauge	NORM	Stopover spot	INN,MOTEL
Statistics	DATA	Stop up	DAM
Statuary piece	TORSO	Stopwatch	TIMER
Statue spot	NICHE	Storage place	BARN
Statute	ACT	Storage space	BIN
Stave	RUNG	Store-ad subject	SALE
Stay	ABIDE,STOP	Store (away)	STASH
Stayed put	STOOD	Storehouse	ETAPE
Stay put	LIE	Storied dog	TOTO
Stead	LIEU	Storied island	TAHITI
Steady	EVEN	Storied mansion	TARA
Steak order	RARE	Storied ship	ARGO
Steal from	ROB	Storm	GALE,RAGE
Stealthy	FELINE	Storm center	EYE
Steam chamber	AGER	Storm sound	ROAR
Steel area	RUHR	Story	SAGA,YARN
Steel city	GARY	Story, Forsyte	SAGA
Steelworker's leader	ABEL	Story, of a kind	ALIBI
Steep	RET	Story teller	AESOP
Steep acclivity	BANK	Stout's kin	ALE
Steeple	SPIRE	Stow cargo	LADE
Steep rocks	CRAGS	Stowe heroine	EVA
Steep slope, in Hawaii	PALI	Stow in a ship's hold	STEEVE
Steinbeck D.P.	OKIE	St. Paul's architect	WREN
Stemless plant	TARO	St. Peter's feature	DOME
Stem, Plant	BINE	St. Pierre, e.g.	ILE
Steno's need	ERASER	Straight	NEAT
Step	GAIT,STAIR	Straighten	ALIGN,ALINE
Step lightly	TRIP	Straightforward	HONEST
Step of a sort	RUNG	Strain	AIR,EXERT,TRY
Stepped	TROD	Strained	TAUT,TENSE
Steps, Takes	ACTS	Straits	NEEDS
Stereo set	HIFI	Strange	ALIEN,EERIE
Stereotyped	TRITE	Strange: Prefix	XENO
Stern	GRIM,REAR	Stranger	ODDER
Sternward	AFT	Stratagem	RUSE
Stevens	INGER	Stratford name	ANNE
Stew	OLIO	Stratum	LAYER,TIER
Stew flavoring	LEEK	Stratum, Coal	SEAM
Stewpot	OLLA	Stravinsky	IGOR
St. Helena or Elba	ISLE	Straw or mile	LAST
Stick	CANE	Stray	ERR
Sticker	DECAL	Streams, Spark	ARCS
Stickum	PASTE	Streetcar	TRAM
Stick up	ROB	"Streetcar" role	STAN
Sticky one	PEST	Street in Gopher Prairie	MAIN
Stiff	RIGID	Street kind	ONEWAY
Stiff collars	ETONS	Street sight	BUS
Stiff hair	SETA	Street sign	ARROW
Stiff square cap	BIRETTA	Street sound	TOOT
Still	YET	Street urchin	ARAB
Stillness	CALM	Strength	NERVE
Stimulate	PROD	Stretch forward	CRANE
Stinger	BEE	Stretch, with "out"	EKE
Stings	BITES	Strife goddess	ERIS
Stingy	NEAR	Strike	CLAP
Stir	ADO,AROUSE,PROD,ROUSE	Strikebreaker	SCAB
Stirred up	AGOG	Strike out	ELIDE
Stir up	INCITE	Strikes	RAPS
Stitch	PAIN,SEW	Stringed instrument	SITAR
Stitching edge	SEAM	Stringed instruments	LUTES
Stithy	ANVIL	Strip	BARE,PEEL
Stock, in cards	TALON	Strip for hot rodders	DRAG
Stockings	HOSE	Strip of cut grass	SWATH
Stocking woes	RUNS	Strip of wood	SLAT
Stock-list group	RAILS	Strived	AIMED
Stock market maneuver	PUT	Stroke, Golf	PUTT
Stock-market pessimist	BEAR	Strong	IRON
Stock-market quotation	LOW	Strong beam	LASER
Stockton's river	TEES	Strongbox	CHEST
Stock word	PAR	Strong current	RACE
Stoicist	ZENO	Strong fiber	RAMIE
Stone	PIT	Strong flavor	TANG
Stone, Gem	OPAL	Stronghold	CITADEL
Stone and Iron	AGES	Strongly asserts	AVERS

Strongly colored DEEP
Strongly presses URGES
Strong man ATLAS
Strong solution LYE
Strong wind GALE
Structural shape TBAR
Structural unit IBAR
Structure SHED
Strudel component APPLE
Struggle TOIL
Stub TAGEND
Student aid TROT
Student's concern TEST
Students' moment of truth EXAM
Student, Training CADET
Study DEN
Study, as clues SIFT
Study course ARTS
Study, Fields of AREAS
Study intently PORE
Study, Musical ETUDE
Stuff CRAM,PAD
Stuff, Abrasive EMERY
Stuffy person PRIG
Stumble TRIP
Stumblebum OAF
Stumbled FELL
Stupid CRASS
Stupid mistake ROCK
Stupid one DODO
Sturdy plant TREE
Style CLASS,GENRE,MODE,TONE
Style of art DADA
Style of potatoes RICED
Style, Type IONIC
Stylish CHIC,SMART
Styptic ALUM
Sub-chaser's device SONAR
Subdue TAME
Subdued SOFT
Subject of a Blake poem TIGER
Subject, Art NUDE
Subject, Arthur Hailey HOTEL
Subject, College ARTS
Subjected to hardship TRIED
Subjective, for one CASE
Subjoin ADD
Submarine docks PENS
Submarine hazards REEFS
Sub-rosa info TIP
Subsequently LATER
Subside ABATE
Subsidy AID
Substance, Powdery TALC
Substance, Seaweed AGAR
Substitute ERSATZ
Subtle emanations AURAE
Subtle stimulus AURA
Subtly catty SNIDE
Subtraction word LESS
Subventions AIDS
Subway entrance STILE
Subway for Rene METRO
Subway grip STRAP
Succeeding AFTER
Succeeds WINS
Successful show HIT
Success signs SROS
Succinct TERSE
Succulent plant ALOE
Sudden attacks ONSETS
Sudden blow CLAP
Sudden break SNAP
Sudden movement START
Sudden outburst FLARE
Sudden pang STAB
Suds ALE
Suey's partner CHOP
Suffered attrition WORE
Suffers disuse RUSTS
Sufficient, to poets ENOW
Suffix, Adjective IAL
Suffix, Chemical ENE,IDE
Suffixes, Enzyme ASES
Suffixes for bone OSTS
Suffixes in chemistry ATES
Suffix, Feminine ESS,INE
Suffix for bleacher ITE
Suffix for cash IER
Suffix for centi PEDE
Suffix for Dixie or auto CRAT
Suffix for a doer ATOR
Suffix for heart or head ACHE
Suffix for sec or pop ULAR
Suffix for thermo STAT
Suffix for tonsil ITIS
Suffix for trick or pun STER
Suffix in chemistry ANE
Suffix in zoology ATA
Suffix, Native OTE
Suffix, Noun EER,ION,NESS
Suffix, Ordinal ETH
Suffix, Plural IES
Suffix, Superlative EST
Suffix with arch or witch ERY
Suffix with journal or Canton ESE
Suffix with press or moist URE
Suffix with usher or kitchen ETTE
Suffusing shade TINGE
Sugar source BEET,CANE
Sugar: Suffix OSE
Suggestion IDEA
Suitable place NICHE
Suited, Perfectly IDEAL
Suiting SERGE
Suit of sorts ARMOR
Suitor BEAU
Suits FITS
Sullies SOILS
Sullivan and others EDS
Sully SPOT,STAIN,TAINT
Sultan of Turkey AHMED
Sultan's decree IRADE
Summarize RECAP
Summer-camp gear CANOE
Summer clock reading EDT
Summer coatings TANS
Summer drink ADE
Summer pest GNAT
Summers, in Paris ETES
Summit TOP
Summit, At the ATOP
Summon CALL,CITE
Summoned, in a way RANG
Sumptuous meal FEAST
Sun, The STAR
Sunbathe LOLL
Sunday fare ROAST
Sunder REND
Sun disk ATEN
Sun-dried brick ADOBE
Sun, for one STAR
Sun god SOL
Sunken fences HAHAS
Sun or moon ORB
Sun Valley gear SKI,SKIS
Sup EAT
Superfluity FAT
Superfluously TOO
Superior AONE,LAKE
Superior to ABOVE
Superjet SST
Superlative BEST
Superlative ending EST
Superman's garb CAPE
Supernatural being TROLL

Supervisor, for short	EXEC	Swatch	SNIP
Supped	ATE	Sway	REEL,RULE
Supplement (with "out")	EKE	Swearing-in formality	OATH
Supplicate	PRAY	Swedish district	LAN
Supplicates	BEGS	Swedish weight	STEN
Suppliers of the ego	IDS	Sweep	OAR
Support	ABET,AID,REST	Sweep of a scythe	SWATH
Supported (with)	SIDED	Sweeten	SUGAR
Supporter of some big wheels	AXLE	Sweeten the pot	ANTE
Supporting beam	TIE	Sweetens the pot	RAISES
Supports	ABETS	Sweetheart	FLAME,HONEY
Suppose	OPINE	Sweet odor	BALM
Supposedly	ASIF	Sweetsop	ATES
Suppressed	SATON	Sweet wine	PORT
Supra	ABOVE	Swelling	EDEMA
Supreme Court Justice	WHITE	Swerve	SKEW
Suppress	ELIDE	Swift and Jones	TOMS
Surface flaw	DENT	Swiftly	APACE
Surface measure	ARE	Swift's nationality	IRISH
Surface mineral deposits	PLACERS	Swimmer's hazard	CRAMP
Surface, Downy	NAP	Swimmers' milieu	TANK
Surfacing	TAR	Swimsuit top	BRA
Surfeits	SATES	Swinelike animal	TAPIR
Surf noise	ROTE	Swing around	SLUE
Surf part	CREST	Swinging section of London	SOHO
Surf sound	ROAR	Swiss artist	KLEE
Surmount	SCALE	Swiss canton	URI
Surname, Uriah's	HEEP	Swiss city	BERN,BERNE
Surpass	CAP,TOP	Swiss river	AAR,AARE
Surplus	OVER	Swoboda	RON
Surprised sound	OOPS	Sword	EPEE
Surrealist painter	MIRO	Sworn statement	OATH
Surrender	CEDE	Sycophant	TOADY
Surrounded	BESET	Sylvan deity	SATYR
Surrounded by	AMID	Symbol, Music	CLEF
Surrounds, with "in"	HEMS	Symbol of Britain	LION
Surveyor's nail	SPAD	Symbol of defeat	TOWEL
Suspenders stand-in	BELT	Symbol of duplicity	OIL
Sustain	AID	Symbol of heaviness	LEAD
Sustains	BEARS	Symbol of redness	BEET
Sustenance	ALIMENT	Symbol of silence	CLAM
Sutherland forte	ARIA	Symbol of strength	IRON,OAK
Suture	SEAM	Symbol on Australian coin	EMU
Swabs	MOPS	Symbol, Printer's	STET
Swag	LOOT	Symbols of peace	DOVES
Swahili tongue	BANTU	Sympathetic response	ECHO
Swallow hastily	BOLT	Symphony instrument	OBOE
Swanky or stout	BEER	Synthetic	ERSATZ
Swan or gainer	DIVE	Syrian city, to Frenchmen	ALEP
Swapped	TRADED	Syria's neighbor	IRAQ
Sward	SOD,TURF	System	ISM,ORDER
Swarm	HIVE,TEEM	System kind	SOLAR
Swarming, with "with"	ALIVE		

T

Tabby	CAT	Take a bus	RIDE
Tablecloths, etc.	LINEN	Take care of	SEETO
Table item	SALT,SUGAR	Take effect	ENURE
Tableland	MESA	Take evidence	HEAR
Table scraps	ORTS	Take a gander	OGLE
Table staple	OLEO	Take hold	ROOT
Tablet	PAD	Take in	ABSORB
Tabletop decor	VASE	Take it easy	COAST,IDLE,LOLL
Tableware, Matched	SET	Take medicine	DOSE
Taboo thing	NONO	Take off	ELOPE
Taboret	STAND	Take out	DELE,ERASE
Tackle's neighbor	END	Takes a drive	MOTORS
Tacloban's island	LEYTE	Takes five	RESTS
Taft territory	OHIO	Takes on	HIRES
Tailless monkey	APE	Takes the stage	ENTERS
Tailor's concern	SEAM	Take steps	ACT,ACTON
Tai tribesman	LAO	Take the stump	ORATE
Taiwan Strait, Island in	AMOY	Take to the ice	SKATE
Taj Mahal site	AGRA	Take top billing	STAR
Take advantage of	USE	Take wing	SOAR
Take apart	UNDO	Taking repose	ABED
Take, as a plea	COP	Tale	SAGA,YARN

Clue	Answer
Tale of adventure	GESTE
Talkative	GLIB
Talk back	SASS
Talk, Certain	SLANG
Talk extravagantly	RAVE
Talk, Friendly	COZE
Talk idly	PRATE
Talk, in a way	CHAT
Talks	RAPS
Talk softly	COO
Talk turgidly	RANT
Tallow	SUET
Tall: Sp.	ALTO
Tall story	YARN
Tally	ADDUP
Tamarisk	ATLE
Tangle	SNARL
Tank contents	GAS
Tan shade	ECRU
Tantalize	TEASE
Tantivy	APACE
Tapered wedge	CALK
Tapestry	ARRAS
Tar	GOB
Taradiddler's tales	LIES
Tara land	EIRE
Target in quoits	HOB
Targets in a game	PINS
Taro paste	POI
Tarry	LAG,STAY
Tarsus	ANKLE
Tarsus or phor, Prefix for	META
Tartan	PLAID
Tarts	PIES
Task	CHORE
Tasse prefix	DEMI
Taste	SAPOR,SIP
Taste: Fr.	GOUT
Tastefulness	TACT
Tatter	RAG
Taunt	TEASE
Taupe	MOLE
Tavern	INN
Tavern offering	BEER
Tavern sign	NEON
Tawny	TAN
Tax	LEVY,SCOT
Taxed	TRIED
Taxi	CAB
Tea	CHA
Teacake	SCONE
Teacher, Hindu	GURU
Team	SIDE
Team, L.A.	RAMS
Team race	RELAY
Team, Shea	METS
Tea or milk	DRINK
Tear	REND
Tear at	CLAW
Tear down	RAZE
Teasdale	SARA
Tease	RAG
Tease repeatedly	RIDE
Teases	RIBS
Teases: Colloq.	RAGS
Tech area	LAB
Teen hairdo	MANE
Teheran resident	IRANI
Telegram	WIRE
Telepathic faculty	ESP
Telephone tone	DIAL
Telescope part	LENS
Telescope's field	SKY
Teller's space	CAGE
Tells whoppers	LIES
Tempest	GALE
Tempest locale	TEAPOT
Temple of old	FANE
Templeton or Guinness	ALEC
Tempo	PACE
Temporary star	NOVA
Tempters	EVES
Temptress	SIREN
Tenant, Marina	YACHT
Tenant's concern	LEASE
Tend	LEAN
10:15, e.g.	TIME
Tennis gear	NET
Tennis-line material	LIME
Tennis nonscore	LOVE
Tennis serve	ACE
Tennis shot	SMASH
Tennis star	ASHE
Tennis stroke	CHOP
Tennis term	LET
Tennis units	SETS
Tennyson, e.g.	LORD
Tennyson heroine	ENID
Tennyson lady	ELAINE
Tennyson's seaman	ARDEN
Tennyson works	ODES
Ten o'clock scholar's hour	NOON
Tenor's specialty	ARIA
Ten: Prefix	DECA
Ten rin	SEN
Tension	STRESS
Tent	TEPEE
Tenting area	CAMP
Ten to ten	TIE
Term, Bridge	SLAM
Term, Golf	TEED
Term, Heraldic	ORLE
Terminal	END,LAST
Term in cookery	ALA
Term in heraldry	UNDE
Term in new math	SET
Term, Math	RATIO,SINE
Term, Nautical	ABEAM
Term of address	MADAM
Term, Pinochle	MELD
Term, Poetic	OER
Term, Poker	ANTE
Term, Printing	STET
Terms of address	SIRES
Term, Tennis	ACE
Terrible tsar	IVAN
Terrier	SKYE
Territory on Adriatic	TRIESTE
Terror	PANIC
Tessera	TILE
Test	ASSAY,EXAM,ORAL,TRY
Testing place	LAB
Teutonic goddess	NORN
Tevere city	ROMA
Texas college	SMU
Texas cottonwood	ALAMO
Texas leaguer	FLY
Texas river	PECOS
Textile fabric	MOIRE
Thai	ASIAN
Thailand king	RAMA
Thailand money	BAHT
Thai language	LAO
Thalia's sister	CLIO
Thames town	ETON
Thanksgiving concern	MENU
Than, Other	ELSE
Thant or Mao	ASIAN
That is: Lat.	IDEST
That, to Cicero	ILLE
Theater box	LOGE
Theater group	ANTA
Theater lights	SPOTS
Theater part	STAGE
Theater scenery	SETS
Theater sign	EXIT,SRO

Theatrical award TONY
Theatrical scenery DECOR
Theda BARA
Their, in France LEUR
Thelonius MONK
Theme ESSAY
Then, in Paris ALORS
Theory ISM
Thereabouts ORSO
Therefore ERGO
Thermometer reading ZERO
The: Sp. LOS
Thespian's goal ROLE
Thessalonian peak OSSA
They're slippery EELS
Thickening agent AGAR
Thick grape juice SAPA
Thick hair MANE
Thick slice SLAB
Thick-soled footwear CLOG
Thick soup PUREE
Thieves' place DEN
Thin RARE
Thine: Fr. ATOI
"Thin Man" dog ASTA
Thin strip SLAT
Thing ITEM
Thing, in law RES
Thing of beauty GEM
Thing of value ASSET
Thing, Revere's RIDE
Things, Taboo NONOS
Things, Tiny ATOMS
Things to be done AGENDA
Things-to-come expert SEER
Things to know ROPES
Things to make meet ENDS
Thing to beat SYSTEM
Thing, unusual, in London ONER
Think OPINE
Think deeply PORE
Thinker's aims IDEAS
Thinks IDEATES
Think-tank in Calif. RAND
Third of a crowd ONE
Third-rate mark CEE
30, to some OLD
Thirst quenchers ADES
This, in Spain ESTA
This, in Toledo ESTE
Thomas SETH
Thomas or Horace MANN
Thoroughfare, French ALLEE
Thoroughly QUITE
Thought: Fr. IDEE
Thought: Prefix IDEO
Thousand: Prefix KILO
Thrash BELT,CANE,FLAIL,TAN
Thread LISLE
Thread, as through shoals REEVE
Threadbare TRITE
Threadlike line STRIA
Thread of a sort YARN
Threefold TRINE
Three, in Italy TRE
Three-pointer in football GOAL
Three: Prefix TRI
3,600 seconds HOUR
Three times: Prefix TER
Three to a side OUTS
Three trios NONET
Throat-clearer AHEM
Throb ACHE,BEAT,PANT,PULSE
Through PER
Through: Prefix DIA
Throw HURL
Throwaway ever since Eve CORE
Throw the lead, at bridge EXIT
Throw off EMIT
Throw out EJECT,EVICT,OUST
Thruway sign EXIT
Thumb and others TOMS
Thumbs down ANTI
Thumbs down, Russian style NYET
Thunder gust THOR
Thurber JAMES
Thus: Lat. SIC
Tibetan beasts YAKS
Tibetan gazelle GOA
Tibetan monk LAMA
Tidal flood BORE,EAGRE
Tide NEAP
Tide, Certain RIP
Tidy NEAT
Tidy the hedge PRUNE
Tie ASCOT,LASH
Tied EVEN
Tiff SPAT
Tiger, for one RAG
Tiger, in India SHER
Tiger star of old COBB
Tighten tackle FRAP
Tight-lipped one CLAM
Tigris meets Euphrates, Where IRAQ
Tijuana friend AMIGO
Till UNTO
Till contents CASH
Till now YET
Tilt LEAN,LIST
Tilted ATIP
Timber tree OAK
Timber trees ASHES
Timber wolf LOBO
Time AGE,HOUR
Time, At any EVER
Time-bomb mechanism FUSE
Time, Long AEON
Time, Of a ERAL
Time of day NOON,SUNUP
Time, Of a geologic ERIAN
Time period ERA,YEAR
Time periods DAYS
Time, Poetic EVE
Times around the track LAPS
Time's companion TIDE
Time, Seasonal LENT
Time spans EONS
Timetable entry ARR
Time, Wear with ERODE
Time zone EDT,EST
Timid SHY
Tiniest LEAST
Tins CANS
Tiny WEE
Tiny amount ATOM,WISP
Tiny creatures ANTS,MITES
Tiny land area ISLET
Tiny one TIM
Tiny Tim word BLESS
Tip END,HINT
Tip's partner TOP
Tipster TOUT
Tipsy: Colloq. OILED
Tipsy one SOT
Tire RECAP
Tire mount RIM
Tire pattern TREAD
Tire word PLY
Tissue TELA
Tissue, Certain SCAR
Tithe TENTH
Titicaca or Geneva LAKE
Title DAME,EARL,SIR
Title, Dostoevsky (with "The") IDIOT
Title, Eastern RAJA,RAJAH,RANEE
Title, Eastern church ABBA

Title for Macbeth	THANE
Title for a rabbit	BRER
Title, French	DUC
Title, Haggard	SHE
Title, Hindu	RANI
Title, Malaysian	TUAN
Title, Melville	OMOO
Title, Moslem	AGA,EMIR,IMAM
Title, Nabokov	ADA
Titles	NAMES
Title, Turkish	AGHA
Title, Zola	NANA
Titter	TEHEE
Tittle	IOTA
To any extent	ATALL
Toasted	FETED
Toasting need	GLASS
Tobacco, for one	ROAD
Tobacco kiln	OAST
Tobacco portion	QUID
To be, in France	ETRE
Tobermory's creator	SAKI
Toboggan	SLED
To boot	PLUS
Toby of "Tristam Shandy"	UNCLE
To the center	INTO
To the city: Lat.	URBI
Tocsin	ALARM
Today in Turin	OGGI
To-do	STIR
Together	ASONE
Together, Fit	NEST
Together, in music	ADUE
Together, Stitched	SEWN
Together, Weld	UNITE
Together with	AMID
To growl	GNAR
To him: Fr.	ALUI
Toil	SLOG
Tokyo, formerly	EDO
Toledo, Love in	AMOR
Toledo, Nothing, in	NADA
Tolerate	BEAR,STAND
Tolled	RANG
Tomboy's knee decor	SCAB
Tom Joad, for one	OKIE
Tommy's ally in W.W.I	POILU
Tone, Certain	DIAL
Tongue, Gaelic	ERSE
Tongue of a wagon	NEAP
Tongue of Pakistan	URDU
Tonic herb	ALOE
Tonsorial gear	RAZOR
Tony of baseball	OLIVA
"Too bad!"	ALAS
Took advantage of	USED
Took a bus	RODE
Took it on the lam	BLEW
Took off	RAN,WENT
Tool	ADZE,AXE,CATSPAW,PICK,RASP
Tool, Digging	SPADE
Tool, Garden	HOE,RAKE
Tool, Pipe	REAMER
Tools, Fencer's	EPEES
Tooth	MOLAR
Tooth, in Tours	DENT
Tooth part	ENAMEL
Top	CREST,LID
Top, Big	TENT
Top billing, Takes	STARS
Toper	SOT
Topic, Ad	SALE
Topic, Steinbeck	OKIE
Top-notch	AONE,ELITE
Topnotcher	ACE
To the point	TERSE
To the point: Lat.	ADREM
Topper	BERET,HAT
Topple	TIP
Tore	RENT
Torero's praises	OLES
Torme	MEL
Torment	AGONY,BAIT,GNAW,HARASS,PANG
Torn	RENT
Toro, Cheer for	OLE
Tortilla	TACO
Toss	HURL
Tosser of a mythical apple	ERIS
Tosspot	SOT
Total	ADD,ADDUP
Total receipts	GATE
Tote	LUG
Tote-board data	ODDS
Totem	POLE
Touch	ABUT
Touches	TAGS
"Touche" weapon	EPEE
Touch lightly	DAB
Toughen	ENURE,INURE
Tourist city	PISA
Tourist mecca	ROME
Tourist's aid	MAP
Tourist sight, Sicilian	ETNA
Tourist stop in India	AGRA
Tours summer	ETE
Toward shelter	ALEE
Tower	SOAR
Tower with an inclination	PISA
Town, Alaskan	NOME
Town, Eskimo	ETAH
Town in Belgium	SPA
Town near Amsterdam	EDAM
Town near Padua	ESTE
Town near Rome	OSTIA
Town, Netherlands	EDE
Town, Norman	STLO
Town on the Thames	ETON
Town on the Tigris	AMARA
Town, Sicilian	ENNA
Townsman: Colloq.	CIT
Town, Venezuelan	AROA
Trace	GLEAM,TINGE
Track event	RACE,RELAY
Track events	MEETS
Track-meet event	DASH
Track, Off the	AMISS
Tracks, Race	OVALS
Track-team member	MILER
Track transaction	BET
Tract	AREA
Trade	SELL,SWAP
Trade discount	AGIO
Trading center	MART
Traffic component	CAB
Traffic sign	SLO,SLOW,STOP
Traffic situation	JAM
Tragic hero	ROMEO
Tragic king	LEAR
Trail, Animal	SPOOR
Trailblazer with Clark	LEWIS
Trail, Deer	SLOT
Trainee	CADET
Train for a bout	SPAR
Trains, Certain	ELS
Trains, Like some	LATE
Train unit	DINER
Tralee's land	ERIN
Trammel	NET
Tramp	HIKE
Trample	TREAD
Trampled	TROD
Transaction	DEAL,SALE
Transfer	CEDE
Transfer design	DECAL
Transfer, Legal	DEED
Transform	ALTER

Clue	Answer
Transfusion material	PLASMA
Transition, Abrupt	LEAP
Translation of amo	ILOVE
Transmit, in a way	RADIO
Transmitted	SENT
Transparent mineral	MICA
Transportations, Certain	ELS
Transported	RAPT
Trap	SNARE
Trapeze insurance	NET
Trapper's quest	PELT
Traubel	HELEN
Travail	TOIL
Traveled	RODE
Traveler's rider	LEE
Traveler's stop	INN
Traverse	ROVE
Trawler gear	NET
Tread and riser	STAIR
Treasure	STORE
Treasury	CHEST
Treat a wound	DRESS
Treated (with "with")	DEALT
Treatment	USAGE
Tree	ASH,CEDAR,ELM,PALM,PINE
Tree dweller	TOAD
Tree feature	LIMB
Tree genus, Asian	THEA
Tree, Linden	TEIL
Tree mammal	LEMUR
Tree, Northern	ALDER
Tree of Brazil	ASSAI
Tree of life site	EDEN
Tree, Palm	ARECA
Tree, Philippine	IPIL
Tree, Rubber	ULE
Tree, Sandarac	ARAR
Tree sight	NEST
Tree, Tamarisk salt	ATLE
Tree, Willow	OSIER
Tree with poisonous sap	UPAS
Trevino's game	GOLF
Trial	TEST
Triangle sides	LEGS
Tribe in Nigeria	IBO
Tribe or thermy prefix	DIA
Tribesman, African	BANTU
Tribesman, Peruvian	INCA
Tributary of the Po	ADDA
Tributary of Seine	OISE
Tributes to skylarks, et al.	ODES
Trick	RUSE
Trick or prank suffix	STER
Trickster	ROGUE
Tricksy spirit	ARIEL
Tricky actions	ARTS
Tricorns	HATS
Tried	ESSAYED
Tries	TESTS
Trifle, in Paris	RIEN
Trifles	TOYS
Trifle with	TEASE
Trifling	IDLE
Trig	NEAT
Trig word	SINE
Trim	NEAT,PRUNE
Trim the lawn	MOW
Trimming	LACE
Trimming, Coat	LAPIN
Trim a photo	CROP
Trinity Church feature	SPIRE
Trio, Biblical	MAGI
Trio of children's story	BEARS
Trio of myth	FATES
Trio, Scoreboard	OOO
Triple-Crown horse	OMAHA
Trips, Auto	SPINS
Trite	STALE

Clue	Answer
Tritons	EFTS
Triumphant cry	AHA
Triumphs	WINS
Trojan or Crimean	WAR
Trojan War figure	PARIS
Trojan War name	HELEN
Troll	GNOME
Troop entertainers	USO
Troops, Turkish	ALAI
Trophy	CUP
Tropical bird	ANI,MACAW
Tropical fruit	DATE
Tropical resin	ELEMI
Tropical staple	TARO
Tropical tree	EBOE
Tropical vine	LIANA,LIANE
Trouble	AIL
Troubles	ILLS
Troublesome	HARD
Trouble's partner	TOIL
Truck feature	CAB
Truck, for short	SEMI
Trudge	PLOD,SLOG
True	REAL
True olives	OLEA
True's companion	TRIED
Truly	YEA
Trumpeters	SWANS
Trunk	TORSO
Trunk, Arterial	AORTA
Try	ESSAY,TEST
Try: Colloq.	STAB
Tryout	TEST
Try sorely	TAX
T-shaped cross	TAU
Tube, Kind of	INNER
Tubers, Dried	SALEP
Tuck away	STOW
Tuckered out	TIRED
Tude or meter prefix	ALTI
Tug's tow	SCOW
Tuileries Gardens, e.g.	PARC
Tula's river	OKA
Tum bad	SOUR
Tumbled	FELL
Tumbler	GLASS
Tumbrel	CART
Tumult	RIOT
Tumultuous sound	DIN
Tune	LILT
Tunes	AIRS
Tung tree product	OIL
Tunisian ruler	BEY
Tunisian seaport	SFAX
Tunnel, Mine	ADIT
Turf	SOD
Turin money	LIRA
Turin three	TRE
Turkey's neighbor	IRAN
Turkeys	TOMS
Turkish capital	ANKARA
Turkish city	ADANA
Turkish coin	ASPER
Turkish coins	LIRAS
Turkish decree	IRADE
Turkish inn	IMARET
Turkish leader	AGHA
Turkish leaders	AGAS
Turkish president	INONU
Turkish regiment	ALAI
Turkish sultan	AHMED
Turkish title	BEY,EMEER
Turkish weight	OKA
Turmeric	REA
Turn away	AVERT
Turner	LANA,LATHE,NAT
Turnpike feature	TOLL
Turnpike sign	EXIT

Turn right GEE
Turn thumbs down VETO
Tuscan island ELBA
Tuscany river ARNO
Tusked animal BOAR
TV ailment SNOW
TV comic Wilson FLIP
TV group PANEL
TV offering NEWS
TV offerings DRAMAS
TV phenomenon SNOW
TV's King ALAN
TV's Mary Tyler MOORE
Twain MARK
Tweed BOSS
Tweed's nemesis NAST
12-point type PICA
Twenty bob, in England QUID
29th, The IOWA
Twenty: Prefix ICOSI
Twenty quires REAM
Twice BIS
Twice-told STALE
Twinge PANG
Twining stem BINE
Twins et al. NINES
Twist COIL,OLIVER,SLEW,WARP
Twists SLUES
Twitchings TICS
Twittery AGOG
Two handfuls TEN
Two horses SPAN
Two, in Mexico DOS
Two-master BRIG
Two of a kind BRACE
Two semesters YEAR
Two-toed sloth UNAU
Two-wheeled carriage TRAP
Type KIND,SORT
Type measures ENS
Type of arch OGEE
Type of auto SEDAN
Type of beam MOON
Type of berth UPPER
Type of bread RUSK
Type of can TIN
Type of coal SOFT
Type of coffee IRISH
Type of curl SPIT
Type of eye EVIL
Type of flu ASIAN
Type of hammer CLAW
Type of hold TOE
Type of ink INDIA
Type of machine LATHE
Type of moss PEAT
Type of muffin BRAN
Type of oak HOLM
Type of painting NUDE
Type of plant ENAMEL
Type of race RELAY
Type of raft BALSA
Type of remark SNIDE
Type of rock SHALE
Type of rubber PARA
Type of sandwich HERO
Type of seal EARED
Type of shoe BAL
Type of ski lift TBAR
Type of soil LOAM
Type of spoon LADLE
Type of star NOVA
Type of test ORAL
Type of theater ARENA
Type of ticket MEAL
Type of train LOCAL
Type of type AGATE
Type of verse meter IONIC
Type of writing IRONY
Typesetting instruction ITAL
Type size ELITE
Typist's type choice PICA
Tyrants NEROS

U

U.A.W. output CARS
U-boats SUBS
Ugly woman CRONE
Ukase's relative IRADE
Ukrainian city KIEV
Ukrainian council RADA
Ule, for one TREE
Ulna, for one BONE
Ultraviolet, for one RAY
Ulysses or Cary GRANT
Umbrella part RIB
Umpire's call BALL,SAFE
Umpire's decision OUT
Unadorned PLAIN
Unaided ALONE
Unalloyed PURE
Unaspirated LENE
Unassisted SOLO
Unattached LOOSE
Unbalanced ALOP
"Un Bel Di" for example ARIA
Unbelievable TALL
Unbend RELAX,THAW
Unbridled action ORGY
Unburdens EASES
Uncanny EERY
Unchanged ASIS,SAME
Unchanging STATIC
Uncle SAM
Uncle, in Scotland EME
Uncle of fiction TOBY
Unclose, to poets OPE
Uncommon, More ODDER
Uncommunicative MUM
Uncouth RUDE
Uncouth one CAD
Uncover BARE,STRIP
Unctuous OILY
Undeceived ONTO
Undeniable TRUE
Underdone RARE
Underhand ploy RUSE
Under, in Italy SOTTO
Underling AIDE
Undermine ERODE,SAP
Underpinnings LEGS
Understand SEE
Understanding KEN
Understanding response ISEE
Understood SEEN,TACIT
Undertake TRY
Under the weather, Is AILS
Underworld figure SATAN
Undiluted NEAT
Undisguised BALD
Undone, Leave OMIT
Undressed NUDE
Unearthly EERY
Une saison ETE
Uneven EROSE
Unexciting TAME
Unfailing TRUE
Unfamiliar NEW
Unfermented grape juice STUM
Unflappable SEDATE
Unfledged bird EYAS

Unfrequented LONE
Unhurt SAFE
Unicorn fish UNIE
Uniform EVEN
Uniform part CAP
Unimproved ASIS
Unique ALONE
Unique guy ONER
Unit ONE
Unit, Corn EAR
Unite WED
United ASONE,ATONE
Unit, Farm BARN,STY
Unit in physics ERG
Unit, Medical DOSE
Unit of length ELL
Unit of weight CARAT,TON
Units, Time ERAS
Unit, Thai money BAHT
Unit, Time YEAR
Universal: Prefix OMNI
Unkempt SEEDY
Unless: Latin NISI
Unlike a mustang TAME
Unlocalized hatrack HOME
Unmask BARE
U.N. member IRAN
Unmixed PURE
Unmoving INERT
U.N. name LIE
Unnatural EERIE
Unoccupied IDLE
Unoriginal one APER
Unpalatable fare SLOP
Unphilosophic NAIVE
Unpin LOOSE
Unpleasant person OGRE
Unpolished CRUDE,RAW,RUDE
Unproductive ARID
Unqualified UTTER
Unrefined COARSE,CRASS,GROSS
Unrehearsed ADLIB
Unruffled COOL,EVEN
Unsophisticated NAIVE
Unspoken TACIT
Unsubstantial AIRY
Unsuccessful VAIN
Untidy MESSY
Until UPTO
Until: Sp. HASTA
Untrained RAW
Untrustworthy one LIAR
Untypical RARE
Unusual NOVEL
Unusual bloke ONER
Unusual, More RARER
Unvaried EVEN
Unvarying SAME
U.N. vote NYET
Unwatered NEAT
Unwelcome one PEST
Unwieldy craft SCOW
Unyielding HARD,RIGID
Up ARISEN
Up and about ASTIR
Up and about, Not ABED
Upbeat, in music ARSIS
Upbraids RATES
Upcoming NEXT
Update an atlas REMAP
Up, Ham it EMOTE
Up, in baseball ATBAT
Up in years AGED
Up, Let EASE
Up, Line QUEUE
Up, Lock JAIL
Up, Match PAIR
Upolu seaport APIA
Upper crust ELITE
Upper: Ger. OBER
Upper or lower CASE
Upper space ETHER
Uppity habits AIRS
Upright ERECT,HONEST,ONEND
Uproar RIOT,TODO
Upset IRATE,RILE
Upsets TIPS
Upshot END
Upstate N.Y. city OLEAN
Up to ABLE,UNTIL
Up to, Look ADORE
Up-to-the-minute LATEST
Up until ASOF
Uraeus ASP
Urban blight SMOG
Urbane BLASE
Urban problem NOISE,RIOT
Urban railways ELS
Urban vehicle TAXI
Urchin ARAB,TAD,TOT
Urge PRESS,PROD,YEN
Urges on ABETS
Urge, with "on" EGG
Uriah HEEP
Uris's hero ARI
U.S. agents TMEN
U.S. anthropologist MEAD
U.S. architect STONE
U.S. author URIS
U.S. author-critic AGEE
U.S. budget outlay ARMS
U.S. capitalist ASTOR
U.S. carrier WASP
U.S. coins, Word on UNUM
U.S. composer CAGE,IVES
U.S. department STATE
U.S. desert sight SAGE
U.S. dramatist INGE,ODETS
U.S. duck SMEE
Use a bike PEDAL
Used a strop HONED
Used a tiller STEERED
Used up ATE
Use an eraser RUB
Useful Latin phrase ETAL
Useful quality ASSET
Useless IDLE,VOID
Use the library READ
U.S. engineer EADS
Use of a pencil's other end ERASURE
Use the phone DIAL
Uses the bridal path RIDES
Uses a pencil top ERASES
Use a spray AERATE
Use a straw SIP
Use a stylus ETCH
Uses the teeth BITES
Use up EAT,SPEND
Usher's quest SEAT
U.S. historian BEARD
U.S. humorist ADE,NYE
U.S. Indian ERIE,SAC,UTE
U.S. inventor HOWE,YALE
U.S.M.A. figure PLEBE
U.S. missile NIKE,THOR
U.S. novelist OHARA,WEST
U.S. painter HOMER
U.S. patriot OTIS
U.S. physicist RABI
U.S. playwright ALBEE,RICE
U.S. poet BENET
U.S. portrait painter PEALE
U.S. President ADAMS,TAFT
U.S. satellite ECHO
U.S. Senator BAYH
U.S.S.R. city OREL

U.S.S.R. range URAL
U.S. tennis star ASHE
Ustinov PETER
Usual bill footer DAD
Usually 72, in golf PAR
U.S. violinist STERN
U.S. writer POE
Utah's lily SEGO
Utensil POT,TOOL
Utmost NTH
Utopian IDEAL
Uttar Pradesh city AGRA
Utter EMIT
Utter disasters LOON
Utters SAYS
Utters sharply, with "out" RAPS

V

Vacant INANE
Vacation spot CAMP
Vacation times in Paris ETES
Vacillate TEETER
Vagrant NOMADIC
Vain IDLE
Vain fancy DREAM
Vainglory POMP,PRIDE
Vale DELL
Valhalla man ODIN
Valley DALE,DELL,GLEN
Valuable horse ARAB
Value, Things of ASSETS
Vamoose SCRAM
Vamp BARA
Vampire LAMIA
Vandyke, for one BEARD
Vanish FADE
Vanishing gas-station gift MAP
Vanity EGO
Vanity case ETUI
Vanquished one LOSER
Vapid writings PAP
Vapor STEAM
Vapor: Prefix ATMO
Vaquero's rope REATA
Variation of fabulist ESOP
Variation of habituate ENURE
Variation of novice TIRO
Variation of rockfish RENA
Variation of Siamese TAI
Variegated PIED
Varieties of plums GAGES
Variety act TURN
Variety, Cabbage KALE
Variety of ink INDIA
Variety of oak HOLM
Variety of palm SAGO
Variety of pear BOSC
Variety of quartz SARD
Variety's Green ABEL
Variety, Tea CHA
Varnish base LAC
Varnish ingredients ELEMIS
Vase URN
Vase: Fr. URNE
Vaudeville act TURN
Vault DOME,LEAP
Vaulted recess APSE
Veers SLUES
Vegas or Palmas LAS
Vegetable BEET,KALE
Vegetable, familiarly SPUD
Vegetable liquid OLEIN
Vegetable, Pungent ONION
Vegetables PEAS
Vegetables, Nursery-rhyme PEASE
Vehemence HEAT
Vehicle CAR,SLED,TAXI
Vehicle for stage DRAMA
Vehicles CARS
Vehicles, Public BUSES
Veins LODES
Veld covering GRASS
Veld sight ZEBRA
"Venerable" historian BEDE
Venetian sky CIELO
Veneto or Corso VIA
Venezuelan copper center AROA
Venezuelan state LARA
Venice, Money in LIRE
Veni, translated ICAME
Veni, ubi, amo, etc. LATIN
Venner or Dinsmore ELSIE
Venomous snakes ASPS
Vent EMIT
Ventilate AERATE
Venture RISK
Ventured DARED
Venturous RASH
Veranda LANAI
Verb ending ING
Verb form, French ETES
Verb, French ETRE
Verb, Latin ESSE
Verdant GREEN
Verdi heroine AIDA
Vergil word ARMA
Verify AVER
Verily AMEN,YEA
Verne's captain NEMO
Versailles, Very, in TRES
Verse STAVE
Verse maker BARD
Verse, Of a ODIC
Versifier POET
Verve ELAN
Very, in France TRES
Very, in music ASSAI
Very little DROPINTHEBUCKET
Very recent Mrs. BRIDE
Very spacious VAST
Vessel EWER,LINER,TUN
Vessel of 1492 NINA
Vessels ARKS
Vessels at Anzio landing LSTS
Vessels, Heating ETNAS
Vessel, Two-masted BRIG
Vessel, W.W.I UBOAT
Vestibule ENTRY
Vestige TRACE
Vestment ALB,MANIPLE,ROBE
Vestment, Papal ORALE
Vetch ERS,TARE
Veteran OLD
Veto word NYET
Vex RILE,ROIL
Vexes IRKS
Via PER
Via Veneto's city ROMA
Vibrant ALIVE
Vibrate TRILL
Vibration TREMOR
Vic's radio partner SADE
Vichy or Bath SPA
Vicinity AREA
Victim PREY
Victory margin NOSE
Vietnam city HANOI
Vietnamese holiday TET
Vietnamese port HUE
View SEE
Viewed EYED
View from Taormina ETNA

View halloo	CRY	Visit frequently	HAUNT
View, Kind of	DIM	Visit a mall	SHOP
Vigilant	ALERT	Vista	SCENE
Vigor	ELAN	Visualize	SEE
Vigorous denial	NONO	Vital fluid	PLASMA
Village, African	STAD	Vitality	ELAN
Village, Irish	TARA	Vital statistic	AGE
Village, Russian	MIR	Vivacious	AIRY,ANIMATE
Villain	OGRE	Viva voce	ORAL
Villain's cry	AHA	Vivid	LIVE
Villain's greeting	HISS	Vivid events	DRAMAS
Villain, Shakespearean	IAGO	Vladimir Ulyanov	LENIN
Villainous look	LEER	Vocal	ORAL
Villa near Rome	ESTE	Vocal presentations	CANTATAS
Vincent's theme	NOLA	Vocal range	ALTO
Vindicate	AVENGE	Vogue	RAGE,TREND
Vine	LIANA	Voice	EMIT
Vineyard valley of California	NAPA	Voice, Choir	ALTO
Violated a traffic law	SPED	Voiced	ALOUD
Violates a commandment	STEALS	Voice of Moscow	TASS
Violation	SIN	Voice part	TENOR
Violent desire	MANIA	Voices, Choir	ALTI
Violent, Extremely	RABID	Void	INANE
Violently	AMAIN	Voided escutcheon	ORLE
Violent rush	TEAR	Voids	QUASHES
Violinist Bull and others	OLES	Volcanic matter	ASH
Violinist Isaac	STERN	Volcanic rock	TRASS
Violin maker	AMATI	Volcano	ETNA
Violin-string material	GUT	Volcano that erupted in 1902	PELEE
V.I.P.	LION	Volstead's opponents	WETS
V.I.P., Arab	EMEER	Voluble	GLIB
V.I.P., Eastern	RAJA	Volume	TOME
V.I.P. of silents	HERO	Voodoo	MAGIC
V.I.P.'s spot	DAIS	Voodoo deity	LOA
Viper	ADDER	Vote	NAY
Vipers	ASPS	Vote, Affirmative	YEA
Virago	SHREW	Voters, Certain	MEN
Virginia, for instance	REEL	Votes	AYES
Virginia willow	ITEA	Votes against	NOES
Viscount	PEER	Votes for	YESES
Viscount's superior	EARL	Vowels, Greek	ETAS
Viscous liquid	TAR	Voyage	TRIP
Vise and cast prefix	TELE	V.P. under Nixon	AGNEW
Vishnu's incarnation	RAMA	Vulgar	COARSE,RANK
Visionary	AIRY,SEER		

W

Wabash or Ohio	RIVER	Wallach	ELI
Wac's cousin	SPAR	Wall and Canal	STREETS
Wader	HERON	Wall appliance	OVEN
Wading bird	IBIS,RAIL,STORK	Wallet items	ONES
Wad of tobacco	QUID	Wallflower's kinsman	STAG
Wagner heroine	SENTA	Wall hanging	ARRAS
Wagnerian cycle	RING	Wallop	CREAM
Wagnerian god	WOTAN	Wall Street men	TRADERS
Wagnerian work	OPERA	Wall St. word	ASKED,PAR
Wagner role	ERDA	Wander	ROVE,STRAY
Wagon pole: Dial.	NEAP	Wandered	ERRED
Waif	STRAY	Wanderer	NOMAD
Waikiki's island	OAHU	Wane	EBB
Waipahu, Wreath in	LEI	Wanes	FADES
Waistband	OBI	Want	NEED
Waiter's burden	TRAY	Wanting	NEEDY
Waiter's expectancy	TIP	Wapiti	ELK
Waiter's offering	MENU	Warble	TRILL
Waken	AROUSE,ROUSE	Ward off	AVERT
Wake-robin	ARUM	Ware, Enameled	TOLE
Wake rudely	ROUST	Warehouse	DEPOT,ETAPE
Waldorf	SALAD	War god	ARES
Walk	STEP	Warm	TEPID
Walked	TROD	Warm attachment	LOVE
Walk heavily	PLOD	Warmth	ARDOR
Walk in	ENTER	Warning	ALERT
Walk nervously	PACE	Warning device	FLARE
Walk or pace	GAIT	Warning, Word of	DONT
Walks	MALLS	Warplanes	MIGS
Walks fast, with "it"	LEGS	Warren	EARL

Warship equipment	RADAR	Webfooted animal	OTTER
Wartime group	OSS	Webster	NOAH
Wartime Secretary of State	HULL	Weddell and Ross	SEAS
Was eminent	SHONE	Wedding-account word	NEE
Was "in"	RATED	Wedding feature	RICE
Was: Lat.	ERAT	Wedding notice	BANNS
Was off guard	SLEPT	Wednesday, Certain	ASH
Was sore	ACHED	Wee	TEENY
Wash	LAVE	Wee bit	MITE
Washes down	HOSES	Weed	TARE
Wash finale	RINSE	Wee, in Glasgow	SMA
Washington bills	ONES	Weekdays, Forty	LENT
Washington figure	SENATOR	Wee one	TAD
Wash up	CLEAN	Weep	SOB
Waste allowance	TRET	We: Fr.	NOUS
Wasteland	SAHARA	Weight	OUNCE,TON
Wasteland tracts	MOORS	Weight deduction	TARE
Waste product	DROSS	Weight of India	SER,TOLA
Waste time	IDLE	Weight system	TROY
Watch	EYE	Weight unit	CARAT
Watchful	ALERT	Weir	DAM
Watch holder	FOB	Weird	EERIE,EERY
Watch over	TEND	Welcome call by bridge partner	RAISE
Water animal	OTTER	Welcoming wreath	LEI
Water bird	EGRET,ERNE,LOON	Weld	UNITE
Water birds	ERNS	Well-coordinated	AGILE
Water color	AQUA	Well disciplined	TAUT
Watercourse	RACE	Well fuzzed	HAIRY
Watercraft	BOAT	Well-known Briton	EDEN
Watered silk	MOIRE	Well-known college	SMITH
Water, in France	EAU	Well-known Loch	NESS
Waterless	SERE	Well-known nickname	ARI
Water lily's milieu	POND	Well-known tune	TAPS
Water or gas carrier	MAIN	Well ordered	NEAT
Water or musk	MELON	Welsh name	EVAN
Waterproof	SEAL	Went	LEFT
Waterproof covering	TARP	Went astray	ERRED
Waters	HOSES	Went bathing	SWAM
Water, Spanish	AGUA	Went first	LED
Waterway	CANAL,INLET	Went for the hook	BIT
Watery fluids	SERA	Went into second base	SLID
Watterson or Dana	EDITOR	Went together	DATED
Waugh or Templeton	ALEC	Weskit	VEST
Wave, in France	ONDE	West	MAE
Waver	TEETER	West Coast campus	UCLA
Waves	SEAS	Western alliance	OAS
Wave top	CREST	Western bean	PINTO
Wavy, in heraldry	UNDE	Western bulrush	TULE
Way	MODE,ROAD	Western capital	SALEM
Way, Habitual	USAGE	Western cat	PUMA
Way, In any	ATALL	Western city	OMAHA,RENO
Way of speaking	ACCENT	Western farm	RANCH
Way out	EXIT	Western hero	EARP
Way-out	ULTRA	Western house	ADOBE
Ways	ROADS	Western Indian	CREE,OTOE,SAC,UTAH,UTE
Wayside, for one	INN	Western lake	MEAD
Weak	ANILE	Western lily	SEGO
Weaken	SAP	Western movie	SHANE
Weapon	LANCE	Western or ham	OMELETTE
Weapon, British style	SABRE	Western pact	NATO
Weapon, Fencer's	EPEE	Western park	ESTES
Weapon, in France	ARME	Western plant	SAGE
Weapons	ARMS	Western range	TETON
Weapons: Lat.	ARMA	Western show	RODEO
Wear away	ERODE	Western sight	CANYON,MESA
Wear, Gym	SNEAKERS	Western style, opposed	AGIN
Wear, Halloween	SHEET	Western weed	LOCO
Wearing apparel	HATS,HOSE	Western wine valley	NAPA
Wear, Opera-box	TIARA	West, Indian of	OTO
Wears	LASTS	West Indian shrub	ANIL
Weary	TIRE	West Indies magic	OBEAH
Weasels	STOATS	West Pointer	CADET,PLEBE
Weather forecast	HAIL,RAIN,SNOW	West role	LIL
Weather report	SMOG	West Virginia product	COAL
Weather term	SLEET	Wet, Dripping	ASOP
Weather word	CLEAR,HOT,ICE	Wetland	FEN
Weave	SPIN	Whack	RAP
Weaver's reed	SLEY	Whale	ORCA

Whaler AHAB
What deltas are made of SILT
What "de novo" means ANEW
Whatever ATALL
What Italian's ella means SHE
What Jack did FELL
What Johnnie can't do READ
What Mae West wanted peeled GRAPE
What a Manx lacks TAIL
What non-swimmers do WADE
What Oliver Twist wanted MORE
What "phage" means EATER
What pigs do ROOT
What she wants, she gets LOLA
What's left REST
What some actors do EMOTE
What some gamblers hope to get EVEN
What some lovers do ELOPE
What to do with four aces RAISE
What trouble-makers raise HOB
What "veni" means ICAME
Wheat by-product BRAN
Wheedles BEGS
Wheel projection CAM
Wheel shaft AXLE
Whenever ONCE
Where the action is ARENA
Where the Adige flows ITALY
Where all roads meet ROME
Where "Avast!" is heard ASEA
Where Chillicothe is OHIO
Where Cnossus is CRETE
Where esthetes meet SALON
Where figleaf was skirt EDEN
Where Fort-Lamy is CHAD
Where Galileo taught PADUA
Where Gaugin painted TAHITI
Where the girls are HAREM
Where the heart line is PALM
Where: Lat. UBI
Where the Liffey flows EIRE
Where lovers toss coins TREVI
Where Mosul is IRAQ
Where Muscat is OMAN
Where one's asleep ABED
Where Provo is UTAH
Where Singaradja is BALI
Where the Styx flows HADES
Where Surabaya is JAVA
Where Tabriz is IRAN
Where toffs wander SOHO
Wherewithal MONEY
Where the Yalu flows KOREA
Where Zeno taught STOA
Wheys SERA
Whilom ERST
Whip FLAIL,LASH
Whippersnapper SNIP
Whirlpool EDDY
Whiskies RYES
Whisky drink SOUR
Whisper, Stage ASIDE
Whistle time NOON
Whistle-wetters ALES
Whit ATOM,IOTA
White frost RIME
White House name ADAMS
White House nickname IKE
White House room OVAL
White lie FIB
White or Blue NILE
White or fire events SALES
White poplar ABELE
Whitetail DEER
Whitney or Wallach ELI
Whodunit name ERLE
Who, in Italy CHE
Whole ENTIRE
Whole lot SLEW
Wholly ALL,QUITE
Whooping cranes, Like RARE
Whopper LULU
Wicked EVIL
Wicker basket CREEL
Wide-mouthed jar OLLA
Widely, Search COMB
Widespread RIFE
Widow's coins MITES
Wield EXERT
Wields USES
Wife, Hitler's EVA
Wife, Knight's DAME
Wife of Aegir RAN
Wife of Athamas INO
Wife of Cuchulainn EMER
Wife of Geraint ENID
Wife of Henry VIII ANNE
Wife of Menelaus HELEN
Wife of Osiris ISIS
Wife of Zeus HERA
Wigglers and spinners LURES
Wight ISLE
Wild FERAL
Wild asses of Asia ONAGERS
Wildebeest GNU
Wild game DEER
Wild goat IBEX
Wild guess STAB
Wild habitat LAIR
Wild hog BOAR
Wildly enthusiastic: Slang GAGA
Wild ox ANOA
Wild plum SLOE
Wild sheep of India SHA
Wild time ORGY
Wiles ARTS
Will Brandt negative NEIN
William H. or Robert TAFT
William, Playwright INGE
William R. or Stephen V. BENET
Williams ROGER
Willie of baseball fame MAYS
Willing GAME
Willing's companion ABLE
Will item ESTATE
Willow ITEA,OSIER
Will V.I.P. HEIR
Wilson's predecessor TAFT
Win GET
Winchester RIFLE
Wind BORA,COIL,GALE
Wind direction ENE,NNE,SSE
Wind indicator VANE
Wind instrument OBOE
Window ORIEL
Window part SASH,SILL
Window sign TOLET
Wine PORT
Wine additive STUM
Wine and dine TREAT
Wine city of Italy ASTI
Wined and dined FETED
Wine, Dry, as SEC
Wine, Like good AGED
Wine measure TUN
Winery refuse MARC
Wine's tagalong DINE
Wine vessels AMAS
Wing ALA
Wing, Building ELL
Winglike ALATE
Winglike part ALA
Wings ALAE
Wing-shaped ALAR
Winks BATS
Winners INS

Clue	Answer
Winning	ONTOP
Winning margin	NOSE
Win over	ENDEAR
Wins	GETS
Winter hazard	SLEET
Wipe off	ERASE
Wiper	RAG
Wire measure	MIL
Wisdom	SENSE
Wise	ONTO
Wise man	NESTOR
Wise men	MAGI
Wise ones	SAGES
Wish one hadn't	RUE
Witch city	SALEM
Witches'-brew ingredients	TOADS
Witch's hex	CURSE
With	ALONG
With "a-tete", cozy meeting	TETE
With "Abba", Israeli statesman	EBAN
With "Bator", Asian city	ULAN
With "Eban", Israeli statesman	ABBA
Withered	SERE
Withers	FADES
With "Friday" and "thirteenth", a time for caution	THE
With full force	AMAIN
With "gestae", legal acts	RES
With "Happy is the house" and "shelters a friend", a homely quote	THAT
With "He serves his party best" and "serves the country best", a Presidential quote	WHO
With, in Arles	AVEC
Within: Prefix	ENDO,ENTO
With, Invest	ENDUE
With lance in hand	ATILT
With "mens", clothing	WEAR
With "one", street sign	WAY
Without frills	PLAIN
Without, in France	SANS
Without a mate	ODD
Without: Suffix	LESS
With "out", supplement	EKE
With reference	ASTO
With "Queen Anne's", wild carrot	LACE
With "tete", cozy meeting	ATETE
With "way", street sign	ONE
With "wear", clothing	MENS
Witness	SEE
Witness-box response	IDO
Witness of a sort, with "best"	MAN
Witness of a sort, with "man"	BEST
Witticism	MOT
"Wizard of Oz" dog	TOTO
Woe sound	SOB
Woeful cry	ALAS
Woes	ILLS
Wolf	LOBO
Wolf or card unit	PACK
Wolfert and Gershwin	IRAS
Wolfish, Be	OGLE
Wolframite et al.	ORES
Woman	EVE
Woman, Arthurian	ENID
Woman, Indian	RANI
Womanish, Old	ANILE
Womanly weapon	TEAR
Women's lib mecca	RENO
Women: Slang	DAMES
Won	GOT
Wonder	AWE
Wood	FIR
Wood burr	KNAR
Wooden shoe	SABOT
Wood file	RASP
Wood product	PAPER
Wood, Ship	TEAK
Wood support	SLAT
Wood tool	ADZE
Woodwind	OBOE
Woody fiber	BAST
Woody or Mel	ALLEN
Wooed Morpheus	SLEPT
Woof's companion	WARP
Wool cloth	LLAMA
Wool: Lat.	LANA
Wool: Prefix	LAN
Word	PROMISE
Word, Attention-getting	AHEM
Word, Auction	SOLD
Word before deep or high	KNEE
Word before humbug	BAH
Word before sorry	OOPS
Word, Common Latin	ESSE
Word, Doll's	MAMA
Word ending, Biblical	ETH
Word for Adenauer	ALTE
Word for Cassius	LEAN
Word for a fille	ELLE
Word for heavenly gates	AJAR
Word for invading Mongols	HORDE
Word for a Mohican	LAST
Word for N.Y. State	EMPIRE
Word for a piper	PIED
Word for a quick exit	SCAT
Word for a Ranger	LONE
Word for a ship	SHE
Word for a shoppe	OLDE
Word for some halls	IVIED
Word for some stories	TALL
Word for some whisky	AGED
Word for a strikebreaker	SCAB
Word for a tie, in tennis	ALL
Word for Wellington	IRON
Word, French menu	ROTI
Word, Freudian	EGO
Word, Gambler's	ODDS
Word, Golf	FORE
Word heard in the back room	ANTE
Word in Einstein's equation	MASS
Word in a Hemingway title	ARMS
Word in a palindrome	MADAM
Word in a Salinger title	RYE
Word in a Thomas Wolfe title	RIVER
Word in "Wanted" circular	ALIAS
Word in a wedding notice	NEE
Word in a Williams title	ROOF
Word, Judge's	ORDER
Word, Nautical	ABEAM,ALEE
Word of the Aeneid, First	ARMA
Word of agreement	YES
Word of approval	AMEN
Word of cheer	OLE
Word of contempt	TUT
Word of disgust	PSHAW,RATS,UGH
Word of regret	ALAS,SORRY
Word of respect	SIRE
Word, Omar	ENOW
Word on "Arrivals" board	LATE
Word on a bill, with "please"	REMIT
Word on a proof	STET
Word on a quarter	UNUM
Word on the wall	MENE
Word, Pinball	TILT
Word, Poetic	EEN,EER,ERE,TIS
Word, Poet's	OER
Word, Poker	POT,SEE
Word, Quaker	THEE
Word, Rocket	AGENA
Word, Sandy's	ARF
Words, Certain	NOUNS
Words for a bit more	ORSO
Words for an egoist	III
Words for an interim official	PROTEM

Clue	Answer
Words from Caesar	ETTU
Words from Gertrude Stein	AROSE
Words, New-math	SETS
Words of assent	IDO
Words of comprehension	ISEE
Words of dismay	OHNO
Words of warning	NONO
Words of wisdom	DICTA
Words, Sale	ASIS
Word to children	DONT
Word to a lady	MAAM
Word to a lifeguard	HELP
Word, Traffic-sign	SLO
Word under a red light	EXIT
Word used with "chic"	TRES
Word, Weather	HAIL,SMOG,SNOW
Word with bahn or mate	AUTO
Word with black and boot	STRAP
Word with blight or renewal	URBAN
Word with brass or banana	TOP
Word with circle or rehearsal	DRESS
Word with cracker or hatch	NUT
Word with fangled	NEW
Word with him or her	SELF
Word with home or bed	STEAD
Word with horse and comic	OPERA
Word with maid or master	OLD
Word with man or mat	DOOR
Word with play or run	END
Word with sand or cobble	STONE
Word with snow or corn	FLAKE
Word with stone or star	LODE
Word with "trial offer"	FREE
Word with up or lively	STEP
Work	OPUS
Work animals	OXEN
Work, Art	OIL
Work at	PLY
Work by Stravinsky	AGON
Worker, Bakery	ICER
Worker, Bookcover	LACER
Work for	EARN
Work, Lyric	EPODE
Work of David	PSALM
Work, O'Neill	DRAMA
Work on mss.	EDIT
Workplace	SHOP
Work, Rousseau	EMILE
Works, The	ALL
Works, Choral	CANTATAS
Workshop items	TOOLS
Works, Poetic	ODES
Work unit	ERG
Work, Wagnerian	RING
World area	ASIA,EAST
World power	USSR
World War II corps	WAC
World-weary	BLASE
Worm, Silk	ERI
Worn	USED
Worship	ADORE
Worsted	SERGE
Worth	MERIT
Worthless	IDLE
Worthless stuff	TRIPE
Worthless trifle	FIG
Wounded vanity	PIQUE
Wrap	STOLE
Wrap in cloth	CERE
Wrapped garments	SARIS
Wrath	ANGER,IRE
Wreath	LEI
Writer Deighton	LEN
Writer for Friday	DEFOE
Writer, French: 1823-92	RENAN
Writer Gardner	ERLE
Writer James	AGEE
Writer Leon	URIS
Writer Munro	SAKI
Writer Murdoch	IRIS
Writer Norman	MAILER
Writer of light verse	LEAR
Writer of success stories	ALGER
Writer Paton	ALAN
Writer St. Johns	ADELA
Writer Waugh	ALEC
Writer Wolfert	IRA
Writes	PENS
Writing, Vapid	PAP
Written pledge in law	AVAL
Wrongful act	TORT
Wrong, Go	ERR
Wrong: Prefix	MIS
Wrongs	EVILS
Wrote	PENNED
W.W.II battleground	STLO
W.W.II coalition	AXIS
W.W.II conference site	YALTA
W.W.II marine threat	UBOAT
W.W.II service group	WAAC
W.W.I spy	HARI
Wyoming range	TETON

XYZ

Clue	Answer
Xanthippe	NAG,SHREW
Xmastime	YULE
Yacht-club sights	SAILS
Yak away	JAW
Yakutsk's river	LENA
Yale	ELIHU
Yale men	ELIS
Yangtze tributary	HAN
Yardarms	SPARS
Yarn	STORY,TALE
Yarn measures	LEAS
Yarn spindle	HASP
Year, A	LEAP
Yearly record, old style	ANNAL
Yearn	ACHE,LONG,PINE
Year of Nero's first marriage	LIII
Years and years	EONS
Years, for Caesar	ANNI
Yell	RAH,SHOUT
Yellowish white	CREAM
Yellow journal: Slang	RAG
Yemen capital	SANA
Yen	ITCH
Yens	URGES
Yes	ISEE
Yes-man	TOADY
Yesterday, in Arles	HIER
Yesterday's child	ADULT
Yesterday tomorrow	TODAY
Yet, to poets	EEN
Yield	RELENT
Yielded	GAVE
Yields	CEDES
Yields under pressure	SAGS
Ymir's slayer	ODIN
Yonder	THERE
Yonkers event	TROT
Yore, Command, of	HEST
Yore, Formerly, of	ERST
Yorkshire river	AIRE,OUSE,URE
You: Ger.	SIE
You love: Lat.	AMAS
Young fish	FRY
Young mule	FOAL
Young one	LAD
Young oyster	SPAT
Young salmon	PARR
Young whale	CALF

Youngest Cratchit	TIM
Youngster	TAD
Youth	LAD
Youth goddess	HEBE
Yugoslav name	TITO
Yul Brynner's kingdom	SIAM
Yutang	LIN
Zaharias	BABE
Zany	FOOL
Zealot's enterprise	CRUSADE
Zenith	ACME,NOON
Zeno's building	STOA
Zero	NIL,NONE
0900, for example	HOUR
Zest	TANG
Zesty	TANGY
Zeus, Son of	ARES
Zhivago's love	LARA
Ziegler or Nessen	RON
Zither's ancestor	ASOR
Zodiac sign	ARIES,CRAB,RAM
Zodiac sign and others	LEOS
Zola	EMILE
Zola heroine	NANA
Zone	AREA,BELT
Zoo animal, for short	ORANG
Zoo animals	DEER
Zoo attraction	HIPPO
Zoo attractions	SEALS
Zoo features	APES
Zoo sound	ROAR
Zounds!	EGAD

The following is a list of the clues we have researched that contain abbreviations. We find that almost all crossword puzzles contain clues that either say "Abbr." or have an abbreviation in them, such as "Brit. fliers" (RAF).

Clue	Answer
Abbreviation for incoming mail	RECD
Abbreviation in a date book	APPT
Abbreviation on an envelope	ESQ
Abbr. on a business letter	ENC
Abbr. on a spoon	STER
Abed: Abbr.	RET
Accepted: Abbr.	RECD
Acronym, Army	AWOL
Acronym for short take-off craft	STOL
Addresses, G.I.	APOS
Addresses: Abbr.	STS
African country: Abbr.	ETH
After Aug.	SEPT
After Feb.	MAR
Agency, Gov't	REA
Agency, Gov't.	USIA
Agency, W.W.II	OPA
Agency of U.N.	ILO
Ages: Abbr.	YRS
Aide: Abbr.	ASST
Aides to M.D.'s	RNS
Airline abbreviation	ETA
Airman's initials	USAF
Air pilot's concern: Abbr.	ALT
Amusement: Abbr.	REC
And more: Abbr.	ETC
And others: Lat.	ETAL
And others, Main: Abbr.	STS
Animal org.	SPCA
Annapolis abbr.	ENS
Annapolis initials	USNA
Anne or Marie: Abbr.	STE
Appendant abbreviation	ETC
Appended: Abbr.	ATT
Appraisals: Abbr.	ESTS
Approximations: Abbr.	ESTS
Areas, Store: Abbr.	DPTS
Area, W.W.II	OSS
Army girl of W.W.II	WAAC
Army initials	AWOL
Army man: Abbr.	NCO
Army men: Abbr.	SGTS
Army officers: Abbr.	LTS
Army school: Abbr.	ROTC
Army V.I.P.	GEN
Art course: Abbr.	ANAT
Arteries: Abbr.	AVES,STS
Art process: Abbr.	ENGR
Assn.	ORG
Astronauts' org.	NASA
Athletic org.	NCAA
Auditing initials	CPA
Aunt or uncle: Abbr.	REL
Author's group: Abbr.	PEN
Author's monogram	RLS
Author's output: Abbr.	MSS
Autoist's org.	AAA
Aviation initials	STOL
Banking abbreviation	INT
Basketball tourney: Abbr.	NIT
Baton Rouge initials	LSU
B.B. league	NAT
Benelux member: Abbr.	BELG
Between Fri. and Sun.	SAT
Bible book: Abbr.	ISA
Biblical song: Abbr.	PSA
Big shot: Abbr.	VIP
Blue Eagle initials	NRA
Body of troops: Abbr.	DET
Book, Bible: Abbr.	PSA
Bookkeeping abbr.	BAL
Book of the Bible: Abbr.	ISA
Book reviewer, of a sort: Abbr.	ACCT
Book supplement: Abbr.	ADD
Bordeaux miss: Abbr.	MLLE
Boston and others: Abbr.	SPTS
Branches of a school org.	PTAS
Branch of medicine: Abbr.	PATH
Branch of physics: Abbr.	ELEC
Breathing: Abbr.	RESP
Bridge builder: Abbr.	ENGR
Brief moments: Abbr.	SECS
Brisk, in music: Abbr.	ALLO
Brit. fliers	RAF
British money: Abbr.	STER
British title: Abbr.	BART
Broadway group: Abbr.	ANTA
Brookings, for one: Abbr.	INST
Bro. or sis.	REL
Business course: Abbr.	ECON
Business letter abbr.	INST
Business letter notation: Abbr.	ENC
Bus or train term.	STA
Cabinet post: Abbr.	AGR
Calculator: Abbr.	CPA
Calendar abbr.	SAT
Calendar abbreviation	SEPT
Calendar abbrs.	WEDS
Cal Tech, for one: Abbr.	INST
Campus mil. group	ROTC
Canadian province: Abbr.	ALTA,ONT
Can. province	QUE
Capitol Hill man: Abbr.	REP,SEN
Catch-all abbr.	ETC
Catch-all abbreviation	ETAL
Catherine, Mary and: Abbr.	STES
Certain carriers: Abbr.	RRS
Certain cities: Abbr.	SPTS
Certain newsman: Abbr.	CORR
Certain party: Abbr.	GOP
Certain photo job: Abbr.	ENL
Certain soldiers: Abbr.	PFCS
Certain students: Abbr.	SRS
Certain type: Abbr.	ITAL
Certain voter: Abbr.	DEM
Choice: Abbr.	SEL
Chosen: Abbr.	SEL
Church man: Abbr.	DEA
Circle's width: Abbr.	DIA
Circuitry designers: Abbr.	EES
Civil War initials	CSA,GAR,REL
Clairvoyance: Abbr.	ESP
Classical language: Abbr.	LAT
Classified ad wds.	APTS
Classmen: Abbr.	SRS
Club: Abbr.	ORG
Cobh's land: Abbr.	IRE
Cockpit abbreviation	ALT
College course: Abbr.	ECON
College sports org.	NCAA
College subj.	ANAT
College subject, for short	LIT
Col.'s superior	GEN
Command: Abbr.	ORD
Common abbreviation	ETC
Common Latin abbreviation	ETAL
Commonplace: Abbr.	ORD
Comm. system	TEL
Communication initials	RCA
Complex: Abbr.	SYST

Clue	Answer
Conrail takeover: Abbr.	RRS
Continent: Abbr.	EUR
Cookbook abbreviations	TSPS
Cooling measures, for short	BTUS
Copy: Abbr.	IMIT
Corporation V.I.P., for short	EXEC
Corp. or sgt.	NCO
Cost of borrowing: Abbr.	INT
Country, Mideast: Abbr.	ISR
Course, Med.	ANAT
Court-case figure: Abbr.	RESP
Cpl. or sgt.	NCO
Dallas college: Abbr.	SMU
Data, Pitching: Abbr.	ERA
Date: Abbr.	APPT
David's songs: Abbr.	PSA
Day: Abbr.	MON,SAT
D.C. men	SENS
D-Day leader	DDE
Debtor's initials	IOU
Defendant in a suit: Abbr.	RESP
Defense arm: Abbr.	NAV
Defense initials	USN
Defense unit: Abbr.	USAF
Degree: Abbr.	LLD
Dental degree: Abbr.	DDS
Dep., Opposite of	ARR
Depot: Abbr.	STA
Depression-era letters	CCC
Depression initials	NRA
Detroit-based union: Abbr.	UAW
Developer's abbr., Photo	ENL
Digits: Abbr.	NOS
Dike country: Abbr.	NETH
Direction: Abbr.	ENE,ESE,NNE,NOR,SSE
Disengaged: Abbr.	DET
Diversity: Abbr.	VAR
Doctors' org.	AMA
Documents: Abbr.	MSS
Doorway: Abbr.	ENT
Dover's state: Abbr.	DEL
Draft abbr.	SSS
Dublin initials	IRA
Dyed: Abbr.	OLD
Eastern state: Abbr.	DEL
Edition: Abbr.	ISS
Educators' org.	NEA
E.g., Sgt.	NCO
Electronics initials	RCA
Elec. unit	AMP
Emeritus: Abbr.	RET
Envelope, Abbr. on a	ESQ
Et al., Jean d'Arc	STES
Etc., Sgts.	NCOS
Eur. country	NETH,NOR
Eur. country: Abbr.	GER
Executive: Abbr.	PRES
Expatriate poet's initials	TSE
Fake: Abbr.	IMIT
Familiar author: Abbr.	ANON
Familiar initials	USSR
Famous fifty: Abbr.	USA
Farming: Abbr.	AGR
Fast plane: Abbr.	SST
Fast, to slow: Abbr.	ANT
F.B.I. men: Abbr.	AGTS
F.D.R. agency	OPA
Figure, Ring: Abbr.	REF
First letter: Abbr.	INIT
Fixed: Abbr.	STA,STAT
Flat: Abbr.	APT
Flight arm: Abbr.	SAC
Flight word: Abbr.	ARR
Flying initials	USAF
Follower of H.S.T.	DDE
Football scores: Abbr.	TDS
Former Govt. agency	ECA
Former Mideast org.	UAR

Clue	Answer
Form of precognition: Abbr.	ESP
For one, Cal Tec: Abbr.	INST
For short, Electrical units	AMPS
For short, flats	APTS
For short, Party man	DEM
For short, Prosecutors	DAS
For short, Shells	AMMO
40th, the: Abbr.	SDAK
Founded: Abbr.	EST
France's neighbor: Abbr.	BEL
French co.	CIE
French divine: Abbr.	STE
French miss: Abbr.	MLLE
French women: Abbr.	MMES
Furnace tender: Abbr.	STO
Future books: Abbr.	MSS
Game officials: Abbr.	REFS
Gateway: Abbr.	ENT
Gender: Abbr.	MASC
Genetic initials	DNA
Genuine, Not: Abbr.	IMIT
Georgia, etc.: Abbr.	USSR
Gettysburg initials	DDE
G.I. address	APO
G.I. initials	USA
G.I.'s friend	USO
Gob's monogram	USN
Good name, for short	REP
Got: Abbr.	RECD
Government agency: Abbr.	USIA
Gov't agency	CIA
Gov't. agency	REA,SSS
Gov't agency of 1933	CCC
Gov't units	DPTS
Go, Way to: Abbr.	RTE
Gridiron plays: Abbr.	TDS
Group: Abbr.	ASSN,ORG
Group, Educ.	NEA
Groups, School: Abbr.	PTAS
Group, W.W.I: Abbr.	AEF
Group, Waterfront: Abbr.	ILA
Group, Workers': Abbr.	ILO
Guesses: Abbr.	ESTS
Gun group: Abbr.	NRA
Handbook: Abbr.	MAN
Handy Latin abbr.	ETAL
Hanky decor: Abbr.	INIT
Heat units: Abbr.	BTUS
Height: Abbr.	ALT
Helper: Abbr.	ASST
Highway: Abbr.	RTE
Holy woman: Abbr.	STE
Home: Abbr.	RES
Hosp. people	RNS
Hostess's letters	RSVP
Humane group: Abbr.	SPCA
Inactive: Abbr.	RET
Individual: Abbr.	PERS
Initials, Draft	SSS
Initials, Eletronic	RCA
Initials for a fast plane	SST
Initials on an airport board	ETA
Initials on an audit	CPA
Initials, Postal	RFD
Initials, Power	TVA
Initials, Ref. book	NED
Initials, W.W.I	AEF
Initials, W.W.II	ETO,OPA,OSS
In the same place: Abbr.	IBID
Insect study: Abbr.	ENT
Insurance men: Abbr.	AGTS
Integers: Abbr.	NOS
International org.	NATO
Intuition, for short	ESP
Invitation letters	RSVP
Island off Italy: Abbr.	SAR
Italian island: Abbr.	SAR
Item on a handbag: Abbr.	INIT

It hath 30 days: Abbr.	SEPT
Jargon: Abbr.	DIAL
Jeanne or Marie: Abbr.	STE
Journalist, Certain: Abbr.	CORR
Kind of mention: Abbr.	HON
Kind of plane: Abbr.	SST
Kind of power: Abbr.	ELEC
Kind of pronoun: Abbr.	PERS,REL
Kind of type: Abbr.	ITAL
Kind of verb: Abbr.	IRR
Knowledge source: Abbr.	ENC
Labor initials	CIO
Labor org.	ILO
Land area: Abbr.	ISL
Landing craft: Abbr.	LST
Land mass: Abbr.	EUR
Land, Mideast: Abbr.	ISR
Language: Abbr.	ENG,GER,LAT
Language study: Abbr.	GRAM
Lat. abbr, Namely	VIZ
Latin abbr.	IBID
Latin abbr., Common	ETC
Latin abbreviation	ETAL
Latin abbr., Of age	AET
Law: Abbr.	STAT
Lawyer: Abbr.	ATT
Lawyer's group: Abbr.	ABA
Lectures: Abbr.	SERS
Ledger entry: Abbr.	ACCT
Legal abbreviation	INRE
Legal man: Abbr.	ATT
Letter, of a kind: Abbr.	INIT
Library list: Abbr.	CAT
Life or theft item: Abbr.	INS
Line, N.Y. subway	IRT
Liquid meas.	GAL
Literary initials	RLS
Lively, in music: Abbr.	ALLO
L.P. for one: Abbr.	REC
Machinist: Abbr.	ENGR
Madrid woman: Abbr.	SRA
Mailing address, G.I.	APO
Main et al.	STS
Man, Big: Abbr.	VIP
Manhattan, for one: Abbr.	ISL
Man or Bermuda: Abbr.	ISL
Map abbr.	LAT,RTE
Marie, for one: Abbr.	STE
Math branch: Abbr.	TRIG
Mat. time	AFT
Measure: Abbr.	GAL
Measures: Abbr.	INS
Measures, Heat: Abbr.	BTUS
Medical org.	AMA
Medit. island: Abbr.	SAR
Medit. land	ISR
Med. study	ANAT
Meeting: Abbr.	SESS
Member of a church group: Abbr.	UNIT
Member of U.S.N.	ENS
Members, Party: Abbr.	DEMS
Men, army: Abbr.	NCOS
Men, Audit: Abbr.	CPAS
Men, Capitol Hill: Abbr.	REPS,SENS
Men, Law: Abbr.	ATTS
Menlo Park monogram	TAE
Men of letters, for short	EDS
Method: Abbr.	SYS,SYST
Metric unit, for short	KILO
Middle East land: Abbr.	ISR
Middlemen: Abbr.	AGTS
Mideast initials	UAR
Midwest state: Abbr.	ILL,IND
Military abbr.	ULE
Military acronym	AWOL
Military address: Abbr.	APO
Military group: Abbr.	ROTC,SAC
Military wear: Abbr.	ODS

Mil. officers	LTS
Mil. title	GEN
Mil. unit	DET
Moments, for short	SECS
Money back: Abbr.	REF
Monogram part: Abbr.	INIT
Motoring org.	AAA
Mrs., in France	MME
Ms. men	EDS
Mus. direction	RIT
Musical direction: Abbr.	RIT
Mus. piece	SEL
Namely: Abbr.	VIZ
Native of a sort: Abbr.	CIT
NATO member: Abbr.	USA
Nautical initials	USS
Naval initials	USS
Naval off.	ENS
Naval vessel: Abbr.	LST
Navigation abbr.	SHA
N.C.O.'s	SGTS
Neighbor of Ark.	OKLA
Neighbor of Ger.	DEN
Neighbor of Ill.	IND
Neighbor of It.	SIC
Neighbor of Mass.	CONN
Neighbor of N.B.	QUE
Neighbor of Neth.	BELG
Neighbor of Nev.	OREG
Neighbor of Que.	ONT
Neighbor of U.S.	CAN
Network: Abbr.	SYS
New Deal initials	NRA
News agency, Gov't.	USIA
New World resident: Abbr.	AMER
New York time: Abbr.	EST
No longer active: Abbr.	RET
Nos. expert	CPA
Notation, Map: Abbr.	RTE
Not crooked: Abbr.	STR
Note in a date book: Abbr.	APPT
Not an orig.	IMIT
Not public: Abbr.	PERS
Numbers men: Abbr.	CPAS
N.Y. and S.F.	SPTS
N.Y.C. subway	IRT
N.Y., Ill., Cal., etc.	USA
N.Y. summer hours	EDT
N.Y. time	EST
Ocean vessel: Abbr.	STR
Of age: Abbr.	AET
Offense, Military: Abbr.	AWOL
Office copy, for short	STAT
Old draft agency: Abbr.	SSS
Older ones: Abbr.	SRS
Old Mideast initials	UAR
Old Wash. players	NATS
One of the leagues: Abbr.	NAT
One, Helpful: Abbr.	ASST
Ont., Neighbor of	QUE
Opening lines, for short	INTRO
Opponents of Reps.	DEMS
Opposite of civ.	MIL
Opposite of fem.	MASC
Opposite of lv.	ARR
Opposite of plu.	SING
Opposite of syn.	ANT
Organization: Abbr.	ASSN
Org., Auto	AAA
Org., Civil War	GAR
Org., Detroit-based	UAW
Org., Draft	SSS
Org. founded in 1890	DAR
Org., Humane	SPCA
Org., Military training	ROTC
Org., Postwar U.S.	ECA
Org., Service	USO
Org., Space	NASA

Orgs., School	PTAS
Org., Teachers'	NEA
Oslo resident: Abbr.	NOR
O.T. book: Abbr.	ISA
Others, And: Abbr.	ETAL
Ottowa's prov.	ONT
Parent org. of N.B.C.	RCA
Parisian co.	CIE
Park or Madison: Abbr.	AVE
Part: Abbr.	SECT
Particularly: Abbr.	ESP
Part of CBS: Abbr.	SYS
Part of M.I.T.: Abbr.	INST
Part of a monogram: Abbr.	INIT
Part of N. Amer.	CAN,USA
Part of Old World: Abbr.	EUR
Parts of cens.	YRS
Parts of yds.	INS
Party initials	GOP
Party man: Abbr.	REP
Party men: Abbr.	DEMS
Pen pal: Abbr.	CORR
Periods, Time: Abbr.	YRS
Personnel, Hospital: Abbr.	RNS
Pertinent: Abbr.	REL
Philatelist's concern: Abbr.	ISS
Phone book abbreviation	RES
Photo lab abbr.	ENL
Physicist's concern: Abbr.	ATNO
Piano part: Abbr.	PED
Pier group: Abbr.	ILA
Pierre's state: Abbr.	SDAK
Pitchers' statistics: Abbr.	ERAS
Place, Stopping: Abbr.	STA
Plainclothesman: Abbr.	DET
Pls. reply	RSVP
Political group: Abbr.	ADA
Political initials	GOP
Political party: Abbr.	DEM
Pol. party	GOP
Post: Abbr.	STA
Postal abbreviation	RFD
Posting, Airline: Abbr.	ETA
Post-season basketball tourney: Abbr.	NIT
Postwar U.S. agency	ECA
Power source: Abbr.	ELEC
Power-project initials	TVA
Presidential initials	DDE
Presidential monogram	DDE
Printing style: Abbr.	ITAL
Professional men: Abbr.	ATTS
Prosecutors: Abbr.	DAS
Protective group: Abbr.	SPCA
Province, Can.	ONT
Province of Can.	ALTA
Psychic initials	ESP
Publication: Abbr.	ISS
Pulpit talk: Abb.	SER
Pulpit talks: Abbr.	SERS
Punctuation mark: Abbr.	APOS
Quantities: Abbr.	AMTS
Rail complex: Abbr.	SYST
Railroad stops: Abbr.	STAS
Ranking ones: Abbr.	SRS
Recipe abbr.	TSPS
Red letters	USSR
Ref. book	ENC
Reference work: Abbr.	NED
Region: Abbr.	TER
Relative of et al.	ETC
Relative of etc.	ETAL
Relative of NATO	SEATO
Relative of an org.	ASSN
Relative of sra.	MME
Relative of sts.	AVES
Relatives of aves.	STS
Relatives of mos.	YRS
Relatives of qts.	GALS
Religious abbr., French	STE
Religious discourse: Abbr.	SER
Remainder: Abbr.	BAL
Representatives: Abbr.	AGTS
Request, Invitation: Abbr.	RSVP
Researcher's abbr.	IBID
Researcher's aid: Abbr.	ENC
Residences: Abbr.	APTS
Resident: Abbr.	CIT
Respect, Title of: Abbr.	ESQ
Response: Abbr.	ANS
Right-hand man: Abbr.	ASST
Ring arbiters: Abbr.	REFS
R.N. to M.D.	ASST
Road map abbreviation	RTE
Rough calculation: Abbr.	EST
Rubbing fluid: Abbr.	LIN
Rulers: Abbr.	EMPS
Sacred people, French: Abbr.	STES
Safeguard: Abbr.	INS
Savings-book abbreviation	INT
School course: Abbr.	ENG
School group: Abbr.	NEA
School org.	PTA
Science course: Abbr.	ANAT
Sea-going initials	USS
Seagoing initials	USN
Secret nationalist org.	IRA
Sellouts: Abbr.	SROS
Send back: Abbr.	RET
Sens' colleagues	REPS
Service branch: Abbr.	NAV,USN
Service club: Abbr.	USO
Service-mail initials	APO
Sgts.	NCOS
Shells, bullets, etc.	AMMO
Ship: Abbr.	STR
Ship initials	USS
Ship pilot: Abbr.	NAV
Shipping initials	FOB
Ships, W.W.II	LSTS
Short time, for short	SEC
Signature on some writings: Abbr.	ANON
Silver: Abbr.	STER
Sixth sense: Abbr.	ESP
Sleuth, for short	TEC
Slight difference: Abbr.	VAR
Sloping lawn: Abbr.	TER
Slow, in music: Abbr.	AND
Solution: Abbr.	ANS
Southern state: Abbr.	FLA
Sovereigns: Abbr.	EMPS
Space initials	NASA
Spanish ladies: Abbr.	SRAS
Spanish lady: Abbr.	SRA
Special kind of airport: Abbr.	STOL
Sports officials: Abbr.	REFS
Sports org.	NCAA
Staff member: Abbr.	ASST
Standard: Abbr.	NOR
State: Abbr.	ALA,ALAS,CAL,CONN,DEL,FLA, IND,OKLA,ORE,OREG,PENN,PENNA,SDAK
State and Main: Abbr.	STS
Statement: Abbr.	ACCT
Statistics, Pitching: Abbr.	ERA
Statue support: Abbr.	PED
Statute: Abbr.	ORD
Stop, Railway: Abbr.	STA
Store divisions: Abbr.	DPTS
Style, Type: Abbr.	ITAL
Subj., School	ENG
Subway, N.Y.	IRT
Sums: Abbr.	AMTS
Sunday talk: Abbr.	SER
Sundry: Abbr.	VAR

Teacher's org.	NEA
Term: Abbr.	SESS
Terminals: Abbr.	STAS
Teutonic: Abbr.	GER
Theater org.	ANTA
Theodore White subj.	PRES
Third book of O.T.	LEV
Thoroughfares: Abbr.	AVES,STS
Timetable abbr.	EST
Timetable abbreviation	ARR,STA
Timetable, for short	SKED
Time units: Abbr.	SECS,YRS
Time zone: Abbr.	EST
Title: Abbr.	ESQ,HON
Train stop: Abbr.	STA
Transport systems: Abbr.	RRS
Trial figures: Abbr.	ATTS
Trigonometry abbr.	COT
Type of type: Abbr.	ITAL
Type of verb: Abbr.	IRR
Undergraduates: Abbr.	SRS
Union, Pier: Abbr.	ILA
Units, Elec.	AMPS
U.N. member	USSR
U.S. agency	CIA,NASA,SSS
U.S. agency: Abbr.	REA
U.S.A., Mex., etc.	AMER
U.S. dept.	AGR,HUD
U.S. dry group: Abbr.	ATS
Useful abbr.	ETAL,ETC
USMA's rival	USNA
U.S.O., for one: Abbr.	ORG
U.S. 1 and others: Abbr.	RTES
U.S. spy org.	CIA
U.S. troops	GIS
Vacation state: Abbr.	FLA
Vessels, W.W.II	LSTS
V.I.P.	EXEC,PRES
V.I.P., Capitol	SEN
Voters, Certain: Abbr.	DEMS
Wall St. watchdog	SEC
Wartime group: Abbr.	OSS
Wash. people	SENS
Waterfront union: Abbr.	ILA
Way: Abbr.	RTE
Weapons: Abbr.	ORD
Weather abbr.	TEMP
Western group: Abbr.	OAS
Western nation: Abbr.	BELG
Western org.	NATO
Western state: Abbr.	ORE,OREG
Western univ.	UCLA
Western world: Abbr.	AMER
West of Sask.	ALTA
Where Haarlem is: Abbr.	NETH
Where S.F. is	CAL
Where the Shannon flows: Abbr.	IRE
White House initials	DDE
Wilmington's state: Abbr.	DEL
Wire: Abbr.	TEL
Women's org.	DAR
Word, Photo-developer's: Abbr.	ENL
Word, Savings-bank: Abbr.	INT
Words, opening, for short	INTRO
Worker's group: Abbr.	ILO
Worldwide: Abbr.	INT
World workers' group: Abbr.	ILO
W.W.II area: Abbr.	ETO
W.W.II craft	LST
W.W.II fliers	RAF
W.W.II group	OSS
W.W.II mil. woman	WAAC
W.W.I outfit	AEF

The next few pages contain fill-in-the-blank clues. These are probably some of the most repetitive clues in the crossword business. For example, the word LESE occurred in 16 of the puzzles we researched, and every time it was clued as "__ majesty". Who has ever seen a puzzle entirely free of fill-in-the-blank clues? Probably no one. However, we have not yet seen a dictionary that gives a full treatment of this type of clue.

Clue	Answer
A as in __	ALFA
__ Ababa	ADDIS
Ab __ (from the beginning)	OVO
"Able was I __ ..."	ERE
__ Abner	LIL
"__ aboard!"	ALL
__ about	ONOR
Acadians' Grand __	PRE
__ acid	AMINO
Actor Beerbohm __	TREE
Ad __	HOC
"__-a-Dale"	ALLAN
__ Adams	EDIE
__ adjudicata	RES
The __ Affair in 1797	XYZ
"The Age of __"	REASON
Agnus __	DEI
__ the air	UPIN
__ Alamos	LOS
Alfred Thayer __	MAHAN
"All about __"	EVE
"All __ go"	SYSTEMS
"All __, I'm so ..."	ALONE
All __ piece	INONE
Alma __	MATER
"__ Alone"	ALL
Alpha and __	OMEGA
Also-__	RAN
__ Alte	DER
Amino __	ACID
__ ammoniac	SAL
Amo, amas, __	AMAT
"Ancient of __"	DAYS
__ and all	ONE
"And all I ask is a __ ship"	TALL
"... and baby makes __"	THREE
__ and carry	CASH
__ and desist	CEASE
"__ and forget"	FILE
__ and image	SPIT
"__ and Lovers"	SONS
__ and sane	SAFE
"... and so __ you"	ARE
"__ and the Swan"	LEDA
__ and terminer	OYER
__ Angelico	FRA
"The __ Animal"	MALE
__ Anita	SANTA
"Anitra's __"	DANCE
Anthony __	EDEN
__ antiqua	ARS
__ Antony	MARC
Apostle James the __	LESS
__ appetit	BON
"The Apple __"	CART
__-a-prayer	DIAL
"Apres __ ..."	MOI
__ Arbor	ANN
__ arms	UPIN
"__ around the house"	AMAN
__ artium	ARS
__ asinorum	PONS
As like __ (probably)	ASNOT
__ as a rock	HARD
"__ as a Stranger"	NOT
As __ (usually)	ARULE
"At __!"	EASE
__ at ease	ILL
__ at hand	NEAR
At __ (in any case)	LEAST
At long __	LAST
__ at the switch	ASLEEP
__ au rhum	BABA
"Auld Lang __"	SYNE
"Auntie __"	MAME
Ave atque __	VALE
__ avis	RARA
__ Aviv	TEL
"A votre __"	SANTE
__ away	SALT
__ Baba	ALI
__ back (reinvests)	PLOWS
"Bad __ to you!"	CESS
Baked __	ALASKA
"Ballad of the __ Cafe"	SAD
__ basin	TIDAL
__ Bator	ULAN
"__ a bat out of ..."	LIKE
Beau __	GESTE,IDEAL
Beerbohm __	TREE
__ bellum	ANTE
Below the __	SALT
__ ben Adhem	ABOU
__ bene	NOTA
"__ bet!"	ITSA
Between the __	LINES
Beyond the __	PALE
Bide __ time	ONES
__ bien	TRES
__ bill	DUE
__ Bill	PECOS
Bitter __	ALOES
Black __	CAT,MAGIC
Black or evil __	EYE
__ blanche	CARTE
Blind __ bat	ASA
__ blue	CADET,TRUE
__ bodikins	ODS
Bon __	MOT,SOIR,TON
Bonne __	AMIE
__ bonne heure	ALA
__ bonnet	EASTER
Book __	END
"__ boy!"	ATTA,ITSA
Brass __	HAT
__ Bravo	RIO
__, Bravo, Charlie	ALFA
__ breve	ALLA
"__ Britannia"	RULE
"Brother __"	RAT
"Brown October __"	ALE
"__, Brute"	ETTU
Bucket __	SEAT
"Buenos __" (good morning)	DIAS
Buenos __	AIRES
__ buffa	OPERA
Bum __	RAP
"... __ burning bright"	TIGER
Busy as __	ABEE
"__ but the brave ..."	NONE
"The butcher, the __ ..."	BAKER
"__ but the Lonely Heart"	NONE
"__ but you"	NOONE
By __	EAR

"__ by any other name ..."	AROSE
__-cake	PATA
__ Caliente	AGUA
__ California	BAJA
Call __ day	ITA
"Call Me __"	MADAM
"__ Camera"	IAMA
__ Canals	SOO
"__ can it be?"	WHO
Canterbury's Saint __	ANSELM
__ canto	BEL
__ capita	PER
__ carte	ALA
__ cat	ONEA
Caught __-handed	RED
Caught in the __	ACT
__-ce pas?	NEST
"C'est __"	LAVIE
Charlotte __	RUSSE
Chere __	AMIE
__ chic	TRES
Chou __	ENLAI
Chou En-__	LAI
__ citato	LOCO
__ Claire	EAU
Clean __	SLATE
Clear the __	AIR
__ clear	ALL
__ clocks	TIME
"__' clock scholar"	TENO
"Cogito, __ sum"	ERGO
__ a coin	FLIP
"__ a cold, ..."	FEED
Cole __	SLAW
Collector's __	ITEM
"__ Columbia"	HAIL
"... come at __'clock"	TENO
Come to the __	POINT
Commedia dell'__	ARTE
__ cone	NOSE
Conrad's "__ Jim"	LORD
__ contendere	NOLO
Con __ (tenderly)	AMORE
Coq __	DOR
__ corner	AMEN
__ costs	ATALL
County __	SEAT
Coup d'__	ETAT
__ Cruces	LAS
__ cry	AFAR
__ culpa	MEA
__ Curie	MME
__-da-fe	AUTO
__ Dame	NOTRE
__ damnee	AME
__ dare	ONA
Dark __	AGES
__ day now	ANY
Days __	ONEND
__-day service	SAME
"__ a deal!"	ITS
"Dear __"	SIR
"Dear Sir or __"	MADAM
Debussy's "La __"	MER
__ de corps	ESPRIT
__ de deux	PAS
Deep __ well	ASA
De __ (fancy)	LUXE
"The defense __"	RESTS
__ de France	ILE
__ de la Cite	ILE
"De mortuis __ ..."	NIL
__ de Pinos	ISLA
Dernier __	CRI
Der __ (old one)	ALTE
__ de tete	MAL
__ de vie	EAU
De __ (you're welcome): Sp.	NADA

Dial __	TONE
Diamond __	LIL
"Did you __!"	EVER
"Did you __ see ..."	EVER
__ die	SINE
__ diem	PER
Dies __	IRAE
__ diet	ONA
__ dieu!	MON
Disaster __	AREA
"Ditat __," motto of Arizona	DEUS
__ dixit	IPSE
__ does it	EASY
Dog __	DAYS
"Do it or __"	ELSE
__ Dolorosa	VIA
__ dolorosa	MATER
__ Domini	ANNO
Done to __	ATEE
Don't care a __	RAP
"Don't pin that __"	ONME
"Don't tread __!"	ONME
"Do __ open umbrellas indoors."	NOT
"Do __ others"	UNTO
Dos-__	ADOS
__-do-well	NEER
Down __	EAST
__ Downing St.	TEN
D'Oyly __	CARTE
__ a dream	ASIN
"__, drink ..."	EAT
__ drive	LINE
"... __ a drop to drink"	NOR
The __ Duke (Wellington)	IRON
"__ a dull moment	NEVER
Dumb __	DORA
Dutch __	TREAT
__ eagle	BALD
"East of __"	EDEN
__ eaten (shabby)	MOTH
Eau-de-__	VIE
Ecce __	HOMO
El __	CID
__ 'em	SIC
En __	MASSE
"... end __ perfect day"	OFA
__ en point	ENTE
"__ en Rose"	LAVIE
Entr'__	ACTE
Entre __	NOUS
"... ere I __ Elba"	SAW
__ escape	NARROW
__ estate	REAL
__ est percipi	ESSE
Et __	ALII
__ et orbi	URBI
__-European	INDO
__ even keel	ONAN
__-evident	SELF
Evil __	EYE
__ exempli	MALI
__ ex machina	DEUS
__ extra cost	ATNO
__ eye	EVIL
__ eyed	SLOE
"Fables in __"	SLANG
__ facto	IPSO
__ Faithful	OLD
"__ the Fall"	AFTER
Family __	TIE
Fat __ pig	ASA
__ favor	ASKA
__ Fe	SANTA
Feel one's __	OATS
"__ fellow well met"	HAIL
"__ the fence is out"	OVER
Fer-de-__	LANCE
__ fide	BONA

Clue	Answer
Fire __	ALARM,EATER,ENGINE
First __	AID
First and __ (football term)	TEN
Fits to __	ATEE
Five and __	TEN
__ fixe	IDEE
Fly the __	COOP
Fond du __	LAC
"__ fool"	IMA
"A Fool There __"	WAS
For a __	SONG
For all __	THAT
"__ for All Seasons"	AMAN
"__ for the birds"	ITS
Foreign __	AID
"For I am poor and __"	NEEDY
"For __ a jolly good fellow"	HES
"For the love of __"	PETE
__ for one's money	ARUN
"__ for the show"	TWO
"For 2 cents __"	PLAIN
Forty-__	NINER
"For want of a __ the shoe is lost"	NAIL
"__ for your money"	ARUN
__ France	ILEDE
__ free	SCOT
A friend in __	NEED
__ fun!	SOME
__ Gail, Derby winner, 1952	HILL
__ Gang	OUR
__ Gardner	AVA
Gare du __	NORD
Gates __	AJAR
__ Gatos	LOS
Gay __	PAREE
__ generis	SUI
Gentle __	BEN
Geodesic __	DOME
__ gestae	RES
"Get __!"	AHORSE
Get the __	GATE
Get in under the __	WIRE
"... a giant __ for mankind"	STEP
Gil __	BLAS
__ gin	SLOE
"__ girl!"	ITSA
"__ Girls"	LES
Give the __	AIR
Give __ (berate,scold)	ITTO
Give __ (listen)	EARTO
"Give __ try"	ITA
__ glance	ATA
"__ gloom of night ..."	NOR
__ go	LETS
"__ go!"	LETS
"__ go bragh"	ERIN
"Go climb a __!"	TREE
"God's Little __"	ACRE
"__ goes!"	HERE
Go __ (fail)	UNDER
Golden __	RULE
"... gold in __ thar hills"	THEM
__ Goodfellow	ROBIN
"Goodnight, __"	IRENE
Good Queen __	BESS
Go to __ of trouble	ALOT
"__ got you under my skin"	IVE
Graf __	SPEE
__ Grande	CASA
"Grand Old __"	FLAG
__ grata	NON
__ gratia	DEI
__ gratia artis	ARS
"__ a Grecian Urn"	ODEON
__ green	PEA
__ the ground	EARTO
An __ the ground	EARTO
__ guard	HONOR
Gum __	ARABIC
__ Gynt	PEER
Gypsy __ Lee	ROSE
__ h'ai	BALI
__ a hand	LEND
__ Harbor, N.Y.	SAG
Hard __	ALEE
Hardly __	EVER
__ hat	OLD
__ Haute	TERRE
Have __ at it	AGO
Have __ to grind	ANAX
Have __ (watch out)	ACARE
"The __ heard ..."	SHOT
__ a heart	HAVE
__ hejirae	ANNO
__ the helm	EASE
He's __ it	HAD
Hic, haec, __	HOC
High __	NOON,SEAS
__ Hill	NOB
His __	NIBS
Hit the __	SPOT
Hit it on the __	NOSE
"__ ho!"	LAND
__ hold	TOE
Hole __	INONE
Holy __	SEE
Home __	PLATE
"Home, __"	JAMES
"Home of the bean and the __"	COD
"__ a homer!"	ITS
Homme d'__ (statesman)	ETAT
"__ homo"	ECCE
"__ horse"	GETA
"__ a horse!"	GET
__-horse town	ONE
Hot __	AIR,RODS
Hot from the __	OVEN
"How have you __?"	BEEN
"How sweet __!"	ITIS
Human __	BEING
__ hurry	INNO,INA
Huxley's "__ Hay"	ANTIC
Ibn-__	SAUD
__ the icebox	RAID
"Ici on __ francais"	PARLE
"__ I didn't already know"	ASIF
"__ if by sea"	TWO
"... if __ cares for me"	NOONE
"If this __ love"	ISNT
"I'll be __"	THERE
Ils __	SONT
"I'm all __"	EARS
"I'm __ hurry"	INNO
__ impulse (be imprudent)	ACTON
In and __	OUT
In any __	EVENT
__ incognita	RHEE
"... in corpore __"	SANO
In days of __	YORE
In __ (existing)	ESSE
In the lap of the __	GODS
__ in a lifetime	ONCE
"__ in a manger ..."	AWAY
In medias __	RES
In __ (mired)	ARUT
"__ in my heart"	DEEP
__ in one	HOLE
__ in one's bonnet	ABEE
__ in the saddle	TALL
"__ in the Sun"	DUEL
Inter __	ALIA
In a __ (upset,angry)	SNIT
__ in wait	LIES
In __ (wholly)	TOTO
"A __ in Winter"	LION

In __ words OTHER
"__ is forgiven" ALL
"__ is it?" WHAT
Isle of __ MAN,PINES
Isle of Man's House of __ KEYS
"Is __ promise?" ITA
"The __ is silence" REST
"Is __ so?" THAT
"Is there anyone __?" ELSE
"The __ is yet to come" WORST
Italy's Aldo __ MORO
"It's been __ time" ALONG
"It's __ to tell a lie" ASIN
"I've been __!" HAD
"I want __ just ..." AGAL
__ Jack UNION
Jai __ ALAI
Jane __ DOE,EYRE
"The jawbone of an __" ASS
__ Jeanne STE
Jet __ SET
__ jiffy INA
"__ John" DEAR
Johnny __ REB
"__ a jolly good ..." HES
__ Juana TIA
__ jure IPSO
"Just __ and serve" HEAT
"__ Karenina" ANNA
Keats's "__ Insolence" ODEON
Keats's "__ of St. Mark" EVE
Keep __ cool ONES
Keep __ on (watch) TABS
Kicking __ UNIT
__ kick out of GETA
Kiddie __ CARS
__ king ALA
__ King Cole NAT
"Kings __" ROW
__ the knot TIED
__-la TRA
"La __" MER
"__ La Douce" IRMA
__ lamp ARC
"__ the land of the free" OER
Lao-__ TSE
__ late TOO
"__ a laugh!" WHAT
"__ la vie" CEST
Leap __ YEAR
"Le Coq __" DOR
Le dernier __ CRI
__ Leeds, O'Neill heroine NINA
Lend __ ANEAR
"L'etat __" CEST
Library __ PASTE
__ lie BALD
Life __ SAVER
__ lift SKI
__ light NEON
Light __ under AFIRE
Like __ ITIS
Like a bump on __ ALOG
Like __ of bricks ATON
Like peas in __ APOD
Like __ (probably) ASNOT
Lincoln's __ INN
__ the line TOE
Little __ EVA
"__ little maids from school" THREE
"__ little prairie flower" IMA
"Little things mean __" ALOT
"__ live and breathe" ASI
"__ lively, please" STEP
"Lizzie Borden took __ ..." ANAX
Long __ AGO
__ Longa, ancient city ALBA
"__ long, long way to ..." ITSA

Look __ INON
Lose __ cool ONES
__ loss ATA
Love __ NESTS
"Love __ Marriage" AND
__ low (hide) LIE
Lucia's "Mad __" SCENE
Ma chere __ AMIE
__ Maggiore LAGO
__-Magnon CRO
__ majesty LESE
Major-__ DOMO
Make __ at APASS
Make __ meet ENDS
Mal de __ MER,TETE
"Mamma __!" MIA
__ man YES,TOA
The __ man INNER
"The Man __" ILOVE
__ manana HASTA
"The __ Man and the Sea" OLD
__ a manger SALLE
"__ man of ..." IMA
__ man to another ASONE
__ many words INSO
Mare's __ NEST
"__ Maria" AVE
__ the mark TOE,TOES
Marquis de __ SADE
Marshall __ PLAN
Mata __ HARI
__ mater ALMA
Matinee __ IDOL
Mats. __ and Sats. WEDS
Mauna __ LOA
Maurice __ EVANS
__ meeting MASS
"__ me impune lacessit" NEMO
"__ Melancholy" ODEON
__ meridiem ANTE
__ me tangere NOLI
"__ M for ..." DIAL
Middle __ AGES
__ Miguel SAO
__ Minor URSA,ASIA
__ a minute AMILE
__ the minute UPTO
__ miss NEAR
__ mode ALA
"__ moi, le deluge" APRES
__ Moines DES
__ moment INA
Mona __ LISA
__ monde BEAU
"Mondo __" CANE
__ monster (lizard) GILA
Moth-__ EATEN
Mount __ IDA
"Much __ About ..." ADO
__ much as INAS
__ mundi ANNO
Muscat and __ OMAN
"My end draws __, 'tis time ..." NIGH
"My heart __ up ..." LEAPS
"My kingdom for __" AHORSE
"My __ Lady" FAIR
"My Name Is __" ARAM
"__ my words" MARK
__-Nazi NEO
Neat as __ APIN
__-Neisse line ODER
Ne plus __ ULTRA
"Never __ of money spent" ASK
Nez __ (Western Indian) PERCE
Night __ OWL
"... __ nisi bonum" NIL
Norman Vincent __ PEALE
N. or S. __ AMER

__ nostrum MARE
"__, not again!" OHNO
Not __ bet ONA
Not the __ bit LEAST
Not care __ ARAP
Not give __ ARAP
Not __ in the world ACARE
"Not on __!" ABET
"Not __ Stranger" ASA
"Not __ to stand on" ALEG
Not touch with __ foot pole ATEN
__ nous ENTRE
"__ no use!" ITS
__ nova, music style ARS
Nova Scotia's Grand __ PRE
__ novel DIME
__ now UPTO
__ now (so far) ASOF
__ numeral ARABIC
__ nutshell INA
"The __ of Amontillado" CASK
__ of Aquarius AGE
"__ of bricks" ATON
__ of Cleves ANNE
A __ of color RIOT
__ of Court INNS
__ of the covenant ARK
"__ of Eden" EAST
__ of the game NAME
__ of Gilead BALM
__ of guns SONS
"__ of Hoffmann" TALES
__ of humor SENSE
"__ of India" SONG
__ of India STAR
__ of iniquity DEN
"Of __ I sing" THEE
__ of laughter GALE
__ of love LABOR
__ of luxury LAP
__ of March IDES
"__ of my dreams" GIRL
__ of Nantes EDICT
__ of (rather) SORT
__ of roses ATTAR,ABED
__ of sanctity ODOR
__ of Sharon ROSE
__ of steam AHEAD
__ of theives DEN
__ of thumb RULE
__ of Tranquillity SEA
__ of woe ATALE
"Oh, how __ to get up ..." IHATE
Old __ SOL,SALT
"... a __ o'livin'" HEAP
On __ TIME
On a __ SPREE
On the __ SPOT
"On __ by a river ..." ATREE
Once __ a time UPON
"__ One" ACT
One and __ ALL
"__ on earth ..." PEACE
One at __ ATIME
"One giant __ for mankind" LEAP
One-hoss __ SHAY
One __ million INA
__ a one (none) NARY
"One __ or two?" LUMP
__ one's hand TRY
"__ one's life depended on it" ASIF
__ one's piece SPEAK
__ one's words EAT
One __ time ATA
"One __ under God" NATION
On the __ (fleeing,hiding) LAM
On its last __ LEGS
__ on (manages) GETS
On one's __ TOES
"__ on parle francais" ICI
"On a wing __ prayer" ANDA
On __ with APAR
Op. __ CIT
Or __ ELSE
__ orange OSAGE
__ organs VITAL
__ Oro RIODE
__ out NOSE
__ out (made do) EKED
__ out (supplements) EKES
__ out (survived) RODE
__ out (won closely) EDGED
Out of __ SORTS
Out of a clear __ SKY
__ out of it SNAP
Out on a __ LIMB
"Over __" THERE
__ over lightly ONCE
Paar's "I Kid You __" NOT
Paar's "I __ You Not" KID
__ Pacific UNION
__ pajamas CATS
__ Palmas LAS
"__ a Parade" ILOVE
"... paradise __" ENOW
__ Park, Colo. ESTES
__ part ACTA
__ Passos DOS
Pathet __ LAO
__ patriae AMOR
__ Paulo SAO
Pay through the __ NOSE
Peace __ PIPE
__ Peninsula UPPER
__ penny ONEA
Petits __ FOURS
__-pie CAPA
Pig __ IRON
__-pipe cinch LEAD
__ pity SELF
__ Plaines DES
Plain or Spanish __ OMELET
Play __ APART
Play by __ EAR
Pliny the __ ELDER
__ poetica ARS
Point of __ ORDER
__ polloi HOI
"__, poor Yorick" ALAS
__ porridge PEASE
__ portico SOTTO
__ port in a ... ANY
__ precedent SETA
"Pretty maids all in __" AROW
__ price LIST
Private __ EYE
Pro __ RATA
__ pro nobis ORA
Punta del __ ESTE
__ pupil STAR
Put on __ AIRS
Put one's __ in OAR
__ qua non SINE
"The Queen's __" NAVEE
Quod __ ... ERAT
__ rabbit WELSH
__ Rabbit BRER
Rabbit __ EARS
Raison d'__ ETRE
__-ran ALSO
__ Rapids CEDAR
Rara __ AVIS
Rat-__ ATAT
__ Raton BOCA
"The Razor's __" EDGE
Ready __ ORNOT

__ red	SEE
__-relief	BAS
Rembrandt __	PEALE
__ a reputation	EARN
"__ Rheingold"	DAS
"__ Rhythm"	IGOT
"... ring I thee __"	WED
Rio __	RITA
Robert __	ELEE
"Robin __"of old song	ADAIR
__ rooms	REC
__ rose	OLD
"Rose __ rose"	ISA
Rouge et __	NOIR
Round __ ball	ASA
__ Royale	ISLE
__ rule	ASA
"... ruler of the Queen's __"	NAVEE
Run __	AMOK
Run a __ ship	TAUT
Saddle __	SORE
Saint-__, Channel port	MALO
__ sanctum	INNER
Santa __	ANA,ANITA
__ sapiens	HOMO
Sarah __ Jewett	ORNE
Sargasso __	SEA
Sault __ Marie	STE
__ scout	GIRL
__ scouts	TALENT
Sea of __	JAPAN
"__ the season ..."	TIS
__ second	INA
"The Secret of __ Vittoria"	SANTA
"__ seen everything now"	IVE
"The Seven Year __"	ITCH
Shake a __	LEG
Shake __ (hurry)	ALEG
__ share	LIONS
__ shoestring	ONA
"Shropshire __"	LAD
Sidereal __	YEAR
Sierra __	LEONE
"__ silly question ..."	ASKA
Sixth __	SENSE
"__ Skylark"	TOA
Sleep like __	ALOG,ATOP
Slippery __	ELM
Small __	FRY
"__ small world"	ITSA
Smart __	ALEC
Smell __	ARAT
Snake __	EYES
Sneaky __	PETE
Snick-or __	SNEE
"__ so brave"	NONE
Soft __	SOAP
__ soldier	TIN
Son __ sea cook	OFA
__ song	SWAN
"Song of __"	INDIA
"__ so to bed"	AND
__ souci	SANS
__ space	OUTER
Spare the __	ROD
Spin like __	ATOP
__ spree	ONA
__ spumante	ASTI
Spy __	GLASS
Stand in good __	STEAD
__ standstill	ATA
Start from __	SCRATCH
__ statesman	ELDER
Step __	ONIT
St. __, French port	MALO
__ stick	POGO
Still and __	ALL
Stop __ dime	ONA

St. Philip __	NERI
"The strife is __"	OER
__ Strip	GAZA
Sub __	ROSA
Suit __ tea	TOA
Suit to __	ATEE
Sultan of __	SWAT
Sum, __, fui	ESSE
"__ Sunday afternoon"	ONA
__ supra	UBI
"Sweet are the __ of ..."	USES
Sweetheart of Sigma __	CHI
Sweet __ of success	ODOR
"Sweet __ O'Grady"	ROSIE
"__ Sylphides"	LES
__ system	SOLAR
__ table	END
"__ Tag"	DER
"Take __ from me"	ATIP
Take it like __	AMAN
Take it on the __	LAM
"Take Me __"	ALONG
"Take __ Train," jazz classic	THEA
__-tat	RATA
Teacher's __	PET
Teen-__	AGER
"Tell it like __"	ITIS
"Tell __ the Marines"	ITTO
Terza __	RIMA
Tete-__	ATETE
Tete-a-__	TETES
"Thanks __"	ALOT
"Thanks __ so much"	EVER
"That's __, folks"	ALL
"That's a good __"	LAD
"Then __ dash of ..."	ADDA
"Then there were __"	NONE
"__ There"	OVER
"There __ any more"	ISNT
"Thereby hangs a __"	TALE
"They __ thataway"	WENT
"The __ thickens"	PLOT
__ thief	SNEAK
"This __"	ENDUP
"This one's __"	ONME
"This __ recording"	ISA
"This __ surprise!"	ISA
"Thy will be __"	DONE
__ tidings	GLAD
"Tiger __"	RAG
__ time	ATNO
__ a time	ONEAT
Time __ half	ANDA
__ time (instantly)	INNO
Tin Pan __	ALLEY
Tiny __	TIM
Tit for __	TAT
__ tizzy	INA
"To be __ to ..."	ORNOT
To __ (everyone,everybody)	AMAN
"__ to get up ..."	IHATE
__ to the good	ALL
__ to high heaven	REEK
"__ told by an idiot ..."	ATALE
__ ton	BON
"... __ too late ..."	NEVER
To __ (perfectly)	ATEE
__ to terms	COME
__ to a turn	DONE
Toujours l'__	AMOUR
"__ Town"	OUR
__ trap	SETA
__ tree	UPA
"True __"	GRIT
"__ trust a stranger"	NEVER
__ Tse-tung	MAO
__ tube	INNER
Two __ kind	OFA

Two on the __	AISLE
Uncle __	SAM
__ up	ACT
Up a __	TREE
__ up (appears)	CROPS
__ up (completes)	SEWS
__ up (develop)	SHAPE
"__ upon a time"	ONCE
__ up (prearranged)	SEWED
Up __ (stumped)	ATREE
Up to one's __	EARS
__ value	PLUS
Van Druten's "__ Camera"	IAMA
Vasco da __	GAMA
__ Vegas	LAS
__ Veneto	VIA
"The very __!"	IDEA
Vingt-__	ETUN
__ virilis	TOGA
"__ virumque cano ..."	ARMA
Vissi d'__	ARTE
Viva __	VOCE
"Vive le __!"	ROI
__ voce	SOTTO
__ volente	DEO
__ Volta	UPPER
"... volume of forgotten __"	LORE
"Von Stroheim: The man you love to __"	HATE
Vous __	ETES
__ vous plait	SIL
Vox populi, vox __	DEI
__ vult, crusaders' cry	DEUS
Wagon-__	LIT
Walking __	ONAIR
Want __ of	NONE
"__ was saying ..."	ASI
Washington & __	LEE
"__ Water fowl"	TOA
__ wave	TIDAL
__-way street	ONE
"__ we all?"	ARENT
__ wear	MENS
"__ we forget"	LEST
"__ we got fun?"	AINT
Weigh __	ATON
"__ well"	ALLS
"... were __ enow"	PARADISE
"__ Were King"	IFI
"__ were you"	IFI
What __	AMAN
"Whatever __ wants ..."	LOLA
"What a good boy __"	AMI
"What have __ to show for it?"	IGOT
"__ what I eat"	ISEE
"What's the big __?"	IDEA
"What's __ for me?"	INIT
"__ what she used ..."	AINT
"__ what was coming to me"	IGOT
Whether __	ORNO,ORNOT
__ whiz	GEE
"Who's __?"	THERE
Wild __	OATS
Winnie __ Pu	ILLE
Witches' __	TALES
"With the blue ribbons __"	ONIT
__ with (favored)	SIDED
"__ With Me"	ABIDE
__ with pride	POINT
__ world	ONE
"... ye who __ here"	ENTER
__ year	LEAP
"Yes, __"	MAAM
"You're the __"	ONE
"__, you're dead!"	BANG

This is the most important part of the book for the novice puzzler. These fifteen lists are each equivalent to one word of a crossword puzzle. On the average, one of the words in the first list of words and clues will appear in a standard, 15x15 puzzle. Thus, if you memorize this list, you can usually solve one word of a puzzle. If in addition you memorize the second list, you will be able to solve another word in the crossword. Normally, about fifteen words in a daily puzzle will appear in this list (about twenty to thirty percent of a puzzle). No other crossword puzzle dictionary provides anything similar to these lists.

LIST # 1

ala According to; Between chicken and king; In the manner, style of: Fr.; King's predecessor; State: Abbr. Term in cookery; Winglike part; ___ bonne heure; ___ carte; ___ king; ___ mode.

alai Asian, Kirghiz, Soviet range; Turkish regiment, troops; Jai ___.

ale Bar order; Beverage; Bitter brew; Cakes' companion; "Drink of Englishmen"; Partner of 'earty; Pub item; Stout's cousin, kin, relative; Suds; "Brown October ___"

alee Away from the wind; Boating term; Downwind; Helm position; Mariner's word; Nautical direction; Opposite of aweather; Protected; Robert E., for one; Sailor's call; Toward shelter, at sea; Hard ___.

aloe African, century, lily family, medicinal, succulent plant; Bitter drug-yielder; Lily; Tonic herb.

ante Before: Lat.; Certain payment; Feed the kitty; Opposite of post; Part of A.M.; Poker game: join, money, term; Pony, put up stakes; Prefix for bellum, cede, or date; Sweeten the pot; Word heard in the back room; ___ bellum; ___ meridiem.

area Bailiwick; Coded region; District; Environs; Field; Flat surface; Geography word; Location; Neighborhood; Open space; Scope; Section; Square footage; Tract; Vicinity; Zone; Disaster ___.

aria Bell song; Concert passage, selection; Melody; Forte of former star Pons, Sutherland; Met rendition; Nymph loved by Apollo; Operatic bit, feature, solo; Place for high notes; Tenor's specialty; "Un Bel Di," for one example.

ease Assuage; Comfort; Disburden; Freedom from worry; Let up; Leisure; Lighten; Luxury; Mitigate; Move carefully; Naturalness; Quiet; Relaxation; Simplify; Slacken; "At ___!"; ___ the helm.

eden Anthony; Churchill's successor; Earl of Avon; Elysium; First residence; Former Downing St. name; Garden; No pleasant place for apple eating; One bite ended it; Paradise; Site of Tree of Life; Snake's home; Well-known British P.M., statesman; Where figleaf was skirt; Anthony ___; "East of ___".

elan Ardor; Bounce; Dash; Eagerness; Enthusiasm; Impetuosity; Joie de vivre; Spirit; Verve; Vigor; Vitality.

else Besides; Differently; In addition; Otherwise than; "Do it or ___"; "Is there anyone ___?"

erie Amerind; Buffalo's waterfront; Cleveland sight; Canal finished in 1825; Gould's railroad; Great Lake city in the Keystone State; Lackawanna's old partner; One of "H.O.M.E.S."; Pennsylvania port; Sandusky's county; Scene of Perry victory; U.S. Indian tribe.

eros Aphrodite's son; Asteroid; Cupid; Greek god; Olympian; Psyche's lover.

esse Actual, essential being; Common Latin infinitive, "to be", verb; Existence, in philosophy; First word of N.C. motto; ___ est percipi; In ___ (existing); Sum, ___, fui.

oleo Cooking fat; Corn-oil product; Dairy surrogate; Grocery item; Margarine; Market purchase; Shortening; Spread; Table staple.

one Digit; Individual; Likeminded; Person; Pronoun; Rare score on a golf hole; Single; Third of a crowd; Unit; With "way", street sign; ___ and all; ___-horse town; ___-way street; ___ world; "You're the ___".

see Ascertain; Behold; Bishopric; Comprehend; Episcopacy; Grasp; Observe; Poker term, word; Regard; Understand; View; Visualize; Witness; Holy ___; ___ red.

star Arcturus; Antares, e.g.; Be the best; Betelguese, Rigel, or Spica; Canopus or sun, for one; Dog or North; Flower or fish; Headliner; Hero; Julie Andrews movie; Hero; Kind of pupil or gazer; Luminary; Mariner's guide; Marshal's badge; Outstanding one; Play the lead; Pollux; Regulus or Polaris; Take top billing; ___ of India; ___ pupil.

stir Ado; Agitate; Be in motion; Begin to wake up; Calaboose; Cooking, culinary, recipe direction; Disturb; Enliven; Excite; Fix martinis; Move; Pother;

Prison; Roil; To-do.

tree Abele or Teil; Ash; Bring to bay; Christmas decoration; Clothes rack; Corner; Cradle locale; Elder or alder; Elm or oak; English actor Beerbohm; Larch or carob; Mango or colima; Sapling; Sassafras; Shoe preserver; Sturdy plant; Ule, for one; Actor Beerbohm ____; "Go climb a ____!"; Up a ____.

LIST # 2

abet Aid's companion; Assist; Back up; Collude with; Encourage; Foster; Give aid to; Help in a way; Incite; Second in evildoing; Support; "Not on ____!"

alas Ach!; "Ah, dear me!"; Exclamation; Lack-a-day; Lamentation sound; "Oh, my!"; State: Abbr.; "Too bad!"; Woeful cry; Word of pity, regret; "____, poor Yorick".

alec Fish sauce; Guinness or Templeton; Smart one; Writer Waugh; Smart ____.

alto Choir member; Chorus part; Countertenor; Kind or horn or sax; Singing voice; Tall: Sp.; Vocal range.

anil Dye plant; Indigo source; West Indian shrub.

anon After, in a while; Familiar author: Abbr.; Later; Popular signature on some writings; Prolific writer; Shortly; Soon.

arab Ali Baba, sheik, for one; Bedouin; Hussein subject; Mecca native of Yemen; Mideast league; Omani; Street peddler; Urchin; Valuable speed horse.

asea Addled; Befuddled; Bewildered; Confused; Cruising; Lost; Off on the briny Elizabeth 2; Outward bound; Sailing; Where "Avast!" is heard.

ear Attention; Audience; Auricle; Corn on the cob unit; Fruiting spike; Heed; Often-lent thing; One of a pair; Otologist's concern; Place for a ring; Play by ___.

end Boundary; Butt; Culmination; Denouement; Finale; Finish; Football player, position; Goal; Limit; Objective; Purpose; Result; Scrap; Tackle's neighbor; Tip; Upshot; Word with play or run; Book ___; ___ table.

enter Door sign; Enroll; Go onstage; Join; Pierce; Play, script direction; Post; Record; Register; Share, walk in; "... ye who _____ here".

ere Before, poetically, verse style; Palindrome, poetic word; Present, roll-call reply in Soho; Sooner than; "Able was I ___...".

erle Dashiell's contemporary; First name for an author, detective fiction, mysteries, whodunit; One writer Gardner.

erne Large marine, water bird; Irish lake, river; Sea eagle.

erse Celt; Gaelic tongue; Irish; Scottish.

ess Feminine ending, suffix; Letter Road curve; Sigmoidal figure.

etal And others; Catch-all abbreviation; Common, handy, useful La- notation; Relative of etc.

evil Bad; Corruption; Devilish; Harmful; Injurious; Kind, type of eye; Maleficence; Offensive; Pernicious; Sinister; Wicked; ____ eye.

idea Brainchild; Brainstorm; Concept; Hunch; Impression; Inkling; Inspiration; Intention; Invention; Notion; Plan; Result of cerebral activity; Seminar product; Suggestion; "The very ___!"; "What's the big ____?"

idle Empty; Frivolous; Groundless; Inactive; Kind of talk; Loaf; Nonworking; Not in use; Otiose; Take it at ease; Trifling; Unoccupied; Useless; Vain; Waste time; Worthless.

iran Abadan's, Isfahan's, Meshed's oil country; Afghanistan, Iraq's, Pakistan's, Turkey's neighbor; Asian, Mideast, Shah's land on Caspian city; Persia, today; U.N. member; Where Tabriz is.

ire Anger; Asperity; Choler; Cobh's land: Abbr.; Emotion; Exacerbate; Pet; Pique; Spleen; Where the Shannon flows; Wrath.

ness Cape; Elliot; Headland; Monster's, Scottish, well-known Loch of note; Noun ending; Promontory; State of being: Suffix.

odor Aroma; Bouquet; Fragrance; Hint; Perfume; Quality; Redolence; Reputation; Scent; ____ of sanctity; Sweet ____ of success.

omar A caliph's, Eastern name; Famous poet; Gen. Bradley; Khayyam; Moslem leader; Oft-quoted Persian; Sharif.

oral By, in words; Evangelist Roberts; Exam; Kind of agreement, surgeon; Not written; Of the mouth; Spoken; Type of test; Viva voce; Vocal.

oran Algerian city, naval base; Mediterranean, North African seaport.

rare Distinctive; Exceptional; Hard to find; Infrequent; Lightly cooked; Like a June day, whooping cranes; Scarce; Steak instruction, order; Thin, as gas; Underdone; Untypical.

LIST # 3

all Entirely; Games in a sweep; Inclusive word; One's companion; Wholly; Word for a tie, in tennis; The works; "___ aboard!";

"___ Alone"; ___ clear; "___ is forgiven"; One and ___; Still and ___; "That's ___, folks"; ___ to the good.

are Common verb; Exist; Live; Metric land surface measure; "... and so ___ you".

arid Barren; Desertlike; Dull; Excessively dry; Jejune; Lacking interest; Like the Gobi, Mojave; Parched; Sere; Unproductive.

ashe Commander in Revolution; County in N.C.; Court champ; Laver opponent; Present-day netman; U.S. Tennis ace, name, player, star Arthur.

ate Broke bread; Consumed; Devoured; Dined; Downed; Goddess of infatuation, retribution; Had a bite of brunch; Partook of; Snacked; Supped; Used up.

elia Author linked with roast pig; Director Kazan; Essayist; Familiar pen name; Hazlitt's contemporary; Lamb; Literary signature.

eras Ages; Christian and Elizabethan; Geologic time units; Good Feeling, Mesozoic, et al.; Historic periods; Pitching statistics: Abbr.

erase Clean, clear a blackboard; Efface; Make disappear; Obliterate; Remove; Rub, take out; Wipe off.

ese Compass point; Direction: Abbr.; Inhabitant, locality, resident of: Suffix with Canton or journal; Nautical reading.

este Italian city; Princely family; Spanish direction; This, in Madrid, Toledo; Town near Padua; Villa near Rome; Punta del ___.

eton British school; English town on the Thames; Kind of collar; Short jacket.

etre Being, in Bordeaux; Common French exist, infinitive, to be, verb; Raison d'___.

ette Diminutive, feminine ending meaning small; Suffix with din, kitchen, pal, or usher.

even Balanced; Divisible by two; Equitable; Fully paid; On the level; Steady; Tied; Uniform; Unruffled; Unvaried; What some gamblers hope to get.

exit Barnum's egress; Familiar door, theater, thruway, turnpike sign; Fire escape, e.g.; Red-letter word, under a light; Stage direction; Throw the lead, at bridge; Way out.

ile Capability: Adjective suffix; France's Corse, for one; Land, river, Seine area; Miquelon; St. Pierre, e.g.; ___ de France; ___ de la Cite.

inre Apropos of; As to; Concerning; Legal abbreviation, term; Regarding.

isee Common response to an explanation; Comprehending, crystal-gazer's, fortune-teller's first words; Conversational phrase; Savvy remark; Understanding reply; Yes; "___ what I eat".

near Approach; Close-fisted, by; In the vicinity; Intimate; Kind of beer, miss; Stingy; ___ at hand; ___ miss.

neat Adroit; Exactly suited; Great, to the younger set; Pure; Relative of groovy; Straight; Tidy; Trig; Trim; Undiluted; Unwatered; Well ordered.

ogee Architectural double curve; Kind, type of pointed arch; S-shaped molding.

ole Arena, Cadiz word of cheer for toro, in Madrid; Bravo; Bullfight cry, sound; Chemical suffix; Corrida kudos; Norse name; Spanish exclamation.

ones Certain, some, Washington bills; Individuals; Numbers; People; Persons; Poss. pronoun; Singles; Wallet items; Bide ___ time; Keep, lose ___ cool.

orate Do a political chore; Emulate Bryan; Grandiloquize; Harangue; Make a speech; Sound forth, off; Speechify pompously; Take the stump.

ore Assayer's concern; Bauxite; Cinnabar; Danish, Norwegian coin; Galena; Lode yield; Mine output; Mineral; Neighbor of Ida; Scandinavian money; Western state: Abbr.

ossa Bones: It.; Fabled Hellenic mountain; Greek peak; Pelion's companion; Thessalonian sight.

rest Breather; Caesura; Coffee break; Doctor's frequent advice; Halting place; Kind of cure; Musical sign; Part of R and R; Pause; Recline; Relaxation; Remainder; Repose; Support; Take it easy; What's left; "The ___ is silence".

she Haggard heroine; Novel title; Pronoun; Ship designation, word; What Italian's ella means.

sse Compass point, reading; Mariner's heading; Wind direction: Abbr.

ten Big casino; Bowling, commandment, K.O. number; Decade; Honor, playing card; Lacrosse team; Sawbuck; A scholar's arrival hour, time; Two handfuls; ___ Downing St.; First and ___ (football term); Five and ___.

tsar Autocrat; Despot; Emperor; Former ruler; Ivan the Great; Monarch; Nicholas; Peter I, for one example; Ruler.

LIST # 4

able Code word for A; Competent; Fit; Grade, kind of seaman; One of an eager trio; Qualified; Skilled; Up to; Willing's companion.

amen Closing, final, last prayer word of agreement, approval; Egyptian deity; Ending; Kind of corner; Sabbath utterance; So-beit; Solemn assent; Verily; ____ corner.

anne Bancroft; Boleyn; British, English queen; Girl's, Stratford name; Henry VIII's second, fourth wife; Miss Baxter; Mrs. Lindbergh; Princess; ____ of Cleves.

ares Greek war god; Land measures; Olympian; Son of Hera, Zeus.

aril Pericarp; Seed coating, covering, husk, part.

asia Continent; Eastern, global, map area; Europe's neighbor; Home for two billion or so; Largest one land mass of a world seven; Part of SEATO; ____ Minor.

ata Mindanao native; Suffix in zoology, plural; ___ glance; ___ loss; One ___ time; ___ standstill.

earn Deserve; Gain; Get the hard way; Make a living; Merit; Work for; ____ a reputation.

echo Friend, lover of Narcissus; High-low card signal in bridge; Imitate; Kind of chamber; Nature's replay; Nymph of myth; Rebound; Repetition; Resound; Reverberation; Sound phenomenom; Sympathetic response; U.S. satellite.

emit Discharge; Eject; Give, throw off; Issue; Put into circulation; Send out; Utter; Vent; Voice.

ends Aims; Book holders, items; Closes; Companion of means; Conclusions; Fragments; Is done; Linemen; Remnants; Results; Terminuses; Things to make meet; Upshots; Make ____ meet.

ene Chemical suffix; Compass point; Nautical reading; Wind direction: Abbr.

eons Ages; Eternities; Geological time spans; Long periods; Years and years.

est East, in Naples; Founded: Abbr.; He is: Lat.; New York Time zone, table abbreviation; Rough calculation; Superlative ending, suffix.

ete After printemps; French, Jeanne's, Loire, Tours summer; Gallic, Midi, Nice, Paris season; Juin, juillet, et aout; Une saison.

etes Arles, Midi summers; Bordeaux, Nice, Seine seasons; French verb form; Vacation times in Paris; Vous ____.

etna Heating vessel; Lab equipment; Lamp; Lava source; Sicilians' landmark, Mongibello, peak; Tourist sight, view from Taormina; Volcano.

ever At all; Constantly; Continuously; Eternally; In, by any chance, time, way; Incessantly; "Did you ____ see ...!"; Hardly ____; "Thanks ____ so much".

into Division word; Preposition; To the center.

iota Bit; Greek letter; Jot; Smidgen; Speck; Tittle; Whit.

neo Latest, modern, recent: Prefix for classic, Gothic, or mycin; ___-Nazi.

nile Abukir's, famous, Giza's, Khartoum's, Luxor's river of Africa; Blue or White; El Bahr; Historic waterway; Shade of green.

oboe Double-reed; Hautboy; Mitch Miller's, musical, symphony instrument; Orchestra member; Woodwind.

omit Fail to do, mention; Ignore; Leave out, undone; Neglect; Overlook; Skip.

oner Ace; Distinctive, extraordinary, outstanding, rare, redoubtable person; Expert; Standout; Unique guy, individual; Unusual bloke, fellow, thing, in London.

oven Baking need, equipment; Destination for Hansel; Dutch or brick; Hot place; Kiln; Kitchen feature, item, unit; Oast; Wall appliance; Hot from the ____.

over Completed; Done; Ended; Excessive; Extra; Finished; In preference to; Past; Radio term; Remaining; Roger's companion; Surplus; "____ the fence is out"; "____ There".

rate Appraise; Be important, "in": Colloq.; Chide; Classify; Deserve; Have it made; Hotel tariff; Make the grade; Pace; Price; Rank high; Scold; Score.

rene Chateaubriand title; Coty; Descartes; Frenchman's, Gallic Name; Netman Lacoste.

sent Caused to go; Consigned; Delighted: Slang; Delivered; Directed; Dismissed; Dispatched; Mailed; Shipped; Transmitted.

spa Baden or Evian; Bath, Hot Springs, Saint-Tropez, or Vichy, for one; Health center; Marienbad, e.g.; Resort; Saratoga; Town in Belgium.

stab Brief, haphazard attempt; Casca's blow; Effort, try: Colloq.; Pierce; Sharp pain; Sudden pang; Wild guess.

ste Anne, holy woman, Marie, or Therese: French divine, religious abbr.; Jeanne d'Arc, for one; ___ Jeanne; Sault ___ Marie.

tar Feather holder, partner, of a sort; Gob; Pitch; Road surfacing; Sailor; Salt; Seafarer; Viscous liquid.

tea Ball or biscuit; Beverage; Bohea; Cha; Drink; English repast; Light snack; Noncocktail party; Oolong; Pekoe; Social affair, doing, occasion; Souchong.

LIST # 5

abel Actor Walter; Adam's son; Biblical brother; Genesis figure, victim; Man's name; Steel worker's leader; Variety's Green.
ace Expert; Golfer's thrill; Goodman or Jane; Hole-in-one; Honor card; King's superior; Red Baron, for one; Skilled hand; Tennis point, score, serve, term; Topnotcher pilot.
aero Lofty, gas: prefix for drome, dynamics, gram, nautics, or space; Of flying.
ages Bronze, Devonian, golden, Iron, Permian, Stone, and others; Centuries; Geologic periods; Gets on; Lifetimes; Matures; Ripens; Dark ____; Middle ____.
alan Actor Ladd; Arkin; Arthur's middle, man's name; Author, writer Paton; Seeger; Shepard of space fame; Short-eared dog, in heraldry; TV's King.
alit Came down to rest; Descended; Dismounted; Got off; Landed; Settled.
amor Cherub; Child in painting; Cupid; A god; Love: Lat., in Madrid, Toledo; ____ patriae.
aone Excellent; First class, rate; Prime; Superior; Top-notch.
ari "Exodus" character; Jackie's former mate; Onassis; Uris's hero, protagonist; Well-known Greek nickname.
art Buchwald; Carney; Craftmanship; Guggenheim Museum offering; Knack; Man's nickname; Painting or sculpture; School subject; Skill.
asset Auditor's entry; Beauty or charm; Ledger plus item; Money, for one; Point in one's favor; Property; Resource; Something of value; Useful quality.
east Bridge hand, position; Far, Middle, or Near; Global, world area; Lynne's direction; New England, New York, Delaware, etc.; Down ____; "____ of Eden".
edam Dutch export; Kind of mild, red-coated cheese; Netherlands town near Amsterdam; Relative of Cheddar.
eire Colleen's, Kerry's land of Baile Atha Cliath, the shamrock, Tara; Cork locale; Galway country; Island republic; Neighbor of Caledonia; O'Casey milieu; Where the Liffey, Shannon flows.
elate Cheer; Elevate the spirits; Excite; Fill with pride; Gladden; Inspire; Make exultant; Puff up; Raise the spirits.
eli Biblical name; Eastern collegian; Hebrew judge; High priest; Ivy Leaguer; New Havenite; Samuel's O.T. teacher; Wallach or Whitney.
ell Architect's concern; Building wing; 45 inches; Hardly 'eaven; House part; Letter; Unit of old length measure.
era Christian, for one; Epoch; Pitching data, statistics: Abbr.; Time period.
iago Cassio's slanderer; "Othello" role; Shakespearean character; Stage villain of drama.
lane Air, ocean, sea route; Alley; Bowling area; Byway; Drury, for one; Highway feature, unit; Passage; Sprinter's pathway.
lese ____ majesty.
nee Born, bridewise: Fr.; Once maiden-named; Society page, Wedding-account, notice word.
nero Black, in Rome, Siena: It.; Character in "Quo Vadis"; Detective-fiction name; Emperor; Hot, infamous fiddler; Pianist Peter; Roman violinits; Seneca's pupil; Sleuth Mr. Wolfe.
nest Aerie; Cozy spot; Cuddle in; Group of objects fitted together easily; Henhouse unit; Kind of egg; Kingfisher's, oriole's home; Retreat; Tree sight; ____-ce pas?; Mare's ____.
ode Canticle; Form of verse; Horatian, for one; Keats specialty, work; Pindaric forte; Poetic form, output.
olio Conglomeration; Hodgepodge; Medley; Miscellany; Mishmash; Mixture; Pastiche; Potpourri; Spicy stew.
orel Russian, Soviet city on the Oka of U.S.S.R. 200 miles south of Moscow.
sea Adriatic; Azov, for one; Black, Dead, Red, or White; Caribbean; Freuchen subject; Huge amount; Main; Mosarrat's cruel domain; North or Ross; Ocean swell; One of a world seven; ___ of Tranquility; Sargasso ___.
snap Bean or dragon; Break quickly; Cinch; Cookie; Easy job; Part, sound suddenly; Photo; Sinecure; ____ out of it.
spar Bandy words; Boom; Box; Coast Guard girl; Crystalline mineral; Mast; Shadowbox; Ship pole; Train for a bout; Wac's cousin; Yard.
step Action; Choreographer's concern; Footfall; Gait; Phase; Procedure; Progression; Rung; Scale degree; Short distance; Stair; Walk; Word with lively, one, two, or up; "... a giant ____ for mankind"; "____ lively, please".
stlo Capital of Manche; French, Normandy town; Site of W.W.II battleground city.
toe Digit; Drive a nail obliquely; Kicker; Kind of dancer; Part of a golf club, shoe; Type of hold; ___ hold; ___ the line; ___ the mark.
unit Army group; Basic thing; Constituent; Determinate amount; Item; Member of a church group: Abbr.; Military body; Monad; One; Section; Specific quanti-

ty; Kicking ____.
ural Asian, Russian, U.S.S.R. range; Caspian tributary; Chkalov's, Eurasian, Soviet river.
urge Aching; Advocate; Be insistent; Desire; Exhort; Goad; Hankering; Importune; Impulse; Instigate; Motivate strongly; Plead; Press.
uses Applications; Consumes; Customs; Employs; Exercises; Functions; Practices; Purposes; Takes advantage of; Wields; "Sweet are the ____ of ...".
yser Belgian, European, Flanders, French river into the North Sea.

LIST # 6

aces Ashe's specialty; Assets for no-trump; Certain serves; Experts; Holes-in-one; Honor cards; Points won by a single stroke; Pros; Some fliers.
aide Adjutant; Assistant; Girl Friday's role; Helper; Military man; Sidekick; Staff member; Underling.
ajar At variance with; Clashing; Discordant; Lacking, out of harmony; Like some doors; Partly open; Word for heavenly gates; Gates ____.
alae Winglike parts: Lat.
ana Collection of data, facts, items, quotes; Literary scraps; Miscellany; Odds and ends; Prefix for gram; Santa ___.
ane Before twa; Chemical suffix; French donkey, in Dijon; Scottish one.
ant Busy fellow; Eciton; Fast, to slow: Abbr.; Hill dweller; Industrious one; Leaf cutter; Opposite of syn.; Pharaoh, for one; Red or black insect; Source of formic acid.
ara The Altar of the sky; Brazilian macaw; Constellation; Goddess of vengeance; Parseghian.
atom Jot; Kind of smasher; Mighty mite; Monad; Particle of a molecule; Power source; Tiny amount, portion; Whit.
atone Agreed; Do penance; Expiate; In harmony; Make amends up for; United.
beer Beverage; Bock, for one; Brew; Drink; German export; Lager; Rarebit ingredient; Swanky or stout; Tavern offering.
elsa Famed lioness; Girl's name; Lioness; "Lohengrin" heroine; Maxwell; Miss Lancheser; Prin-Princess of Brabant; She was born free.
eric Colonizer of Greenland; Early famous explorer; Father of Leif; Norse navigator, pioneer; Portman; The Red.
eris Greek goddess of discord, strife; Sister of Ares; Tosser of a mythical apple.
errs Blunders; Deviates from aim; Goes wrong; Misdoes; Misses a fly ball; Sins; Slips up; Strays.
erst Formerly, in poems; Of yore; Onetime, in old days, style; Whilom.
esne Domestic slave; Early Anglo-Saxon laborer; Old-time flunky; Serf.
ester Acid-alcohol organic compound; Chemical salt.
ewer Big-mouthed vessel; Pitcher.
hare Certain quarry; Constellation Lepus; Hounds' leader; Leporid; Meadow creature; Rabbit's cousin; Rapid rodent; Run swiftly; Small March animal; Speedy one.
hero D.S.C. winner; Good guy; Hellespont girl; Leading, Medal of Honor man of the hour; Leander's love; Play role; Protagonist; Type of sandwich; V.I.P. of silents.
ira Dublin initials; Gershwin; Man's name; Secret nationalist org.; Writer Wolfert.
irene Byzantine empress; Former dancer Castle; Greek goddess of peace; "Goodnight" girl; Miss Dunne; One of the Horae; "Goodnight, _____".
iris Blue flag; Eye part; Rainbow; Spring flower; Writer Murdoch.
iron Do housework; Early age; Golfbag club, item; Mangle; Mashia or wedge; Minnesota product; Press; Symbol of strength; Word for Wellington; The ____ Duke (Wellington); Pig ____.
isle Alderney, Britain, or Man, for one; Atoll component; Key; Land area; St. Helena or Elba; Wight or Capri, e.g.; ____ Royale.
noon Between A.M. and P.M.; Brightest, highest point; Day, whistle time; Opposite of nadir; Ten o'clock scholar's hour; Zenith; High ____.
nor Common correlative; Conjunction; Connective; Direction, Oslo resident, standard: Abbr.; Eur. country; Neither's companion, partner; "... ___ a drop to drink"; "___ gloom of night ...".
nose Cyrano's worry; A kind of dive; Margin of victory, winning, sometimes; Meddle; Pry; Sniff; Something to follow; ____ cone; Hit it on the ____; ____ out; Pay through the ____.
old Archaic; Antique; Dated; Dyed: Abbr.; Like King Cole; Previous; Second-hand; 30, to some; Veteran; Word with maid or master; ___ Faithful; ___ hat; "The ___ Man and the Sea"; ___ rose.
orne Caen's, Normandy, Moselle river; Department in France; Sarah ____ Jewett.
ria Estuary; Narrow, small inlet.
role Aida or Salome; Characterization; Function; Hamlet or Ingenue, for one; Part in a play; Thespian's goal.
scar Bare place on mountainside;

Capone feature; Certain tissue; Cicatrix; Cliff; Do damage; Heidelberg memento; Isolated rock; Mark; Old wound.

seen Experienced; Noticed; Observed; Perceived; Pictured; Realized; Spied; Spotted; Understood.

sere Arid; Burned out; Desert-like; Desiccated; Like the Sahara; Waterless; Withered.

sled Coaster; Cutter; Go-devil; Luge; Pung; Toboggan; Vehicle.

sta Depot, fixed, post, railway road stopping place, timetable abbreviation; Train or bus term.

stet Dele's opposite; Galley notation; Printing direction, symbol, term; Proofreading word.

tier Fastener; Gallery; Pinafore; Row; Shoelace, for one; Stadium feature; Stratum.

tnt Blasting need; Explosive; Handle-with-care material.

ursa Constellation; Little bear; Major or Minor; Sky animal; ____ Minor.

LIST # 7

abed Not up and about; Resting; Retired; Taking repose; Where one's asleep; ____ of roses.

acre Brazilian state; Israeli harbor; Palestine, Mideast seaport; Realtor's, farm unit; "God's Little ____".

acts Biblical book; Decrees; Feigns; Functions; Impersonates; Skits; Takes steps.

ades Beverages; Cool, summer soft drinks; Thirst quenchers.

adit Access; Entrance; Mine approach, tunnel; Passage.

ado Bustle; Fuss; Stir; "Much ___ About ...".

ales Beverages; Brews; Certain festivals; Malt liquors; Pub drinks; Whistle-wetters.

ani Cuckoo's cousin; Tropical blackbird.

ants Aardvark diet, meal; Communal insects; Formicidae; Industrialists of a sort; Leaf-cutters; Picnic spoilers; Tiny creatures.

arena Colosseum, for one; Game place; Kind, type of amphitheater; Retiarus' milieu; Sports area, enclosure; Stadium; Where the action is.

arete Narrow mountain crest; Rocky, sharp ridge; Spur on a peak.

arr Flight word: Abbr.; Opposite of dep., lv.; Timetable entry.

aver Allege; Assert; Claim; Declare; Insist; State positively; Verify.

deed Accomplishment; Activity; Document; Exploit; Gest; Legal paper, transfer; Scout's good objective, thing.

ears Appendages; Corn on the cob; Front-page boxes; Hearing aids; Jug handles, parts; Organs often lent; Pitchers and walls have them; Projections; Spikes; "I'm all ____"; Rabbit ____; Up to one's ____.

eat Chew; Consume; Corrode; Devour; Erode; Mother's command; Sup; Use up; "___, drink ..."; ___ one's words.

elba Historic, Italian, Mediterranean, Tuscan ex-isle scene near Corsica?

elle French pronoun; She, in Paris; Word for a fille.

epic Account of a sort; Heroic; "The Iliad", "Odyssey", for one example; Impressively great; Movie-ad word; On a grand, large scale.

erato Menander's one Muse of poetry; Sister of Calliope.

erin Albion's neighbor; Cork's, leprechaun, limerick, poets', shamrock, Tralee's land; Mavourneen's place; Name for a green island; "____ go bragh".

esau Biblical figure, twin; Brother of Jacob; Genesis character, name; He sold his birthright; Pottage buyer; Son of Isaac.

eve Adam's rib; Apple-giver; Dec. 31, for one; First lady; Holiday time; Miss Arden; Mother of mankind; Poetic time of day; Woman; "All about ___"; Keats's "___ of St. Mark".

halo Angelic aura, feature, I.D.; Circle; Hallmark of the good; Headgear for some; Nimbus; Ring.

imam Caliph; Islamic, Mohammedan priest of Mideast; Moslem leader, title; Mosque official.

inert Indolent; Lacking motion; Like neon, some gasses; Powerless; Sluggish; Unmoving.

late Better than never; Delayed; 11:30 P.M., midnight, to some; Like George Apley, trains; Overdue; Recent; Slow; Word on "Arrivals" board.

lie Be situated; Fabrication; Famous Norwegian; Former name in U.N. lore; Golfer's ball position, concern, situation; Stay put; ___ low (hide).

mess Army hall, meal; Botch; Dinner of a kind; Disarray; Hodgepodge; Jumble; Mix-up; Predicament; Something to clean up; State of snafu.

oar Boat accessory; Propellor; Rowing need, equipment; Scull; Sweep; Put one's ___ in.

oil Alaskan find; Art medium, work; Auto need; Fuel; Iranian export; Kind of lamp; Linseed, tung tree product; Painting; Pomade; Salad topping; Symbol of duplicity.

olla Earthen, wide-mouthed jar; Mexican stew; Spanish pot.

opera "Aida"; Bizet, Donizetti, musical, Wagnerian work; Covent Garden offering; Lincoln Center unit; Lyric drama; Stage fare; Word with horse and comic; _____ buffa.

ora Anglo-Saxon money; Mouths; Border: Lat.; Hour: It.; Old English coin; ___pro nobis.
orle Architectural fillet; Heraldic band, bearing, term; Shield border; Voided escutcheon.
oslo City of the Storting; European, Northern, Olaf's capital; Fiord, port in Norway; Formerly, modern Christiania; Seat of Nobel Institute.
otoe Nebraska, Plains, Western Indian; Siouan.
race Competition; Contest; Derby, for one; Hurry; Marathon; Strong current; Track event; Watercourse.
reed Calamus; Cattail; Clarinet, for Famous former Knicks' star Willis; Loom part; Marsh growth; Musical instrument; Oboe; Papyrus, for one; Six cubits.
ring Arena; Bell sound; Best man's burden; Encircle; Opera cycle; Phone call; Wagnerian series, work.
rule Control; Criterion; General or slide; Govern; Have, hold sway; It's often golden; Precept; Render a decision; "____ Britannia"; Golden ____; ____ of thumb.
set Arranged; Bridge, new-math term; Clique; Determined; Firm up; Fixed; Matched group, tableware; Movie local; Jet ___.
site Locale; Location; Place; Position; Scene of action.
sss Gov't, U.S. agency: Abbr.; Leaky noise; Old draft HQ, initials, org.
talc Barbershop item; Body powdery substance; Chalky mineral; Soft stone.
user Addict; Consumer; Customer; Employer.

LIST # 8

abie Broadway hero, role; Name in long-run play, show; Nichols' character; Rose's beloved mate, spouse; Stage husband.
act Behave; Decree; Function; Operate; Perform; Play the part of; Stage turn; Statute; Take steps; Caught in the ___; "___ One"; ___ up.
adar Hebrew, Jewish month; Shebat's follower.
ade American, U.S. humorist; Beverage; Ending with block or stock; Fruit punch; Soft drink; Summer cooler.
adore Be fond of; Hold dear; Kneel before; Like highly, greatly (informally); Look up to; Love; Worship.
agar Culture, lab medium; Gelling, thickening agent; Pulitzer historian (1934); Seaweed product, substance.
agee American writer James; Askew; Awry, old style; Late critic; Pulitzer winner, 1958; U.S. author.
ago Bygone; In the past; Since; Have ___ at it; Long ___
ali Baba; Boxing, Eastern, Heavyweight, Oriental name; Caliph; MacGraw; Muhammed; ___ Baba.
ami French friend; Paris pal; "What a good boy ___".
anew Freshly; Once more; Over again; What "de novo" means.
aral Asian, Russian sea east of Caspian; Soviet lake.
arno Late cartoonist; Peter; River of Tuscany, Florence, Italy.
ash Certain Wednesday; Kind of blonde; Residue; Rowan shade tree; Volcanic matter.
aura Aspect; Atmosphere; Distinctive quality; Emanation; Nimbus; Subtle stimulus.
cite Adduce; Mention; Name; Quote; Refer to precedent; Specify; Summon.
deer Bambi; Cud chewer; Forest, zoo animals; Red or roe; Ruminant; Rural highway hazard; White-tail; Wild game.
ebon Black; Dark color; Inky.
eel Elusive fellow; Fish; Seafood delicacy; Slippery or electric customer, one; Smorgasbord item.
egad "Heavens!"; Major Hoople's word; Mild expletive; Old exclamation, oath; Zounds!
elite Choice part; Creme de la creme; The Four Hundred; Leading members of a group; Top-notch class; Type size; Upper crust.
emu Big, earthbound, flightless, large bird; Relative of the cassowary; Symbol on Australian coin.
enid Arthurian woman; Bagnold; Feminine name; Geraint's love, wife; "Idylls" heroine; Oklahoman city; Tennyson lady.
enna Formerly Castrogiovanni; Sicilian city, resort, town.
erat Common Latin verb "to be", "was"; He was, in Rome; Part, word of Q.E.D.; Quod ____ ...
ern Fish-eating bird; Man's nickname; Sea eagle.
err Be incorrect, wrong; Blunder; Deviate; Go amiss, astray; Miscalculate; Misdo; Slip.
inane Characterless; Empty; Fatuous; Insubstantial; Pointless; Shallow; Silly; Vacant; Void.
last Certain straw or mile; Endure; Foot model; Hold on; Shoe form, part; Terminal; Word for a Mohican; At long ____.
least Kind of common denominator; Minimal; Part of l.c.m.; Slightest; Tiniest; At _____ (in any case); Not the _____ bit.
lent Afforded; Did a bank job; Forty weekdays; Imparted; Provided; Seasonal time; Spring period.
mete Allocate; Allot; Deal, give, parcel out; Dole.
nne Compass mark, point, reading; Wind direction: Abbr.
onto Aware of; Familiar with; Hep;

Preposition; Undeceived; Wise.

otic About, of the ear; Auditory; Auricular; Producing: Suffix.

oval Athletic field; Face, pecan shaped a certain way; Elliptical; Relative of a circle; Roundish; Sports area; Stadium; A White House room.

ovate Egg-shaped, in a way; Elliptical; Like Humpty Dumpty; Partly roundish.

ran Absconded; Fled; Hurried; Norse sea goddess; Operated; Stood for election; Took off; Wife of Aegir; Also-___.

rant Bombast; Carry, go on; Declaim; Disclaim noisily; Make a scene; Rave's pal; Talk turgidly.

rear Bring, rise up; Erect; Grade of admiral; Hindmost; In the back; Kind of guard; Nurture; Stern.

rein Bridle part of a horseman's gear; Check; Control; Guide; Halter; Hold in; Restraint.

seat Boxoffice quest; Do ushering; Headquarters; Hot or driver's; A kind of belt; Membership; Position; Bucket ____; County ____.

seed Beginning; Bulb's relative; Canary food; Germ; Origin; Plant; Progeny; Rank, as contestants; Sesame product.

sets Bulbs for planting; Collections; Coteries; Defeats at bridge; Match parts, in a game; Matched groups; New-math words; Scenery; Solidifies; Stage designs; Tennis units; Theater scenery.

smog Air-pollution factor; Atmospheric hybrid; City-sky problem, sight; Los Angeles specialty; Urban blight, nuisance; Weather report, word.

tele Distant, far: Prefix with cast, gram, graph, meter, phone, photo, printer, scope, vise, and vision.

tess Fictional girl's nickname; Hardy heroine; Mrs. Dick Tracy.

test Binet-Simon, for one; Examination; Seek to find out; Series of questions; Something to study for; Student's concern; Tryout.

LIST # 9

abou Arabian, Oriental, Eastern name; ____ ben Adhem.

afar At a, from a, in the distance; Out of range; Remotely; ____ cry.

agate Playing marble; Small type size.

air Area of pollution; Broadcast; Ditty; Emptiness; Express; Manner; Publicize; Service station giveaway; Strain; Clear the ___; Give the ___; Hot ___.

also As well; Besides; Furthermore; Likewise; ____-ran.

amid Among; Chemical prefix; During; Encompassed, surrounded by; In the center; Together with.

amie French companion; Gallic, Parisian friend, in Lille; Bonne ____; Ma chere ____.

anti Against; Contra; In disagreement; No-voter; One opposed to pro; Prefix with aircraft, body, freeze, or trust; Thumbs down.

arts Buchwald, Carney, Linkletter, and others; College study course, field, subject; Tricky actions; Wiles.

ase Chemical suffix; Enzyme ending; Grieg, Ibsen character; Peer Gynt's mother.

asst Aide: Abbr.; Helpful one; R.N. to M.D.; Right-hand man; Staff member.

atee Done to ____ (perfectly); Fit to ____; Suit to ____.

can Container; Neighbor of U.S.; Part of N. Amer.; Preserve; Sardine locale.

canoe Birchbark; Hiawatha's small light craft; Kayak or proa; Narrow paddleboat, in a way; Summer-camp gear.

cree Algonquian tribe; American, Canadian, Manitoba, Western Indian.

ede Dutch city; Netherlands commune; Nigerian town.

emote Affect feeling; Emulate thespians; Ham it up; Overact; Play to the gallery; What some actors do in a way in "East Lynne".

eos Aurora; Greek goddess of dawn.

erose Irregular; Notched; Sawtoothed; Uneven.

erred Committed a faux pas; Goofed; Misdid; Misstepped; Mistook; Sinned; Strayed; Wandered; Went astray, wrong.

here Call to Fido; Hither; Now's companion, partner; Present; Roll-call response; "____ goes!"

ice Bartender's need; Chill; Cool; Diamonds, to Lorelei: Slang; Dick Button's milieu; Drinkers' rocks; Footing for Eliza; Frozen dessert; Kind of cube; Weather word.

inn Hostelry; Lodging place; Motel of yore; Tavern; Traveler's stopover spot; Wayside, for one; Lincoln's ___.

irani Citizen, man of Tabriz; Mideasterner people; Native of Isfahan; Shiraz, Teheran resident.

iter Appian Way; Brain channel; Chariot route; Latin journey; Old roman road for Caesar; Passage in anatomy; Relative of via.

lear Father of Goneril, Regan; Shakespearean character, role; Tragic king of Elizabethan drama; Writer of light verse.

nat King Cole; Man's nickname; One of the B.B., Mets' league: Abbr.; Turner; ___ King Cole.

net Cod catcher; Final; Free and clear; Gain; Part of the court scene; See-through material;

Seine; Snare; Tennis, trawler gear; Trapeze insurance.

olea Genus of trees; True olive shrubs.

oles Arena sounds; Bravos; Bull-ring cries; Cheers for a matador; Corrida encouragement, plaudits; Torero's praises; Violinist Bull and others.

omen Black cat, for one; Foreboding; Foretoken; Harbinger; Portent; Prognostic; Sign; Soothsayer's need.

once Beginning of a fairy tale; Formerly; If, whenever; ___ in a lifetime; ____ over lightly; "____ upon a time".

ort Crumb; Food fragment; Morsel; Table scrap.

otis Amos of baseball; Colonial early patriot; First name in stage lore; Revolutionary figure; Skinner of stage; U.S. inventor.

rang Called; Chimed; Pealed; Phoned; Resounded; Summoned, in a way; Tolled.

reap Cut grain; Garner; Gather in; Get a result; Glean; Harvest.

ret Abed, emeritus, no longer active, send back: Abbr.; Soak, as flax; Steep.

rho After pi; Greek letter.

rise Appear; Bullish time; Companion of shine; Emerge; Get up; Hill; Occur; Rear; Rebel; Singer Stevens; Slope.

rite Anglican, for one; Ceremonial; Customary practice; Formality act; Liturgy; Observance; Solemnity.

scan Analyze poetry, verse; Glance, look over; Read meter quickly; Scrutinize.

scene Landscape; Locality; Location; Place of action; Play part; Setting; Vista; Lucia's "Mad _____".

seer Al Capp's Old Man Mose; Augur; Crystal gazer; Farsighted one; Fortune teller; Prophet; Things-to-come expert; Visionary.

shoe Brake part; Brogan; Do a stable job; Loafer; One-two subject; Oxford; Pump.

stag Antlered animal; Buck; Certain kind of party; Dance extra; Deer; Huntsman's quarry; Men's gathering; Wallflower's kinsman.

stay Brace; Check; Collar prop; Command to a dog; Delay; Hang on, in poker; Hold back; Old corset support; Restrain; Sojourn; Stop; Tarry.

stere Cubic meter; Measure of capacity; Metric volume.

tee Golfing accessory, adjunct, aid, area; Launching pad, locale on the links; Letter; Mark in curling; Pagoda ornament; Palmer's need; Pipe joint.

tend Incline; Look after; Mind; Nurse; Watch over.

tra Before la; Musical song syllable; Refrain part; ___-la.

tret Allowance for waste.

undo Bring to ruin; Cancel; Loosen; Nullify; Release; Take apart.

LIST # 10

acme Culmination; Height; Highest point; Peak; Pinnacle; Zenith.

agog Bug-eyed; Eager; Excited; Expectant; Stirred up; Twittery.

akin Allied; Analogous; Cognate; Compatible; Like unto; Related; Similar.

alt Air pilot's concern: Cockpit abbreviation; High in pitch: Mus.

any At all; Before one or body; Indefinite word; One; Some; ___ day now; ___ port in a ....

ape Baboon; Copy; Follow slavishly; Gibbon; Mimic; O'Neill subject; Primate; Tailless monkey.

atlas African range; Father of the Pleiades; An ICBM; Mainstay; Missile; Reference book; Strong man with a load.

atop Above; At the summit; Overhead; Sleep like ____; Spin like ____.

bare Bring to light; Divulge; Empty; Expose; Minimal; Reveal; Show; Strip; Uncover; Unmask.

den Cub Scout unit; Hideout; House part; Neighbor of Ger.; Retreat; Room; Study; Thieves' place; ___ of iniquity; ___ of thieves.

edge Advantage; Cutting part; Move gradually; Plain or deckle; Sharpness; "The Razor's ____".

ego Conceit; Freudian topic, word; I, in Latin; Id's master; Part of the psyche; Psychiatric concern; Self-esteem; Something to bolster; Vanity.

enos Adam's grandson; Biblical name; Ex-Card Slaughter; Genesis man; Seth's son.

eri Biblical name; Much: Prefix; Silk maker worm; Son of Gad.

eta Airport line posting, board initials: Abbr.; Greek letter, vowel.

eva A Gabor; Girl's name; Hitler's love, wife; Le Gallienne; Stowe heroine; Little ___.

event Activity; Happening; Incident; Outcome; Proceeding; Shotput, for one; Sports meet; In any _____.

icon Byzantine art work; Holy, sacred image; Religious object.

ides Caesar's bane; Certain ill-fated dates in the Forum; Chemical suffixes; Roman period; ____ of March.

init First letter, of a kind: Abbr.; Hanky decor; Item on a handbag; Monogram part: Abbr.; "What's _____ for me?"

item Agenda, list unit; Article; Entry; News brief, piece, release; Paragraph; Particular; Thing; Collector's ____.

knee Cypress feature; Genu; Halfback's vulnerable spot; It's above the tibia; Joint; Leg part; Patella; Word before deep or high.

liar Ananias; Deceitful, untrustworthy one beyond belief; Double-talker; Epithet used in politics; Fabulist; Fibber; Misrepresenter; Mythomaniac.

lit Bed, in Paris; Brightened; College subject, for short; Illuminated; Kindled; Started the fire; Wagon-___.

nasa Astronauts' org.; Moonlighting group; Moonshot sponsor; Space initials; U.S. agency.

neap A certain tide; Wagon pole, tongue: Dial.

neon Bright, display, Star's lighting; Gaseous element; A kind of tavern sign; ___ light.

nora Actress Bayes; Girl's name; Ibsen character, heroine, role; Mrs. Helmer; Nick Charles's wife.

oer Anthem contraction; Finished, in verse; Poetic ended, word, term; "___ the land of the free"; "The strife is ___".

onion Breath strengthener; Cocktail additive; Gibson, salad, shish kebab ingredient; Kind of soup; Pearl or Bermuda; Pungent bulb; Vegetable.

otter Aquatic mammal with webbed feet; Badger's relative; Fur-bearing, playful, water animal.

pest Fly, for one; Gnat or rat; Hanger-on; Nuisance; Sticky, unwelcome one.

rain April forecast; Ark weather; Kind of coat, dance; Maugham story; Outing, picnic spoiler; Pour; Shower.

rama Central American Indian; Deity, Epic hero, figure in Hindu myth; Incarnation of Vishnu; Thailand king.

read Enjoy a book; Interpret; Make out; Perused; Register; Scan; Use the library; What Johnnie can't do.

red Buttons, Grange, or Holzman; Florid; Flushed; Morning-after eyes; Roulette bet; Scarlet; Shade; Skelton; Snoopy's Baron; Caught ___-handed.

reel Bobbin; Film part; Lively dance; Relative of a hornpipe; Spool; Sway; Virginia, for instance.

reno Gambling milieu; Land of the would-be free; Neighbor of Virginia City; Nevada, Western city for one-armed bandits in Hoover Dam's state near Lake Tahoe; Women's lib mecca.

res Home: Phone book abbreviation; Legal acts, matters, things, with "gestae"; ___ adjudicata; ___ gestae; In medias ___.

safe Arbiter's decision; Bank fixture; Baseball umpire's call; Dependable; In the clear; Prudent; Unhurt; ___ and sane.

salt Corn; Dead Sea, Utah flats feature; Nautical man; Preservative; Save, with "away"; Season; Table item; ___ away; Below the ___; Old ___.

seem Appear; Feign; Look.

sense Connotation; Feeling in one's bones; Grasp; Hearing, for one; Meaning; One of five; Sight or Touch; Wisdom; ___ of humor; Sixth ___.

ski Alpine, Sun Valley gear; Engage in a sport; Footwear of a sort; Grenoble item; Runner; Schuss; Slalom; Specialized strip of wood; ___ lift.

sol After, follower of fa; Bull-fight-arena section; Coin of Peru; Money of Lima; Musical note; Roman sun god; Old ___.

stat Ending, suffix with gyro or thermo; Fixed, law: Abbr.; Office copy, for short.

stem Arrest; Check; Flower bearer; Originate, with "from"; Plant part; Prow; Restrain; Ski maneuver; Stalk.

stop Crossing sign; Defeat; Interrupt; Kind of watch; Organ part; Period; Stay; Traffic sign at a through street.

sts Addresses, arteries, State and others, thoroughfares: Abbr.; Kitts and Louis; Main et al.; Relatives of aves.

tare Biblical weed; Common vetch; Weight deduction.

tease Annoy; Back-comb hair in a way; Card, as wool; Coquette; Pester; Tantalize; Taunt; Trifle with.

tete Head, in Lyons, Paris: Fr.; Parisian pate; Place for a chapeau, yeux, and nez; With "a-tete", cozy meeting; Mal de ___.

tiara Coronet; Diadem; Headdress; Opera-box sight, wear.

tore Raced; Ran madly; Rent; Ripped; Rushed; Sped.

tre After uno and due; Italian number, numeral; Three, in Turin.

used Accustomed; Handled; Kind of car; Not brand-new; Secondhand; Spent; Took advantage of; Worn.

LIST # 11

aba Arabian cloak, cloth, garment; Camel's-hair fabric, robe; Desert coat; Lawyer's group: Abbr.; Rhyme scheme.

abba Biblical, Eastern-church, Jewish title; Rhyme scheme; With "Mr. Eban", Israeli statesman.

age Birth-certificate item; Iron or teen; Long time; Mature; Mellow; Period; Ripen; Vital statistic; ___ of Aquarius.

agio Exchange premium, rate; Money-changing fee; Trade discount word.

agra Mausoleum, Uttar Pradesh city on the Jumna; Site of Taj Mahal; Tourist mecca, stop in India.

alibi Courtroom defense; "I wasn't there," e.g., for example; Le-

gal excuse; Story, of a kind.
ame French spirit, sentiment; Gallic soul; ___ damnee.
anta Architectural, building pier; Broadway, stage group: Abbr.; Pilaster; Theater org.
apart Aside; Independently; Individually; Into pieces; Isolated; Separated; Play _____.
arose Came into play; Cropped up; Faced the dawn; Rebelled; Words from Gertrude Stein; "_____ by any other name ...".
auto Detroit product; Item from Flint; Kind of suggestion; Limousine; Nader subject; Parking problem; Prefix for mate or graph; Word with bahn, crat, or mat; ____-da-fe.
bar Drinking counter, place; Impediment; Ingot; Keep out; Kind of bell; Legal group; Nineteenth hole; Obstruct; A profession.
cane Chastise in a way; Fix a chair; Fred Astaire prop; Kind of sugar source; Rattan; Stick; Thrash; "Mondo ____"
data Computer fodder, input, need; Facts; Filed material for a punch card; Information; Statistics.
earl British title; Jazzman Hines; Mountbatten or Avon; Nobleman; Peer; Viscount's superior; Warren.
ebro Iberian, Spanish river to the Mediterranean.
edit Blue-pencil; Do a newspaper, city-room job; Prepare copy; Revise; Work on mss.
eerie Frightening; Inspiring fear; Strange; Unnatural; Weird.
eider Sea duck; Soft down.
ente Being: Sp.; Duck, in Germany; Grafted, heraldry word; ____ en point.
epee Fencing foil; Sword; "Touche" weapon.
esp Clairvoyance: Abbr.; Form of precognition; Intuition, for short; Particularly; Psychic initials; Relative of telepathic faculty; Sixth sense.
essen Eat, in Berlin; German port; Home of Krupp; Ruhr city.
evade Baffle; Dodge; Duck; Get around; Give the slip to; Shirk; Sidestep.
gnat Midge or punkie; Proverbially, a trifle; Small insect; Summer picnic pest.
ideal Goal; Model; Paragon; Perfectly suited example, standard; Utopian; Beau _____.
idol Favorite; Hero-worship subject; Image; Joss; Lion; Object of devotion; Revered one; Matinee ____.
iona Hebrides, Scottish island; New Rochelle college.
lava Certain debris; Cinders; Hot fluid rock; In Hawaii it's called aa; Mauna Loa coating, output; Pelee overflow, product; Scoria.
liner Eye cosmetic; Low, hard-hit baseball drive; Ocean vessel; Queen Elizabeth 2, for one; Ship or plane.
mien Air; Appearance; Bearing; Carriage; Demeanor; Manner.
nea Educators', Teachers' org.; School group: Abbr.
need Essential; Exigency; Indigence; Obligation; Privation; Requirement; Want; A friend in ____.
nolo Defendant's plea; I am unwilling: Lat.; ____ contendere.
ona People of Tierra del Fuego; ___ dare; ___ diet; Not ___ bet; ___ shoestring; ___ spree; Stop ___ dime; "___ Sunday afternoon".
oxen Beasts of burden; Bovines; Draft, farm, work animals.
rag Duster; Scrap; Shred; Tatter; Tease; Tiger, for one; Wiper; Yellow journal: Slang; "Tiger ___".
ram Aries; Farm animal; Fordhamite mascot; L.A. athlete, footballer, player; Zodiac sign.
rara ____ avis.
real Authentic; Kind of assets, estate; Old Spanish coin; Sincere; True; ____ estate.
reds Ball, Cincinnati, N.L., Ohio team; Buttons and others, et al.; Cherry, henna, rose, and ruby; Colors; Port and vermilion.
rent Breach; Budget item; Certain payment; Fissure; Lease; Let; Parted; Schism; Tore.
reset Bowling term; Do, repeat a printing chore, job; Fix again, over; Put in, find a new place for; Replace.
riot Act, of a sort; Demonstration; Outbreak; Police, urban problem; Public disorder; Tumult; Uproar; A ____ of color.
scat Be off!; Command to Pussy; "Go away!"; Opposite of "Here, kitty"; "Shoo!"; Word for a quick exit.
sis Family member; Noun suffix; Relative, for short.
snow Alpine sight; English author, novelist, scientist; A job of sorts; Kind of mobile; Skier's quest; Sled's milieu; TV ailment, phenomenon; Weather forecast, word.
sped Broke, violated a traffic law; Expedited; Hied; Hurried; Hustled; Rushed.
stoa Building where Zeno taught; Columned walk; Greek colonnade; Porch; Portico, in Sparta;
store Abundance; Cache; Deposit; Hoard; Outlet; PX; Put away; Set aside; Shopping-mall unit; Treasure.
tab Bar I.O.U.; Cafe bill; Designate, in a way; Dinner, restaurant check; File marker; Flap; License-plate attachment.
tate English gallery; London art name.
tia Spanish aunt, relative; ___ Juana.
tie Bond; Draw; Four-in-hand; Kind of score; Restrict; Standoff; Supporting beam, rail; Ten to

ten; Family ___.
tram British trolley; Coal-mine car, vehicle; London street sight; Loosely woven silk thread.
try Afflict; Beset; Do a judge's task; Endeavor; Exasperate; Good advice; Make a stab at; Strain; Test; Undertake; ___ one's hand.
yes Affirmative; An answer; Certain pro vote; Green light; I do; Kind of man; Reply; Word of agreement; ___ man.

LIST # 12

abut Be next to; Border on; Join; Touch.
acta Recorded court proceedings; ____ part.
adam Bede; Biblical name; Furniture style; Garden occupant; Genesis figure; Personification of man; Seth's father.
aerie Bird's abode, penthouse; Eagle's retreat; High dwelling; Lofty nest; Mountain stronghold.
aha Exclamation; Triumphant, villain's cry.
ails Bothers; Is distressed, out of sorts, under the weather; Pains; Troubles.
alert Awake; Brisk; Civil Defense condition; On the qui vive; Ready to act; Vigilant; Warning signal; Watchful.
amah Eastern maid; Indian servant; Oriental nurse.
anna First name of Mrs. F.D.R.; Held; King Mongkut's teacher, tutor; O'Neill's heroine Christie; Old Pakistani coin of India; "____ Karenina".
apse Cathedral feature; Church part; Semicircular building recess; Vaulted area.
areas Fields of study; Localities; Neighborhoods; Regions; Scopes; Spaces; Vicinities.
asa Botanist gray; King of Judah; Blind ___ bat; Deep ___ well; Fat ___ pig; "Not ___ Stranger"; Round ___ ball; ___ rule.
ask Call for; Emulate Socrates; First man, in Nordic myth; Invite; Request; "Never ___ of money spent"
asps Reptiles; Serpents; Venomous snakes; Vipers.
aten Solar ring; Sun disk; Not touch with ____ foot pole.
axle Auto, car part; Holder, supporter of some big wheels; Shaft.
case Ablative, genitive, or objective; Condition; Legal job; Situation; Subjective, for one; Upper or lower.
dart Dress feature; Move fast, suddenly; Pub weapon; Run swiftly; Scuttle; Seam; Small feathered missile.
dent Depression; Dimple; Feature of some used cars; Fender damage; Nick; Notch; Slight hollow; Surface flaw; Tooth, in Tours.
done Completed; Ended; Finished; Over; "Thy will be ____"; ____ to a turn.
drama Albee's field; Broadway offering; Gielgud vehicle for stage; High action; "Macbeth," for one; O'Neill's work; Soap opera, e.g.
edna Feminine name; Ferber; Poet Millay.
ella Fitzgerald; Girl's name; Miss Cinders, Logan.
elope Abscond; Avoid wedding expenses; Do the Gretna Green bit; Go run off on the q.t.; One way to marry; Slip away; Take a bride; What some lovers do.
ens Abstract being; Annapolis abbr. Letters; Member of U.S.N.; Naval off.; Printers' type measures.
eral Of a time period, age; Pertaining to an epoch.
ers Hesitations; Noun endings; Speech sounds; Vetch.
estes Kefauver; Western park; _____ Park, Colo.
etat French political body, unit; State, in Paris, Saint-Etienne; Coup d'____; Homme d'____ (statesman).
glee High spirits; Kind of club; Merriment; Mirth; Part song.
isis Cow-headed Egyptian goddess; Wife of Osiris.
leap Abrupt change, transition; A kind of year; Saltate; Spring; Vault; "One giant ____ for mankind"; ____ year.
lee F.F.V. name; Light-Horse Harry; Nautical word; Remick; Shelter; Traveler's rider; Washington & ___.
line Ancestry; Cable; Date or party; Equator; Occupation; Part of a football team; Salesman's samples; Seven of eleven on offense; Short message; ____ drive.
mel Allen or Brooks; Cooperstown name; Honey, in pharmacy; Ott; Singer Torme.
natal Brazilian port; South African area, province.
nil Naught; Nothing; Zero; "De mortuis ___ ..."; "... ___ nisi bonum".
oat Cereal grass, plant; Grain seed; Kind of meal.
ogre Blunderbore; Fairy-tale figure; Fearsome, mean one; Frightful fellow; Grimm bad man; Monster; Unpleasant person; Villain.
ores Bauxite and fool's gold; Certain resources; Chalcopyrites; Metals; Mill raw materials; Mine yields; Minerals; Wolframite et al.
rail Corncrake; Denounce (with "at"); Fence part; Racetrack position; Shore, wading bird; Sora.
rapt Absorbed; Caught up in; Deep in thought; Engrossed; In ecstasy; Lost in delight; Transported.
riata Cowboy's equipment; Gaucho

item; Lariat; Lasso; Ranch rope.

rio Cruise port; Rita or Bravo; River: Sp.; Sight, site of Sugar Loaf; Start of the Grande; ___ Bravo.

roe Asian deer; Canape item; Caviar; Fish eggs; Salty relish.

rot Bosh!; Decay; Disitegrate; Go to ruin; Nonsense; Sometimes dry item; Spoil.

sac American, Illinois, U.S., Western Indian tribe; Flight arm, military group: Abbr.; Pouch.

sari Asian, draped, Hindu, Indian, loose garment; Ranee's attire.

sat Between Fri. and Sun.; Calendar day: Abbr.; Held court; Met; Perched; Posed.

sees Espies; Makes a move at poker; Observes; Spots; Understands; Views.

shad Food, river fish; Kind of roe source.

slab Concrete, generous bread piece; Hunk; Pitching plate, rubber; Thick slice.

soap Castile; Fat product; Item that is slippery when wet; Kind of opera; Lather; Some is soft or no; Soft ____.

sos Emergency sea call of sorts; "Help!"; Mayday's relative; Six dits and three dahs.

spat Falling-out; Quarrel; Squabble; Tiff; Young oyster.

stern Austere; Grim; Harsh; Inexorable; Inflexible; Poop deck; U.S. violinist Isaac.

tan Brown; Healthy look; Hosiery shade; Light color; Tawny; Thrash.

tass Russian, Soviet press agency; Voice of Moscow.

tenet Belief; Doctrine; Opinion; Principle; Stand.

toes Digits; Drives slantingly; Golf club parts; Normally five to the foot; On one's ____; ____ the mark.

true Accurate; Authentic; Common choice in an exam; Correct; Kind of blue; Loyal; Precise; Undeniable; Unfailing; ____ blue.

uvea Eye section; Layer, part of the iris.

yrs Ages, time periods, units: Abbr.; Parts of cens.; Relatives of mos.

LIST # 13

ada Girl's name; Nabokov book, character, heroine, novel, title; Oil city of Oklahoma; Political group: Abbr.; Rehan.

agon Ancient, old Greek contest; Dramatic, literary conflict; Work by Stravinsky.

aid Assist; Befriend; Further; Help; Subsidy; Support; Sustain; First ___; Foreign ___

alar Like wing-shaped; Of the shoulder.

alot Many; Go to ____ of trouble; "Little things mean ____"; "Thanks ____".

ames Ben William's middle name; College town; Iowa city; Neighbor lege town; Iowa city; Neighbor north of Des Moines; Singer Ed and brother.

aper Copycat; Imitator; Me-tooer; Mimic; Unoriginal one.

aran Biblical character; Irish Galway bay islands off Donegal.

arow In a line, in poetry; Queued up; "Pretty maids all in ____".

asian Cambodian, Chinese, Gandhi, Mao, or Thant; Kind, type of flu; Mongol, for one; Oriental; Thai.

asp Cleopatra's quietus, finis; Cobra; Reptile; Serpent; Snake; Uraeus.

asto Anent; Apropos; Concerning; Regarding; With reference.

aves Arteries: Abbr.; Class comprising the birds in general; Part of the fauna; Relative of sts.; Salutations; Thoroughfares.

car Because: Fr.; Coach; Flint product; Hudson, Maxwell, or Reo; Sedan; Stanley, for one; Vehicle.

cede Give up in; Grant; Hand over; Relinquish; Surrender; Transfer.

dear Beloved one; Cherished; Costly; Expensive; First word of a letter; High-priced; Relative of honey; "____ John".

dial Call a number; Certain tone; Face; Jargon: Abbr.; Use the telephone part; ____-a-prayer; "____ M for ...".

dont Common contraction; Mother's, parents' word of warning to children; Prohibition.

eats Beanery, diner's, highway sign; Bothers: Colloq.; Gnaws; Has a bite; Uses up.

eke Make do; Piece, scratch, squeeze out; Stretch; Supplement; ___ out.

ela Highest note of Guido.

elon Biblical judge; Southern college in North Carolina.

enow Ample, plenty, rhyme for "thou", word for Omar; Old enough; "... paradise ____" Sufficient, poetically.

ento Inner, internal, within: Prefix.

ernie A Ford; Man's nickname; Pyle.

espy Behold; Catch sight; Detect; Discover; Notice; Perceive; See; Spot.

etas Greek letters, vowels.

etui Carrying, needle, vanity case for odds and ends; Holder for small items; Reticule.

hail Acclaim; Before Columbia; Call; Greet; Precipitation; Weather forecast word. "____ Columbia"; "____ fellow well met".

ite Bleacher, inhabitant, native of, noun, resident: Suffix.

lease Contract; Hire; Legal document, paper; Realty matter; Renter's, tenant's concern.

less Between little and least; Diminished by; Fewer; Inferior; Minus; Slighter; Subtraction word; Without: Common suffix; Apostle James the ____.

list Cant; Careen; Inventory; Itemize; Roster; Shopper's aid, guide; Tilt; ___ price.

melt Disintegrate; Dissolve; Liquefy; Prepare butter for lobster; Relent.

name Appoint; Christen; Dub; Moniker; Reputation; Single out; ___ of the game.

nemo Captain of fiction; Glade: Prefix; Verne character, hero; "____ me impune lacessit".

note Bill; Distinction; Do, for one; Eminence; I.O.U.; Jot down; Memo; Remark.

odin Frigg's spouse; Norse deity, god; Ruler of the Aesir; Valhalla host, man; Ymir's slayer.

omer About 3.7 quarts; Biblical, Hebrew measure; Part of an ephah.

oss Donovan's group; W.W.II initials; Wartime agency: Abbr.

rani Eastern V.I.P.; Hindu queen, title; Indian princess, woman; Rajah's spouse.

redo Change; Decorate again; Fix, make over; Renovate.

rile Exasperate: Colloq.; Get under one's skin; Irritate; Make feisty; Miff; Peeve; Upset; Vex.

rob Commit a crime, holdup; Plunder; Roy; Steal from; Stick up.

ross Antarctic, cold, Southern sea; Banner maker; Barney of ring fame; Betsy.

rte Highway, road map notation, way to go: Abbr.

same Alike; Conforming; Ditto; Duplicate; Equal; Indistinguishable; Unchanged; Unvarying; ____-day service.

sass Impertinence; Impudent back talk; Lip.

sate Appease; Glut; Gorge; Gratify; Overfill; Satisfy.

seal Authenticate; Christmas or Easter item; Close tightly; Fasten; Guarantee; Official stamp; Water, zoo animal; Waterproof.

sera Antitoxins; Evening, in Naples; Immunoliogical items; Watery body fluids; Wheys.

sham Bogus; Counterfeit; Cover of a kind; Feign; Imitation; Kind of battle; Pretense; Put-on; Spurious.

slot Animal track; Deer trail; Machine of a sort; Mailbox part; Niche; Pay phone feature; Place for a coin.

soda Beverage; Chaser; Companion, friend, partner of Scotch; Drink mix; Kind of fountain Pop.

spas Baden and Ems; Baths; Bex and Dux; Health clubs; Hot and Warm Springs; Resorts; Saratoga et al.

sten British ordnance; English kind of gun; Swedish weight.

tall Hard to believe; Improbable; Like a pro cager; Lofty; Unbelievable; Word for some stories; "And all I ask is a ____ ship"; ____ in the saddle.

tap Court-game starter; Draw from, off, on, as resources; Faucet; Kind of dance of sorts; Open a barrel; Spigot.

taxi Futile call, cry on a rainy day; Hack; Kind of dancer; Part of the street scene; Prepare for takeoff; Urban vehicle for Amos of radio.

tile Flooring, roofing material; Game piece; High silk hat; Tessera.

tri Three: Numerical prefix for angle.

upon Atop; Au courant; Between once and a; Immediately; In the know; Part, word of a fairytale beginning; Once ____ a time.

yap Bark; Caroline, Pacific island; Chatter; Jabber; Kennel sound.

LIST # 14

abe Burrows; Daisy Mae's son; Li'l Abner's boy; Man's or Presidential nickname; Mary Todd's husband.

adage Pithy saying; Proverb; Saw.

agile Deft; Dextrous; Limber; Nimble; Spry; Well-coordinated.

aint Common vulgarism; Familiar solecism; Slangy negative contraction of sorts; "____ we got fun?"; "____ what she used ...".

alien Extrinsic; Far removed; Outsider; Strange.

aloha Hilo, Honolulu, Maui, Oahu greeting or farewell; Relative of adieu.

anat Art, science course: Abbr.; College subj.; Pre-med. study.

anent About; As regards to; Concerning; Regarding; Respecting.

arc Bow; Crescent; Curved geometric line; Eyebrow shape; Rainbow; Spark stream; ___ lamp.

aroma Bouquet; Flowers' forte; Fragrance; Redolence; Scent.

att Appendended: Abbr.; Lawyer; Legal man; Old Siamese coin.

casa Acapulco residence; Home, in Veracruz; House, in Mexico, Spain; Senora's place; ____ Grande.

chap Bloke; Fellow; Guy.

core Apple section; Basic, essential part; Center; Heart; Prepare, as fruit; Throwaway ever since Eve.

doe Deer; Distaff rabbit; Female animal; Forest creature, denizen; Jane ___.

ecto External, outside: Prefix for morph or plasm.

eels Congers; Fishes; Smorgasbord items; They're slippery ones.

eer Noun ending, suffix; Poetic contraction, word; Relative of eterne.

epode Aftersong; Lyric poem, work;

Poetic form.
eves Arden and others; Certain poetic times prior to holidays; Important nights before; Tempters.
gila Arizona river; Colorado tributary; Desert lizard; Monster; ____ monster (lizard).
hat Covering; Fedora; Felt or straw; Item to talk through; Medicine or old; Pillbox; Topper; Tricorn; Brass ___.
iced Added frosting; Did a bakery cake job, work; Frozen; Like some kind of tea; Made sure of: Colloq.; On the rocks.
ido Altar, assent, ceremonial, momentous, oath-taker's, rite words; Form of Esperanto; Half a musical title; Witness-box response.
india Asian land; Kind, type, variety of ink or paper; "Song of _____".
inner Kind of circle, sanctum, tube; Secret; The _____ man; _____ sanctum; _____ tube.
irae Dies ____.
ires Angers; Exacerbates; Incenses; Infuriates; Irritates.
ivan Abdul the Bulbul's rival; Grand duke of muscovy; John's relative; Olga's boyfriend; Russian name; Terrible or Great tsar.
lago Como or Maggiore, for one; Lake: It., Sp.; Rupanco or Puyehue; ____ Maggiore.
lair Criminals' hangout; Den; Hideaway place; Wild habitat.
lei Aloha concomitant, item; Garland; Hula wear; Pacific neckpiece; Welcoming wreath in Waipahu.
loge Balcony; Booth; Box; Partitioned-off area; Stall; Theater section.
mane Heavy, thick outgrowth of horse hair; Jungle neckpiece; Lion's pride; Teen hairdo.
mare Belmont entry; Filly's relative; A horse; Old gray animal, one; ____ nostrum.
men Brothers; Certain voters; Chess game pieces; Crew; People; Persons.
naive Artless; Credulous; Ingenuous; Like a babe in the woods; Unphilosophic; Unsophisticated.
needs Demands; Is wanting; Lacks; Obligations; Requires; Requisites; Straits.
odds Advantage; Bettor's, bookmaker's concern; Gambler's word; Probabilities; Race-track term; Rockingham ratios; Tote-board data.
ogle Amorous look; Be wolfish; Emulate a girl-watcher; Eye; Leer; Look, in a way; Take a gander.
ome 'Arry's place; Cockney's flat, pad; Group: Suffix; Residence, shelter, in Soho.
open Certain annual golf match, tourney; Clear; Frank; Initiate; Not shut; On view; Poker term.
oro Ecuadorean province; Loot, treasure on the Spanish Main; Mountain: Prefix; Pirate's gold; ___ y plata.
pisa Galileo's birthplace; Italian tourist city near Leghorn on the Arno known for biased view; Province in Tuscany; Tower with an inclination.
pole Cracow, Lodz man; Item for a vault; North or South; Peary's conquest; Propel a punt; Spar; Star or cat; Totem.
pre Anterior to, before, front: Common prefix for med or meditate; Acadians', Nova Scotia's Grand ___.
rat Coiffure gadget; Despicable one; Lady's hair accouterment, piece, pad; Rodent; Ship stowaway, of sorts; Slum problem; "Brother ___".
remit Forgive; Pardon; Pay up; Postpone; Word on a bill, with "please".
road Course; Highway; Map line; Tobacco, for one; Way.
roi Early Tuileries, Old Versailles resident; French king; Louis XIV, e.g.; Reine's counterpart, husband, spouse; "Vive le ___!"
rue Herb of grace; Regret; Repent; Wish one hadn't.
sale Advertised offering, topic; Deal; Feb. 22 event; Store-ad subject; Transaction.
sassy Fresh; Impertinent; Impudent; Saucy.
seas Deep blue and others; Coral, Red, Ross, and Weddell; Famous seven; High, large waves; High ____.
sect Cult; Cut: Suffix; Denomination; Doctrinal group; Part: Abbr.; Religious division, order.
sen Capitol Hill man, V.I.P.: Abbr.; Change from a yen; Japanese coin; Ten rin.
ses His: French adjective, possessive.
sip Drink slowly; Taste; Use a straw.
snip Cut; Impertinent one; Small amount, bit, piece; Swatch; Whippersnapper.
sort Classify; Kind; Nature; Type; ____ of (rather).
sro Broadway, hit, impresario's favorite, Rialto, theater sign.
stole Article of clothing; Came secretly, with "in"; Did a base-running job; Embezzled; Garment; Mink piece; Purloined; Shawl; Wrap.
tbar Beam of a certain structural shape; Metal piece; Type of skiers' lift, slope equipment.
tens Decades; Folding money; Numbers; Sawbucks; Shoe sizes; Some certain bills.
ton Large amount; Short or long; Unit of weight; Bon ___.
tort Civil, legal wrongful act.
trek Expedition; Journey; Migration.
trot Exam-cheater's, Latin student's aid; Gait; Jog; Kind of horse race; Pony; Yonkers event.
una "Faerie Queen" maiden; Merkel; Spanish article; Spenserian

lady.
year Leap or light, for one; Part of a decade; Time period, unit; Two semesters; Leap ____; Sidereal ____.

LIST # 15

abets Eggs on; Encourages; Is in cahoots with; Supports; Urges on.
ager Antiquing device; Dyeing apparatus; Field, for Cicero; Land: Lat.; Steam chamber; Teen-____.
agora Ancient assembly; Athens sight; Market place; Public square of old.
alga Kelp; Plankton; Rockweed; Sea plant.
alii Hawaiian royalty; Others, in Rome: Lat.; Part of et al.; Et ____.
amos Andy's associate, pal, partner, sidekick; Book of O.T.; Follower of Joel; Hebrew prophet; One of a radio pair; Otis of baseball.
and Besides; Common word; Conjunction; Or's relative; Part of etc.; Plus; Slow, in music: Abbr.; "Love ___ Marriage"; "___ so to bed".
aorta Arterial trunk; Blood vessel.
arcs Bow shapes; Curve parts; Lights for stars; Lines made by compasses; Rainbows; Spark streams.
asor Hebrew lyre; Zither's ancestor.
beta Certain ray; Greek letter.
cat Kind of burglar; Library list: Abbr.; Small sailboat; Siamese, for one; Spiteful woman; Tabby; Black ___.
cola African tree; Fountain soft drink; Kind of caffeine-producing beverage nut; Soda flavor.
die Cutting, shaping device; Dotted cube; Mold; One of a pair; Stamp.
eave House part; Overhang; Roof edge.
edie Actress, songstress Miss Adams; She was a lady; ____ Adams.
een Bard's nightfall; Imitation fabric: Suffix; Yet, poetic adverb, word.
emir Arabian noble, prince; Descendant of Mohammed; Eastern title; Moslem ruler.
erode Destroy slowly; Deteriorate; Eat away; Undermine; Wear with time.
exert Exercise vigorously; Put forth into action; Strain; Wield.
hale Hearty's companion; In fine fettle, good shape, the pink; Nathan; Robust; Sound.
hera Greek Juno; Olympian goddess; Wife of Zeus.
ici Here, in Brest, Guadeloupe, Paris: Fr.; "___ on parle francais".
inca "Child of the sun"; Early South American; Indian; Lake in Andes; Peruvian tribesman; Quechua.
inge American dramatist; Gloomy Dean; "Picnic" author; U.S. playwright William.
int Cost of borrowing: Abbr.; Savings-bankbook word; Worldwide.
irate Choleric; Disturbed; Incensed; Indignant; Provoked; Upset.
ital Certain kind of typesetting instruction; Printing style: Abbr.
lace Do a shoe chore, part; Edging; Fabric; Product of Alencon; Trimming; With "Queen Anne's", wild carrot.
laic Nonprofessional; Secular.
lara Byron poem; Pasternak character; Venezuelan state; "Zhiago"'s girl, heroine, love, name.
lion British symbol; Celebrity; Famous one; Feuchtwanger; Pride member; Social V.I.P.; "A ____ in Winter".
magi Biblical wise men; Christmas trio; Creche, nativity figures; Eastern astrologers; Melchior and companions.
mao Author of sayings; Late Chinese great, leader; Oriental name; ___ Tse-tung.
mede Ancient, early Asian; Old name for one of Irani; Persian ally.
menu Bill of fare; Cafe card, window item; Chef's, thanksgiving concern; Gourmand's reading; Waiter's offering.
nana Dog in "Peter Pan"; Renowned novel character of 1880; Zola heroine, title.
nice Agreeable; Exact; Fastidious; Finicky; French, Mediterranean resort; Fussy; Precise.
odes Certain literary Tennyson works; Poems; Tributes to skylarks, et al.
olive Bar staple; Cocktail additive, fruit; Kind of drab color; Oil source; Part of O.D.; Popular garnish; Relish-tray standby.
opal Blue shade; October gem stone.
opine Allow as how; Believe, old style; Express, present an idea; Suppose; Think: Colloq.
pad Expand needlessly; Hippie's home; Lily part; Lodging of a kind; Part of a dog's foot; Stuff; Tablet.
poi Dish for Kamehameha; Hawaiian food; Luau course, item; Oahu fare; Taro paste.
pore Opening; Orifice; Ponder; Reflect on; Study carefully, intently; Think deeply.
proa Malaysian boat, canoe, vessel; Native craft; Pacific outrigger.
rata Pro ____; ____-tat.
rete Network; Plexus.
rode Did work at Belmont; Got saddle sores; Lay at anchor; Took a bus, cab; Traveled; ____ out (survived).
root Become fixed; Cheer; Etymon; Fountainhead; Kind of beer; 1912 Peace Nobelist; Source; Take hold; What pigs do.

saar European basin; German area, region; River to the Moselle.
sap Enervate; Exhaust; Fall guy; Foolish one; Juice; Ninny; Spring riser; Undermine; Weaken.
scot Britisher; Burns, Lauder, or Sir Walter, for one; Canny, Dundee, Glengarry man; Tax; ___ free.
sec Dry, as wine; Not sweet; Short time div.; Wall St. watchdog.
seep Go through a sieve; Ooze; Percolate; Permeate; Small spring.
ser Hindu, Indian weight; Pulpit, Sunday talk, religious discourse: Abbr.
sess Meeting, term: Abbr.
slam Bridge bid, contract, score, six or seven, term; Impact; Small or grand.
sora Marsh bird; Short-billed rail.
span Bridge; Cross over; Encompass; Measure with the hand; Pair; Reach; Two horses.
stand Bear; Endure; Kiosk; Position; Run, in England; Taboret; Tolerate.
tat Do fancy handwork; Knot lace; Make edging; Tit for ___.
tenor Caruso, for one; General direction, idea; Purport; Quartet member; Stamp; Voice part.
tent Big Top; Camper's home, item; Circus feature; Kind of caterpillar; Loose dress.
tone A flat, for one; Bodily vigor; Elegance; General character; Mood; Resiliency; Style; Dial ___.
tot Add; Child; Drink, as of rum; Kiddie; Little one; Small portion; Urchin.
tres Very, in Rouen, Versailles: Fr.; Word used with "chic"; ___ bien; ___ chic.
ulna Arm bone; Forelimb part; Radius's companion, neighbor.
uso Club, group, mecca, org. serving servicemen: Abbr.; G.I.'s friend; Troop entertainers.

ORDER FORM
for Dictionary of CRUCIAL CROSS WORDS

CrossStar 5334 S. 74th E. Ave. Tulsa, OK 74145
(918) 622-6881

Tear out this form, fill it in, and mail to address above accompanied by proper funds.

			Savings
1 - 20	books	$3.95 ea.	
21 - 50	books	3.55 ea.	10%
51 - 100	books	3.15 ea.	20%
101 or more	books	2.75 ea.	30%

$.60 shipping & handling for each book

Quantity x (Unit cost + ship. & handling) = Price

Example

40 x ($3.55 + .60) = $166

_______ x (_________ + .60) = _______

Sold to:

Name_________________________________Date__________

Address____

City_________________________State_____Zip__________

Phone (______) ______-_____________

Deliver to:

Name____

Address____

____

City_________________________State_____Zip__________

No Credit Cards or C.O.D.s

Make check or money order payable to CrossStar